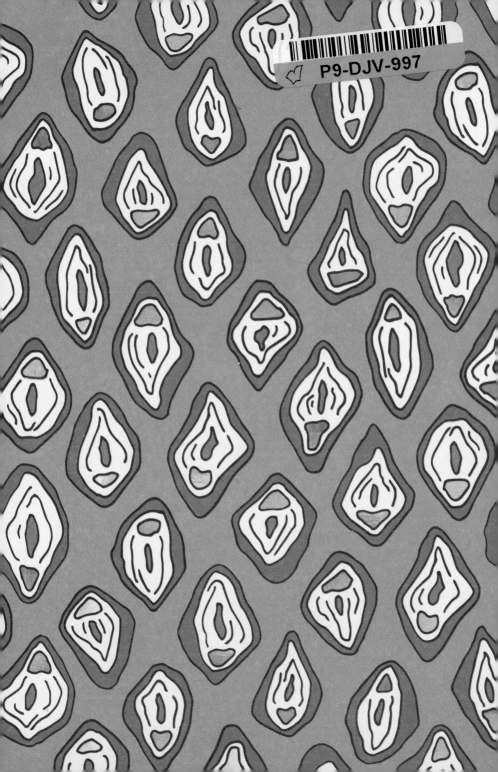

Act Like A Lady

Act Like A Lady

QUESTIONABLE ADVICE, RIDICULOUS
OPINIONS, AND HUMILIATING TALES
FROM THREE UNDIGNIFIED WOMEN

Keltie Knight, Becca Tobin,
and Jac Vanek

RODALE.
NEW YORK

CONT

ENTS

Wanna Hang with the Gang?

Um, excuse us? Are you standing in a bookstore with a mediocre latte in hand asking yourself *Am I That Bitch?* and/or *Do I need a book that speaks to me on a personal level?*

Still questioning your life decisions?

Have you ever accidentally farted during sex?

Have you ever left a tampon in for way too long and lived to tell the tale?

Have you ever ugly-cried rom-com-style in the bathroom at work during your lunch break?

If the answer is yes to any of these questions (as they SHOULD BE) . . . AIN'T NO SHAME. . . . **WELCOME TO THE LADYGANG!**

We started the LadyGang with a simple mission statement: to make women to feel less alone. The three of us were individually fed up with the hyper-curated, bullshit-filled world around us. We were *starving* for something honest, raw, relatable, and a little messy . . . like women actually are. You know when you're sitting around with your girlfriends, sharing your darkest, dirtiest, funniest, most cringeworthy stories, when one of you shouts with a mouthful of tequila and guac, "OMG! We should start a podcast!"? Well, that's basically the idea behind the LadyGang.

Things started off remarkably smooth. Jac made a logo, Keltie created a layout for the show, and Becca called in ten favors with a smidge of blackmail from celebrity friends to come on as our first guests. But don't get us wrong, we've definitely fucked up along the way. Since our podcast launched in December of 2015, we've accidentally erased entire recordings, been in a legal battle that almost cost us all our savings, and unsuccessfully asked John Mayer to come on our show twenty-seven times. (FYI, this officially counts as twenty-eight, John . . . hello???) But with lots of hard work and some tough love with one another, the LadyGang has grown into quite the juggernaut. We have employees, a subscription beauty box, a merchandise store, a podcast network, a touring business, and a TV show! This is our first rodeo, and we're constantly looking at each other thinking, *How the fuck have we not been bucked off and kicked in the head yet?!*

The truth is, the magic happens when the three of us sit in a room and just . . . talk. Much like the show *Teen Mom,* it was something we never planned for and definitely never expected. We all ran in a similar Los Angeles circle but were acquaintances at best and couldn't be more different personality-wise. Keltie is the type-A workaholic whose idea of a good time is an afternoon at Home Depot preparing to DIY shiplap her own bathroom. Jac is the adventurous free spirit, an all-around "good-time girl" who has never met a dartboard, cornhole, or Jenga game she didn't like. And Becca is the cynical, blunt, and usually the most offensive cherry on top. Becca and Keltie had known each other while they were both professional dancers in New York City, and their paths continued to cross again and again. Becca accidentally became a pseudo-star on the hit TV show *Glee* and was interviewed by none other than Keltie on the Hollywood red carpet. Jac and Keltie share a mutual ex-boyfriend, and Jac will constantly remind everyone (and we mean EVERYONE) how Keltie "took her sloppy seconds." But the driving force that brought us together was that all three of us felt stagnant in our careers. Our day jobs were not fulfilling us, not inspiring us, and, quite frankly, we were sick of working for the man.

And so the LadyGang was conceived.

Well, not quite. Before checking the trademark registry, we started the podcast with a different name. (Yes, that's a thing. First piece of advice: don't name a business without checking if someone else owns said business name.) We refuse to say the original name out loud now . . . it's kind of like Voldemort. And after we made custom jackets, did a photo shoot, and launched the show, it became clear that even if we were to pool all our savings together, we would never be able to afford to purchase a trademark someone else owned. Speed bump number one: find a new name.

And so like a phoenix rising from the ashes, the LadyGang was born, *again.*

What started as a celebrity-driven podcast quickly turned inward to the three of us. Within the first few episodes, Becca admitted she dropped her dirty underwear, complete with a "snail trail" (use your imagination), in the parking garage to later be retrieved by her new boyfriend, now husband. And in that moment, Pandora's box was ripped wide open. Nothing was too crude, gross, smelly, or inappropriate for our podcast. Our listeners thrived on our embarrassing stories about stumbling through womanhood, and seemingly overnight we had a worldwide gang of devoted ladies who celebrated our good weeks (like when Jac had a sandwich named after her) and cry-laughed at our bad weeks (like when Keltie was mistaken for Steven Tyler).

Since our show launched, we've had millions and millions of downloads, been nominated and lost both a Webby Award and a People's Choice Award (which is great because losing is more on-brand for us). We've been featured in fancy magazines, walked red carpets, and even drank wine with Kathie Lee and Hoda on the *Today* show. We worked our asses off to make the podcast so radical that the E! network took notice and gave us our own TV show. We were "executive producers," so not only did we have an important say in how our show was made, but we were also able to hire a staff full of radiant and smart women to produce us, film us, and reach down our shirts to mic us.

Although we would never agree on who has been our favorite celebrity guest on the show (Keltie says Ed Sheeran, RuPaul, and Jenna Fischer. Becca says Dorit Kemsley, Ryan Murphy, and Lea Michele. Jac says Nico Tortorella, Karamo Brown, and her mom), we all agree that the very best thing about starting the LadyGang has been meeting all our listeners out in the real world. Ladies stop us at concerts, on the street, and at drugstores while we are buying tampons, and we are constantly in awe of how fucking awesome they are.

The LadyGang has become a community full of smart, accomplished, hardworking, caring, stylish, badass women who have their shit together but might also happen to be wallowing over a bad job, a bad breakup, or a bad spray tan. Maybe your guy does the dishes but won't go down on you; maybe you just spent $2k to be in a wedding for someone you don't even like; or maybe your parents, friends, ovaries, or boss are acting like fucking jerks, and you just need somewhere to vent. The LadyGang has got your back.

This is "technically" an advice book, but we are well aware that we give pretty questionable advice. We hope that by being honest about our struggles, insecurities, breakups, divorces, leaked nude photos, and plastic surgery we can rip the veil off the bullshit that the world is currently selling you. Our mission is to help you feel more normal. You are not the only one who feels as if they have no idea what they are doing. When a fuckening is on the horizon, whether it be in a relationship, at work, or with a shitty friend, it's really easy to feel like no one else has ever experienced the crushing pain you're currently going through. But, in reality, everyone has gone through all of this shit and then some. We've all been full Natalie Imbruglia in the fetal position crying and lying naked on the floor, and all we ever needed was someone to talk to. If we didn't have our ladies to lean on, womanhood would be completely unbearable.

For so long, it has felt like a woman's success has been defined by whether or not she could achieve the "happily ever after" fairy tale. We have been sold this image of happiness as riding off into the sunset with a handsome prince, or living with a white picket fence, or having a dozen kids. Our value has been based far too much on things outside of us, and, frankly, we're sick of it. Women are dynamic and real and messy and smart, and we have so much more to offer than society's bunk-ass expectations of us. And don't worry, we don't hate men. We actually love them to death, but we also love our careers, our friends, sex, and, most important, we love ourselves (well, we're trying to, at least).

So, as modern women, we will focus on the four *significant* relationships you have in your life:

1. Your relationship with your **lover**: current, past, and future, and the important lessons you learn from each one throughout your lifetime.

2. Your relationship with **yourself** (including your body), and all the crazy shit that flows through your mind and out your vagina on a daily basis.

3. Your relationship with your **career**, how to feel fulfilled professionally, and how to navigate the crazy working world.

4. Your relationship with your **friends**, how to find your gang, and understanding the different types of friendships you have over time.

We will share all of the mistakes we've made and lessons we've learned, offer up some unsolicited advice, and suggest a couple of rules we think you should follow. Do we have any idea what we are actually doing? Nope. Will this book fix your life in ten simple steps? Probably not. Use this book as needed: jump around to whatever section speaks to you, Instagram the quotes that you passive-aggressively want others to see, or take us in the bath with you and read us cover to cover. Lady life is messy, hard, and can be heartbreaking, but what we've learned is that the bad stuff isn't as bad when you can laugh about it with your LadyGang.

The next question is, are you a Becca, a Jac, or a Keltie?

Are You a Becca?

I was raised in the land of beauty pageants and Baptist churches: Marietta, Georgia. However, I was unable to participate in either due to my liberal mother and Jewish father. I come from three generations of lawyers and yet I barely broke a thousand on my SATs and fucking hated school . . . hence the reason I took up musical theater.

I got kicked off the cheerleading squad in the seventh grade for flipping off some boys who were heckling us from the stands. Nowadays I could be celebrated for that, but whatever . . . fuck 'em. After the cheer career ended, I threw myself into the arts completely, and my one-track mind was set on Broadway.

After high school, I moved to New York City and took up intense theater training (and chain-smoking). I finally made it onto the Broadway stage at twenty-three, and my parents were legitimately thrilled that I had made something of myself. I proved the naysayers from my hometown wrong and actually didn't end up on a stripper pole with a cocaine addiction, as so many had predicted. However, I *did* play a stripper in said Broadway show, and I may have tried cocaine a handful of times . . . or possibly six handfuls of times, but who's counting?

At twenty-six, I got my big "Hollywood break" (that I honestly was never seeking out) when Ryan Murphy cast me as a bitchy cheerleader on the hit show *Glee*. I spent three glorious seasons on that show. It was certainly where I peaked, and Hollywood doesn't let me forget it. Oh wait, that's a lie . . . Hollywood doesn't even remember.

After *Glee*—and months of consistently losing jobs to people like Demi Moore's kid and some YouTuber from Canada—I decided it was time to find a job no one else wanted (at the time) . . . podcasting!!! And the rest is history.

I'm an insane achiever in disguise. I low-key *love* success, and I'm obsessed with being the best at whatever I'm doing, but I'll never show it. I'm the most resilient person I know, and I will rarely let you see me

I love success
and I'm
obsessed with
being the best
at whatever
I'm doing,
but I'll never
show it.

–Becca

cry. And after years of therapy, I realize that this is actually a fault, so I'm definitely not bragging.

I'm terrified to become a mother (even though I'm pretty confident I will become one) because sometimes I don't have the energy to get out of bed before 9:00 a.m., and I'm worried I may beat up another kid for being mean to my own kid and end up in prison. I also get freaked out by anything pregnancy-related. Would you judge me if I used a surrogate?

I am critical of activities like dressing up on Halloween, bridal showers, and buying adults Christmas presents, but I won't judge you for participating in any of it. I truly believe people should be able to do whatever the fuck they want in life as long as it's not hurting anyone. (Just don't expect me to do any of it.)

I love deeply, but I will rarely say it. I will forget your birthday, but that's because I never know what the date is and I have a weird inability to remember numbers. I will fly across the country to be there for my best friends' births, breakups, whatever. I hate grocery shopping because I don't like having a lot of options. I love cleaning my house. My sister is my best friend on planet Earth, and I feel sorry for anyone who doesn't have one. I hate injustice, and I will pee in your purse if you fuck me or my friends over.

Are You a Jac?

Hi, I'm Jac Vanek. I'm a self-made entrepreneur, CEO, designer, business owner, podcaster, TV host, fashion and music influencer, and now I guess . . . an author? Growing up, I was a nerdy little girl with thick red glasses who always danced to the beat of my own quirky drum, but my life really "began" when I went to my first rock concert at fifteen years old. I pushed my way to the front row against the barricade; my tiny, prepubescent body was getting smashed to oblivion, crowd-surfers kicked me in the head, and I'd never been happier. I finally felt like I belonged for the first time in my life. I finally felt like I found my people. I finally felt like I was home.

"

I'll do
anything
once,
twice if it
involves
booze.

–Jac

From that moment on, every single thing I did was fueled by my love for music. By the time I was halfway through college, most of my friends were in bands touring the world and having the time of their lives, and I wanted that life *so* bad. I didn't have any musical talent, and I didn't want to *just* be some musician's girlfriend (even though I have been multiple times), but I *did* have a degree in graphic design and a pretty substantial following on the internet. So I took out a $200 loan from my parents, made a small batch of rubber bracelets with the word RUTHLESS printed on them, and sold them out of my backpack at concerts and on bulletin boards on my Myspace page. I gave some to friends in bands, they would wear them onstage, and all of their fans jumped to buy them to emulate their favorite rock star. Fast-forward ten years, and my Jac Vanek brand has expanded into an entire message-driven lifestyle brand that has been worn by celebrities like Lindsay Lohan, Demi Lovato, Joe Jonas, Paris Hilton, and Miley Cyrus, and that has been carried in big-box retailers all over the country. I've traveled the world representing my brand on music tours and beyond.

My love for music led me to where I am today, but that's just the tip of the Jac iceberg. Keltie thinks I'm pretty cool, and that's why she and Becca reached out to me to start the LadyGang. I don't give a shit about Hollywood or fame, so I'm kind of the outsider of the three of us. I know nothing about celebrities, but I know literally everything about serial killers. I work hard so I can play harder. I am drama-free, but I *love* gossip and drinking everyone else's tea. I'm curious and spontaneous, and I always want to carpe the fucking diem. I'll try anything once, twice if it involves booze. I am a social introvert and an optimistic cynic and a lot of other oxymorons that probably make zero sense. I hate small talk, and I can't pretend to be interested in your bullshit. I have crippling anxiety around strangers, and I bite my nails until they bleed. I'm extremely picky and specific about everything in my life from the food I eat (hate garlic, sorry) to the clothes I wear (can't have anything tight around my calves) to the men I date (no flip-flops allowed). I always have a hundred outrageous ideas swirling around in my head, and I usually make ninety-nine of them come to life. I am a fiercely loyal friend to six people, and

I consider everyone else an acquaintance. I want to get drunk at 11:00 a.m. and be in bed by 7:00 p.m. I prefer *Seinfeld* over *Friends*, and I'm definitely a Jerry. I'll probably be the one playing with your dog in a corner at parties. I like sunshine and sunsets, and I always want to be outside. The ocean is my forever happy place. I am a bad cook and an even worse dancer. I am insanely competitive, I love playing games, and I will most definitely kick your ass in cornhole. I love *The Bachelor* and country music and Charles Bukowski. I will make any excuse to go on a vacation. I can be really scatterbrained and I currently have 25,482 unread emails in my inbox. My go-to karaoke song is "Bohemian Rhapsody" because my voice sucks, I hate being the center of attention, and I love a good sing-along. I'm sassy as hell, honest to a fault, and my love language is talking shit. I like to jump out of planes and off of tall things for fun. I have a big squishy heart, and I am really fucking hard on myself. The only thing I have in my refrigerator right now is a bottle of prosecco. I'm pretty confident in my own skin, and I honestly don't care what you think about me. I am a lot of things, and I like that about myself.

Are You a Keltie?

While the other ladies will be humble and modest and will hate that they have to write about themselves, this is the part of the book where I will truly shine (being an overachieving Aquarius, Enneagram 3, and lover of to-do lists, goal setting, and organization).

I've been fiercely independent since I could walk, and I went to three different high schools because being "normal" and doing whatever everyone else was doing never interested me. I left my hometown of Sherwood Park, Alberta, Canada, when I was eighteen to follow my far-fetched dreams of becoming a professional dancer. What I lacked in actual technique or talent I made up for in guts and determination. Little old unremarkable me went on to dance for two NBA teams, high-kicked during five seasons with the Radio City Rockettes, performed on *Saturday Night Live*, and danced in oodles of music videos and with famous stars, including Kanye West (for which he has never paid me; Kanye, you owe me $150!), John Legend (ridiculously talented), Beyoncé (very sweet, with an engagement ring so big it will blind you), Taylor Swift (her mom gave me a *Fearless* guitar pic and I still have it—and a matching *Fearless* tattoo), Panic! at the Disco (got a fun ex-boyfriend out of that gig, who I share with Jac, more on that later in the book), and Fergie (one of the prettiest celebrities I've ever met with no makeup on). I was a principal dancer in two movies and even starred in my very own cover of *Dance Spirit* magazine. When I retired from being a dancer, I fell into being a TV host because I loved music so much and knew a bunch of musicians and had a handycam. I've spent the last decade on TV talking about celebrities, working sixteen-hour days, traveling around the world, and getting spray tans. In 2018, I won my first Emmy, and now everywhere I go, people are forced to introduce me as "Emmy Award–winning Keltie Knight," which I think is really chic.

On my best days, I am charming, ambitious, highly effective, charitable, self-accepting, and thoughtful. On my worst days, I am terrified of failure, a social climber, and somewhat of a careerist, always trying to impress others with my superiority, although for the most part I have zero idea what I am doing. I like rules, order, and people who are on time. I think I'm a moderately good wife, a really fabulous friend during major life events like your wedding or your husband cheating on you, and kind of a shitty friend who lets two months go past without checking in. I'm a terrible cook, a great gift giver, and I have my underwear sorted into four different compartments based on their usage. If any of this rings true to you, then you might be a Keltie. Welcome to the K-type way, and please tell your friends about this book so they can be inspired, but mostly so I can become a *New York Times*–bestselling author.

99

I like rules, order, and people who are on time.

–Keltie

THE POWER OF THE LADYGANG

"I feel like you guys are my best friends!"
—everyone

You don't know how often we hear this from complete strangers, and that statement alone is exactly why we do what we do. We've always aimed to make the LadyGang a digital table that everyone can sit at, but not in the living-in-the-clouds, everything-is-perfect kind of way. We are those friends who will celebrate the shit out of you, but we'll also call you out when you're acting like a dick. We'll make sure you like your face before we post a group pic online, but we'll also leave a savage comment on your lovey-dovey photo with your boyfriend.

Even though some people call us vapid, stupid, annoying, and pointless (more on how to deal with jealousy later in the book), we have come together in ways we couldn't have imagined to help and support our ladies around the world. What started with the three of us has taken on a life of its own, and we've empowered women (and a few guys) to use the power of the LadyGang to connect, make friends, and feel less alone. We've helped one another get over breakups, get out of abusive relationships, and navigate depression and anxiety. We've helped one another move to new cities, make friends in adulthood, and ask for raises. We've helped one another through the deaths of parents, friends, lovers, and pets. We've helped one another through abortions, miscarriages, and through the shame of your body not "working the way it should" when you're trying to conceive. We've photoshopped pimples off one another's faces, photoshopped exes out of family photos, and we have even helped one another make the right choice about getting adult braces.

There is a "LadyGang Teachers" group, a "LadyGang Marketplace" to resell your stuff and make extra cash, and we even have 189 members in the "LadyGang Loves Their Doodles" puppy group. Our "LadyGang

Investigates" group has uncovered cheaters, liars, catfishes, and has used Google's reverse image search to find the truth about guys with double lives, wives, and kids.

We don't yell it from the rooftops, but the LadyGang was able to donate supplies to hurricane victims and work with Children's Hospital Los Angeles, the Hollywood Food Coalition, and more. We've granted over $100,000 in college scholarships to our listeners, and Keltie even lent her bridal headpiece to a complete stranger to wear on her big day as her "something borrowed."

Our members have borrowed one another's contractors to remodel their kitchens (and saved $20k). When one lady asked for a recommendation on a furry vest, another gal had one lying around and just sent it to her out of the goodness of her heart! An LG bride got secretly married by a different LG member who got certified to do the ceremony online, and *another* LG member came to be the witness (none of them had ever met in real life before that day)! One of our ladies was down on her luck around Christmas, and when her inflatable mattress broke and she asked for cute doggy pictures to cheer her up, the group all pitched in and sent her $800 for a new bed. One of our gals with cystic fibrosis was looking for ways to make money from home, and another one of our ladies hired her as a remote marketing manager. When one of our members died during childbirth and a fund was set up to help support the widowed daddy and new baby, our ladies helped raise $18,000 for the family. We've laughed with one another when our kids, significant others, or bosses make us want to pull our hair out. All this from a worldwide group of strangers who bonded over listening to three idiots talk about their own lives. Our ladies have banded together by being in a judgment-free zone, because no matter who you are or where you're from, we're all just trying to get through life with two blobs of fat on our chests.

Here's the thing you need to keep in mind while you're reading this book: We have no idea what we're doing. And we totally expect that you have no idea what you're doing. And if you look around the room, there actually isn't a single person who has any idea what they're doing.

EVERYONE IS FAKING IT. Everyone is pretending they have more money and less credit card debt than they really do. Everyone is pretending that their relationship is perfect, that they love their job, and that their life is as flawless as it looks on social media. Everyone is pretending they have a five-year plan and understand how to properly do their taxes. But, in reality, we're all having meltdowns while stuffing our faces with French fries on the ride home from work.

We were once at a dinner party with a bunch of really stuck-up elitist women in Hollywood, and everyone was presenting their most phony picture-perfect selves. The entire conversation was essentially a veiled competition of who was the prettiest, richest, and most successful girl in the room. And right in the middle of a yawn-worthy monologue about some B-lister's next big project, one of the girls asked everyone at the table if they could make a vagina out of their armpit. Insane, right?! Not quite! By her suggesting something so ridiculous, the conversation went from shallow fluff to excruciatingly honest discussions about real-life vulnerabilities and anxieties to fear of failure, infidelity, and affairs. Finally, one girl told us she was at the lowest point of her life earlier that day when she pulled over on the side of the road sobbing due to her postpartum depression.

The moral of the story is that by breaking the ice and opening up about that one time we shit our pants on a date, hopefully it makes it easier for you to talk about your own lady stuff . . . regardless of how silly or serious it is.

So if you're already a member, it's good to see you. Thank you for making the LadyGang so incredible. We couldn't do this without you. And if you are new to us, we hope to open up the door (with our armpit vaginas) and welcome you into our LadyGang.

There's no TMI here.

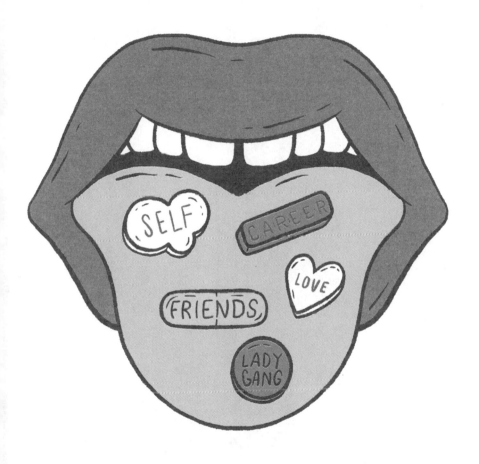

Dick Pics, Death Threats, and Dating 101

We love and celebrate every gender and sexual orientation, but since we are three straight ladies writing about our personal experiences going out with (and being ghosted by) straight men, our perspective will be from our own romantic adventures.

Dating is a terrible, confusing vortex, and we have some LadyGang rules to live by to help you get through to the other side. We are going to share our most cringeworthy and heartbreaking moments, so that you can learn a lesson or two from us. We've been fooled, stuck, lovesick, and embarrassingly obsessed so many times we've lost count, so hopefully you can try to avoid being as pathetic and bamboozled as we have been. We want you to have your happily ever after, whatever that means to you. Although we think our heartbreaks made us who we are today, these rules will help you stay confident, stay focused, and stay out of the dicksand. We know that you won't follow them. In fact, we know you are probably going to do the exact opposite of what we tell you to do. But when you're drinking your fourth glass of pinot and weeping as you watch *Love Actually* for the millionth time, don't forget that *we told you so*.

BE INDEPENDENT. That old saying "How can you love someone if you don't love yourself?" is cheesy as hell, but it's true. You need to be complete on your own before you can enter a healthy relationship. Financially, emotionally, and mentally. Every day, people fall in and out of love, people leave, and, it's dark, but . . . people die. And at the end of the day, you need to be able to be alone with yourself, so make sure you're okay with that.

DO YOUR RESEARCH. If you're meeting a dude off a dating app, get on Google, tap into your inner Nancy Drew, and find those skeletons. Unless he's in the goddamn CIA, he should have at least *some* form of social media you can stalk. Jac got catfished by a guy once who said he didn't have Instagram because he was in the FBI, but shocker . . . he was actually just married. Make sure he hasn't killed anyone or been arrested for tax evasion. Then you're good to go.

HAVE A TWO-DRINK MAXIMUM (OR MINIMUM). We polled our LadyGang, and the results were completely split on how much to drink on a first date. Some girls slam two shots of vodka in the parking lot to take the edge off, and others cut themselves off after a few cocktails to keep a clear head. So the consensus is to do whatever makes you feel the most comfortable, but be safe and share your location with a friend just in case the dude is a serial killer.

PUT YOUR WORST FOOT FORWARD. Okay, don't take this one completely literally, but just be yourself. Don't pretend to be a perfect, buttoned-up, false version of yourself. Don't rehearse the best answers you think he'll want to hear. Don't be scared to say what you think and feel. He's going to figure you out eventually, so it's better to just put your cards on the table and be authentically you from the start. The right man for you is going to love and embrace all of the qualities that may have scared other men off in the past.

RESPECT YOURSELF FROM THE GET-GO. We hate to break it to you, but the way a guy treats you on your first date is pretty much how he's going to treat you for the rest of your time together. Stand your ground and demand respect from the very beginning, and set the stage for how your relationship will grow and progress moving forward.

DON'T PUT ANYONE ON A PEDESTAL. If you're in a dry spell, feeling **dickpressed**, and finally meet someone new, it's easy to get ahead of yourself. Women in general are pretty optimistic and trusting when it comes to love and relationships, and we tend to only see the good in someone and ignore the red flags. You know how it goes: You go on a first date, he tells you a few nice things, and before you know it, you're envisioning what your future kids will look like. You're scribbling his last name on a napkin like you're in seventh goddamn grade. You're completely ignoring his **justache** and the fact that you don't really know what he does for work, because sometimes it's fun to live in the clouds. Here's a pro tip: Just look at his bare feet. It'll bring anybody back down to earth.

GETTING TO KNOW SOMEONE TAKES TIME. We're here to remind you that you barely know a guy after a first date (or five), and you have just as much of a choice to continue dating as he does! This isn't about just hoping he likes you, because the power lies in the hands of both of you equally. The sole reason why we date is to get to know someone and figure out if this person is worthy of committing to. So take your time, be rational, and remember that it takes a while to truly know someone.

KEEP YOUR OPTIONS OPEN. Sometimes we jump the gun and get so excited about a new guy that we throw our rolodicks away too early. Unless you've had the exclusivity conversation, you need to assume by default that everyone is dating and sleeping with other people. Think like a dude, and force yourself to date other people until it gets serious with the guy you're really feeling.

NEVER TEXT HIM FIRST. Keltie and Becca take this one literally and will still never text their husbands first. But this is the LadyGang way of saying, let him court you and chase you a bit. Let him prove he's interested. Call us old-fashioned, but you should never have to always be the one initiating conversation and asking to see him.

UNFOLLOW YOUR EXES. If you start dating someone new, unfollow anyone that you've dated, period. We know you want them to see you live your best life, and we know you want them to be jealous of the new guy, but posting things in the hopes that an old flame will see it is petty, messy, and unfair to the new dude. Also, how gratifying is it to slam that "unfollow" button? SEE YOU IN HELL, TRAVIS.

DON'T RUSH INTO THINGS. If there are problems in your relationship, a ring, a wedding, or children will not solve them. If anything, rushing into these huge life commitments when you're not ready will exacerbate any deep-rooted issues you may have. Instead of putting a Band-Aid on a huge gaping wound, take a long hard look at what is causing all of the distress that is making you want to anxiously jump into something you're not prepared for.

IF THEY CONSTANTLY LEAVE YOU FEELING CONFUSED, THEY'RE NOT THE ONE. You know what mixed signals are? They are disinterest mixed with boredom. If they're stringing you along, or always hot and cold, or one foot in and one foot out, they're just not that into you. We don't care if they text you all the time. We don't care if he's super sweet when you're together. If you want to be with a guy and he's avoiding commitment like the plague, he doesn't want to be with you, period. Men are black-and-white, and if they want you, you'll know.

YOU CAN'T CHANGE A MAN. And you definitely can't change how a man sees you or ultimately loves you. If he enters the relationship with the upper hand, he's probably always going to have the upper hand. You will know in the beginning how a man sees you, and that will probably be how he sees you forever.

YOU DESERVE SOMEONE GREAT! You're worthy of a big love. Don't get **dicknotized**. Only date men who look at you like you are God's gift to the world (because you are). You can tell immediately if a man is going to appreciate and admire your greatness, so stop chasing the unattainable and unavailable. You should only be with a man who makes you feel amazing about yourself *all of the time*. Your confidence and self-worth should never come from a man, but it's pretty damn incredible to constantly be assisted and lifted up by your partner. And you can tell pretty much immediately if you're dating the type of man who will treat you like a queen.

A WHITE LIE NEVER HURT ANYONE. Need to break things off with someone you're casually seeing? Tell them that you recently rekindled a flame with an ex and that "out of respect, you're going to stop seeing other people." We know honesty is usually the best policy, but this is a little loophole that you can use to avoid hurting someone's feelings while not being a total dick and just ghosting. It's pretty iconic, we know.

IF SOMEONE WANTS TO LEAVE, LET THEM. This one is pretty self-explanatory, but you should never have to beg someone to be with you, ever.

HIS NEXT GIRL ISN'T BETTER THAN YOU. And she definitely doesn't have a golden vagina. She just expects less than you did and puts up with more bullshit than you were willing to put up with. It's easy to think you had a profound impact on his heart and trained him to be a better man, but the truth is, he just dated a weaker woman after you. If a guy treated you like shit, you bet your ass he's treating his new girlfriend like shit, too. So congratulations on adding this guy to your **porkfolio**. Time to move on!

LADY THOUGHTS

Fuckboys

JV: How do you spot a fuckboy?

BT: His shoes.

JV: Oooooh ... flip-flops, the telltale sign.

KK: What he orders to drink!

BT: What does a fuckboy order?

KK: Like, a martini.

JV: Or a Jägerbomb.

KK: Or a virgin frozen mixed drink.

JV: Ew ... that's just a fucking weirdo.

It's a Bird, It's a Plane, It's SuperDouche!

Dating in Los Angeles is a bitch. There is this weird sense of entitlement for anyone who moves to LA to pursue their "career" in the entertainment industry. The city is filled with the "next big thing" from every small town in America, but in LA, you're just a stinky little turd in a massive sea of semi-talented, extremely attractive movie star wannabes. But these mediocre douchebags think they're God's gift to women, and they act like their shit don't stink. (Spoiler alert: It smells like a flat vodka Red Bull and Taco Bell Crunchwrap Supremes.) And *every guy* has Peter Pan syndrome (a.k.a. guys who are incapable of growing up into functioning adults and live in a perpetual state of college-frat-boy). Middle-aged men with receding hairlines and sciatica fill the trashiest clubs in Hollywood, trying to fuck Instagram models half their age. How sweet.

I should also mention that none of these morons gallivanting around Hollywood have real, steady, paying jobs. Oh, you're a writer / actor / model / musician / producer / influencer / living in a one-bedroom apartment with four of your friends until one of you makes it? If you're a college student, great! Go chase that dream, boy! But not so attractive when you are in your late thirties. The jig is up. But please tell me more about your groundbreaking screenplay, Hayden. Did you invest all of your savings into Bitcoin, too? Don't even get me started on how many grown-ass men say they're a "Midwestern boy chasing his big dreams in LA." You are forty-six years old, George, STOP CALLING YOURSELF A BOY.

And listen, I'm all about chasing your dreams. I have always been a creative, and I have never had a "real" nine-to-five job other than my two-week stint at Old Navy in high school (more on that later). I lived most of my twenties with no stability, a lot of financial risk, and I have always had to pay my health insurance out of pocket. I have an unconventional professional life, and I constantly juggle a dozen "jobs" at once. I think the difference is that I can tell when it's time to move on. I am perceptive

---

enough to admit when something isn't working, and I know how to pivot my goals without everything crashing and burning. I chase my dreams, but my dreams are to be a boss bitch. So when I'm on a date with forty-four-year-old Jimmy who still has three roommates and has spent his last $50 on improv classes so he can't afford drinks this time . . . there is a bit of a disconnect there, to say the least.

That being said, the number of these losers I've been ghosted by is honestly astounding. The dating app culture of today, mixed with living in a city where everyone thinks they're the next Chris Hemsworth, is an equation for the typical LA dating disaster. Dating apps promote this culture of abundance and replaceability. With the next swipe, there is always someone prettier and younger and more successful than the awesome girl you just took out. If someone is less than perfect, it takes no effort to just toss them in the trash and move on to the next. It's a peak example of our disposable culture at work, and for someone genuinely looking for a potential lifelong partner, it can get extremely frustrating and disappointing. But, lucky for you, I wasn't worn to the ground and jaded at the point when this daring tale takes place, so here we go.

In my first round of adult singledom in my mid-twenties, dating apps were this fun game. I had just gotten out of a relationship, and I wasn't looking for anything serious. I just wanted to have fun, and it was the first time I was meeting new guys outside my group of friends and going on *actual* dates. Tinder was my own cute, fucked-up version of Pokémon, but I was trying to catch all of the superhot, super-unemployed dudes. When dating apps were first released, all of my girlfriends were single, so we would have competitions of who could go out on the most ridiculous date every week. We would meet up every Taco Tuesday and, in roundtable fashion, take turns telling our entertaining yet terrifying tales of dating in Hollywood. I am a sucker for a mimbo, so I usually won these competitions. When I was just looking to smooch a hottie, a nice head of hair and big biceps really outweighed the fact that he didn't know who Neil deGrasse Tyson was.

I tried every new dating app as they were introduced. Tinder was the OG, and, surprisingly, in the beginning there were some semi-decent dudes on there. But it wasn't long before it turned into a dick-pic-sending, douchebag-filled nightmare. I've always said, send me a pic in a suit going to your professional job, and I might be impressed. Bumble is nice because girls make the first move, so it weeded out some obvious creeps, but the ones that slipped through exposed themselves pretty quickly nevertheless. The League, an app originally for Ivy League graduates that expanded to business professionals, seemed appealing, and I actually went out with a few lawyers from there. But they turned out to be just as bad as the actors. Raya is another "super exclusive" app aimed at celebrities and creatives, but in reality it was filled with a bunch of "photographers" trying to creep on young girls and "actors" whose claim to fame was being background in a local Denny's commercial once. However, there were some good celebs on there, including John Mayer, Brett Eldredge, Kevin Durant, and my ultimate dream man, Diplo. I matched with Dane Cook two days after a crazy breakup, and honestly it felt like a gift from heaven. His pictures were more photoshopped than a Kardashian's, and I had to pretend that I didn't know his entire *Harmful If Swallowed* CD by heart (OH YEAHHHHHH), so I think we talked about salt-and-vinegar potato chips instead. He used way too many emojis, so I eventually stopped responding, even though I am a sucker for a good potato chip. But my favorite celeb match was Josh Groban. Ugh, Josh, if you ever read this, I think you were the one that digitally got away.

All jokes aside, I really did put my best foot forward going into the dating scene. I'm a monogamist at heart, I would like to think I'm a good person, and at the end of the day I've always just wanted to find my for-ever dude. But here was one of my biggest problems back in the day: I drank too much on dates. Not in the way you're thinking, though. I was never getting too drunk in a dangerous way, but after a few drinks, I could literally have had incredible chemistry with a brick wall. But, in my defense, there's nothing better than getting tipsy with someone you're crushing on. The nerves and the excitement and the booze: It's the perfect recipe for frivolous fun . . . and, in my case, dating disaster. So I'd go on these mediocre dates with less than mediocre men and leave them drunk and starry-eyed, thinking I met the love of my life *every single time*. Here is my list of dudes I thought I had INCREDIBLE chemistry with:

One-Hit-Wonder Wally had a very popular song on the radio in 1998 and has done nothing of significance ever since, other than get osteoporosis. Mattress Mike was so busy with his acting career that he "never got around" to buying a bed frame, and he actually slept with his mattress on the floor, college-student style. Street-Performer Sam was . . . you guessed it, a street performer. He wrote plays that he performed in public restrooms at subway stations. For free. Messy Michael had exposed, tangled wires all over his house. His mantle decor included a plastic jar of pennies, a single used running sneaker, a signed headshot of *himself,* and a few rogue mummified McDonald's French fries. Never-Grow-Up Ned answered his door on our first date wearing a giraffe onesie and suggested we eat gummy bears for a snack. I was thinking sushi, but to each his own. Hatfish Harry was only hot with his beanie on. Poor-Sport Peter took me to the state fair and had a macho-man meltdown when I kept beating him in all the carnival games. I actually ended up winning a giant four-foot stuffed banana, and he made me carry it while he moped around five feet behind me with his bruised masculinity and fragile ego all night. Screwvenir Steve stole my Nine Inch Nails shirt after we hooked up one time. Poopy-Pants Paul shit his pants on our first date (in his defense, he had food poisoning, and I went out with him again because I felt bad for him, but he still was a bore). Can't-Get-a-Credit-Card Cody was $50,000 in debt and expected me to be his sugar mama. Flaccid-Dick Frank wouldn't stop sending me pictures of his limp penis after a failed first date. D-List Dave was quite a handsome dude in his forties and the villain on a very popular television show. He decided to snort three lines of coke, pop a molly, take five shots of tequila, and then eat an edible in the first fifteen minutes of our date. I excused myself to go to the bathroom, slipped out, and went home an hour into our date. He didn't even notice I had left until the end of the night. Highdea Hank would get stoned before our dates and blab on and on about his life-changing ketchup car-holder invention. Can't-Get-Over-His-Ex Carl ran into his ex-girlfriend on our dinner date. He proceeded to leave with her in the middle of said date and stranded me with a $200 dinner bill. These men were all memorable in their own adorable ways, but I am going to talk about the most "LA" dude I've ever dated.

One night while watching *Seinfeld* in bed and sipping on my third glass of pinot noir, I was feeling kinda frisky and needed some male attention. So I did what any other normal, mildly insecure twenty-six-year-old does: I opened up Tinder. After swiping left on around a hundred duds, an actor who played a supporting role in *She's All That*, and a loser I had hooked up with a few months prior, I finally came across this total freakin' babe. 6'5", forty-one years old, full head of luscious dark brown hair, beefy build, good style (but not TOO good, ya know? He can't be looking better than me), and the best part: he had a *Curb Your Enthusiasm* quote in his bio. He was like a younger, taller, buffer Robert Downey Jr., and he loved Larry David as much as I did. HELLO, HAVE I FINALLY SWIPED TO FIND MY SOUL MATE???

He messaged me immediately with a reference to my picture at Stagecoach (country music fan . . . check!) and we instantly started vibing. He was witty, hilarious, SUPER sarcastic and self-deprecating, didn't take himself seriously—basically everything I was looking for in a man. The banter was quick and smart, which is the biggest turn-on for me.

He didn't have anything on his profile referencing what he did for a job, so I was nervously crossing my fingers that this forty-one-year-old hottie wasn't sleeping on his friend's couch as he chased his impossible dream of being the next Jason Momoa. So, after some flirty back-and-forth, I decided to just rip the Band-Aid off and ask what he did for work. He responded immediately that he was the "voice of Acura" and did some acting on the side. All right, all right, looking good. For those of you outside of the hellhole of Hollywood, you can actually make pretty good living doing legitimate voice-over work. "The voice" of an entire car brand means national commercials. So as long as he had a job bringing in some kind of dough, I can get behind whatever weird acting passion projects he has. Also, fingers crossed for a super sexy voice.

And, boy, did the sexy voice deliver. We connected during a super busy time for both of us, so we didn't actually meet up in person for about a month after we matched. I was traveling to Vegas for a trade show, and he was down in San Diego for Comic-Con, so during this time, we texted nonstop and talked on the phone almost every night. His voice sounded how an expensive Scotch tastes: deep, rich, husky, and extremely intoxicating.

Why was he at Comic-Con, you ask? Well, apparently he was starring in a film about an aspiring washed-up actor who was down on his luck in Los Angeles (sounds familiar) and who transforms into a superhero at night. He was at Comic-Con promoting the film, and he let me know he was even doing a bit with Jimmy Kimmel to promote it. He kept me updated about his activities during the day, sending me pictures of him dressed up in his costume and everything. I know nothing about the Comic-Con world, but it all seemed pretty legit.

I will make a sidenote that, as usual, I immediately googled his name after we matched. Nothing really came up, which was strange, but I knew this was his first actual role in a major movie and they had only begun to start filming. I tried to YouTube the Jimmy Kimmel skit, but it must not have been released yet. I also looked up virtually every Acura commercial and couldn't match his voice to any of them. These were all definitely glaring red flags, but he kept making me laugh, and did I mention he was hot? So I let it slide.

He was kind of hard to get together with in general, because he was working a lot on his movie. We would make plans, and they would fall through at the last minute because he had to work all of a sudden, or he wouldn't get his schedule until the last minute, or it was always changing, or he had to be on call just in case they needed him. The excuses were endless. I didn't work in the entertainment world myself, but I was smart enough to know that filming schedules don't just "change around last minute." There are hundreds of people involved in creating a movie, so you need a schedule and call sheet approved very far in advance. Again, kinda fishy, but whatever.

After a few weeks, our schedules finally aligned, and it was time to meet in person. I was nervous because we had weeks of conversation and amazing banter built up, so my expectations for our in-person chemistry were pretty high. I invited him over to my apartment because it felt like we already knew each other, and, to be honest, I kinda just wanted to get straight to the making-out portion of the night. For some odd reason, I trusted him to NOT be a serial killer.

I put on my favorite pair of leggings that made my butt look extra perky with a cropped T-shirt (no bra, duh). Casual but cute vibes. My Le Labo candle was lit, and James Blake was spinning on my record player (pro tip: ULTIMATE sexy-time music). At 7:00 p.m. sharp, I heard a powerful knock on my front door, and I knew it was my big, husky dude. I downed the rest of my rosé (gotta have that pre-date drink to cut down on the jitters), popped in a piece of gum, and answered the door with an elegantly disheveled, "Oh, hey there, stranger."

He. Was. Beautiful. Almost a foot taller than me and with the body of motherfucking HULK, this man was what my heaven looked like. He effortlessly picked me up and gave me a massive bear hug, and I would have been happy to just be crushed to death by those massive biceps.

I offered him a glass of Johnnie Walker Black Label Scotch (because it matched the voice), and we sat down to get to know each other. It was one of those awkward, "sit on opposite sides of the couch at first and slowly start moving closer and closer toward each other as we get more comfortable" kind of nights. When I finally felt relaxed enough around him, I eventually draped my legs over his ever so coyly, and we dove straight into the hilarious sarcastic banter we had via text. He was just as sexy, masculine, and confident as I had imagined him to be. We talked about everything from our favorite characters on *Lost* (John Locke for the win), to how we both want to be great parents one day, to who would win in a Ping-Pong tournament (me).

The conversation was flowing as smoothly as the cocktails, and once I had enough liquid courage, it was finally time to dive into the confusion I had regarding his career. Being the blunt bitch that I am, I was like, "Hey, I googled you and the movie title you're working on, and nothing really came up." He responds, "Oh, yeah, well, that's just the working title for the film. It's an independent film, though, did I tell you that? My roommate is directing it, it's his first film since he quit working at Chipotle. Oh, and also I'm not getting paid for it." OH GOD, HERE WE GO. Honestly, I wasn't that surprised that this middle-aged man was working pro bono. I should have known. But then it gets worse. I asked him why his schedule was all over the place and why he never really knew his working hours. His response was, "Oh, yeah, I didn't tell you? I'm a method actor. Every afternoon, I get dressed up in my superhero costume and walk around Hollywood Boulevard. I really want to *feel* what my character feels. I want to feel him in my bones. I want to experience the life that he really had. And I'm getting kinda famous out there. I sign at least one autograph every day!" JESUS CHRIST, DUDE. He told me that he drives past Hollywood and Highland every few hours to "feel out" the crowd and decide if it's "worth his time" to get into character. If you really want to be a Hollywood Boulevard character, at least be on-brand and go as Wolverine!

And I bet you're wondering what he was doing at Comic-Con. Well, he went down there to try to crash the parties, and as for the Jimmy Kimmel skit he was boasting about? He was an extra in a crowd of two hundred for a bit on the new Avengers film. He never made the cut. And the best part: he slept in a tent in his friend's front yard while he was there!

So, my mind is spinning as he's explaining all of this to me. He sees the shock on my face and jokingly goes, "I know I kind of bamboozled you. I totally get it if you never want to see me again," and pulls me in for a kiss. I kissed him back because . . . did I mention he was hot???? My big, stupid, lying garbae.

But wait! The voice of Acura, remember? A few weeks after my fateful date with the superhero, I made a quick stop at the mall to grab a face mask from Lush. As I'm strolling through the crowds, I hear this familiar, deep, husky, sexy voice explaining the accessibility features for a new car. I turn around and there he is, dressed in a baby-blue polo shirt with the Acura logo embroidered on the left side of the chest. We make eye contact, he gives me a wink, and he continues to explain the luxury of adding a moonroof to your new car package. The "voice of Acura" sure was a stretch.

I saw him a few times after that, because I'm not *that* shallow. And then two things happened.

He sent me a dick pic. And listen, I actually appreciate a good dick pic every once in a while. And I asked for this one, so it wasn't unsolicited. But this was truly the most mind-blowing dick pic I've seen in my entire life, and it left me dicknotized for a good hour. And the size and shape had nothing to do with it. It was the crazy composition of the picture itself. I wish it wasn't illegal to include a picture of it in this book, because I truly think everyone deserves to see it at least once in their lives. But I will give you the gist of it in the most descriptive way I can. Picture this hulk of a man lying on his back on his bed, phone facing the mirror in front of him. He's wearing a white ribbed tank top, and his pecs are pushed up so high they're covering his face. His legs are spread eagle, and his massive penis is just sitting in the middle of it, looking like the goddamn Washington Monument. My eyes couldn't handle it. The photo was so aggressive and strange-looking that I can't imagine a single woman on this planet being turned on by it.

To accompany said dick pic was the following text:

> I can here my neighbors having sex next door and it makes me think of u. ;)

Really? You can HERE your neighbors having sex??? HERE????? I honestly can accept the weird dick pic. The use of "u" and the creepy winky face was bad enough . . . but the bad grammar had gone too far.

And that, my friends, was the dealbreaker. I never talked to him again after that.

Introducing
Sally Prescott

After months of wallowing in a terrible heartbreak that completely destroyed my confidence, I joined an online dating site. After all, it was impossible to get over my lost love without finding a new love. I was at a point in my life where I was constantly around the same group of people, I was traveling on tour and surrounded by mostly women, I had done enough therapy to have a clear vision of the kind of guy I wanted to meet, and "guys with real jobs" was not a group I found myself in very often. So, I set to work on setting up my dating profile. I clicked away, checking the boxes of all the qualities my dream man would have. The great thing about hiding behind a computer while doing this was that I could be completely honest. I devilishly checked off my age group (twenty-five to thirty-five), height requirement (six-foot-plus), and salary ($100,000-plus per year). I added a little about me, that I love reading, dogs, seeing concerts. Things that were turn-offs: smoking, children, nail-biting. Next, in the "what I am looking for" section, I wrote that I was looking for a nice guy, that I had been burned in the past, and that I really needed someone who was 100-percent honest.

And then I lied.

I used a fake name. Sally Prescott. I don't really know where the name came from. I figured I would be more protected from the possible lover googling if I had an alias. Being Sally, I was willing to talk to anyone who happened to introduce himself to me, I felt safe behind my profile, and I cannot believe how many men looked at my glamorous headshot and thought, "Sally Prescott seems like the lady for meeeee!"

I was essentially homeless at the time, definitely brokenhearted from my last relationship person, and totally NOT ready to fall in love. In the days before everyone single was on a dating app, there was a lot of shame around being "pathetic" enough to sign up for online dating. But, surprisingly, I wasn't the only hopeless and desperate enough romantic looking for love online at all hours of the night.

I chatted away with all types of guys. The attention was creepy and wonderful. Some requested naked photos, who I instantly blocked. Others sent me pictures of their cats, rooms, or faces. I hadn't checked off an area of the country that I wanted to find my date in, because I wanted to keep my options as open as possible. I was that pathetic. My story was semi-true. I was a professional dancer on tour, and I lived anywhere and everywhere. They lived in Texas—I love TEX-MEX! They lived in Miami—I've been there twice and I love the beach!

I connected with a photographer who seemed cool, wrote me constantly, and was an excellent (and pretty hot) distraction. Having never actually met in real life, and after spending hours looking at the two total photos he had on his profile, I was convinced this was THE guy for me. Online stranger man and Sally forever! It just so happened that as the end of the tour loomed, I made the decision that I was going to take a break from my old home in NYC and move to LA. To anyone who asked, I would say that it was because my friends had moved there, or that I wanted a change, but really online "dream man" played a larger part in the move than I care to admit. In a way, I just wanted to feel wanted, and I was willing to move to a new city for that. "You live in Los Angeles, omg! I was just planning to move to Los Angeles. Oh, and by the way, Sally isn't my real name."

Almost as soon as I moved to LA, and as soon as he had been properly introduced to my actual first name, I met long-distance online-dating lover in real life. We went on an awkward first date, where I found out he was recently divorced and very much in the same place emotionally as me (i.e., anyone to fill the space will do). We maybe had a second date, and I remember him cooking dinner for me and talking about himself and his ex-wife incessantly, and then after that, while I was driving around Los Angeles giggling with happiness, singing along to love songs on the radio for my newfound beau, he stopped talking to me. That was the end of that. I never heard from him again. Sad Sally. I was now stuck in a completely strange city with no real purpose for being there, no job, no agent, and, once again, a heavy heart. I couldn't believe that the guy I had met and talked to online for six weeks and went on two dates with after lying about my name and life's purpose didn't fall madly in love with me instantly! Can you imagine? I was out of my mind. In a way, it was a wake-up call for me. I said goodbye to my fake profile, and I never went back to dating online.

I decided to stop trying to find love as Sally, and I started working on falling in love with Keltie.

Ask a Dude

What do guys really think?

WE ASKED THE MEN IN OUR
LG COMMUNITY TO ANONYMOUSLY
ANSWER OUR MOST NSFW QUESTIONS.
HERE'S WHAT WE FOUND OUT:

DO MEN NOTICE MY CELLULITE AS MUCH AS I DO?

- Do you even have cellulite?
- Is that a type of makeup?
- Yes, and I love your booty, cellulite and all.

WHAT DOES IT FEEL LIKE TO GET A BONER?

- Squeeze your finger super hard and cut off all the circulation. It feels like that, but goooooood.
- Exciting and you just want to touch it.
- Swelling in my pants that could potentially get embarrassing if I have to get up or move around.
- Imagine your nipples getting hard, but it's a giant dick.
- Honestly pretty uncomfortable if you've got anything but sweatpants on.
- Anticipation on Christmas morning.

HOW DO YOU KNOW WHEN YOU'VE FALLEN IN LOVE WITH A WOMAN?

- When you would rather be with them than anyone else.
- When they fart in your face and you still have a twinkle in your eye for them.
- For me, it felt like a haze was lifted all around me and I could see my future clearly for the first time.
- I stop thinking about the past and think about the future.
- My heart feels stupid.
- I become less productive because I spend all my time thinking about her.

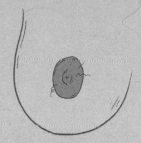

DO YOU EVER NOTICE MY NIPPLE HAIR?

- Not unless you point it out.
- Only if it's ridiculously long.
- Can't say that I have, now I will be looking, though!
- Huh?
- If I did, I wouldn't say anything.
- Yes, pluck it.

WHAT IS THE MOST COMMON THING WOMEN DO TO MAKE YOU LOSE INTEREST?

- Smoking.
- Break up with me.
- Nag.
- Being superficial.
- Attitude and bitchiness.
- Constant accusations of stuff that I didn't do.
- Lying.
- If she does not care about what I do for her.
- Not independent.
- Cry about basic things that will be fine in the end.
- Play games or act batshit crazy.
- Cheat.

ARE MEN INSECURE ABOUT THEIR PENIS SIZE?

- Hard to compare other than by asking other women. So it seems like we are always asking.
- Not me, can't speak for others.
- DEFINITELY.
- I'm sure guys with a small penis are.
- In high school, yes.
- Other men, maybe.
- Absolutely. Every guy is scared of being inadequate.
- No, every guy thinks his is huge.
- Yes, some are, which is why they lift their trucks.
- Up to a certain age, until you realize most dudes don't have a ten-inch penis and all the dudes who said they did were full of shit.

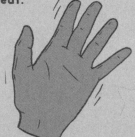

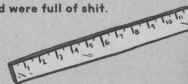

WHAT WOULD YOU THINK ABOUT A WOMAN WHO SLEPT WITH YOU ON A FIRST DATE?

- Sounds like it was a good date.
- Probably not serious about a relationship.
- I would think she's my girlfriend.
- Fine by me.
- This woman's awesome.
- I would think the same as if it was second, third, whatever.
- It depends how the rest of the date went.
- It all depends on the chemistry. You shouldn't script it. It should happen when it happens.
- That she likes me.

DO MEN NOTICE ALL OUR DOUBLE CHINS WHEN WE ARE ON TOP DURING SEX?

- That is definitely not what I'm thinking about, so no.
- Nope, too busy looking at boobs.
- Yeah, sorry . . .
- Yes, but there are better things occupying our time.
- No, there are a few things getting in the way.
- No, but I'll look out for it now!
- No! That's the last thing I'm thinking about.
- LOLOLOL wtf? Never noticed this.
- What? That's a thing?
- How could you know what you look like from underneath yourself while having sex?
- Only if there's a pearl necklace on it.

WHAT DO YOU THINK ABOUT A WOMAN MAKING MORE MONEY THAN YOU?

- Hell yeah, do it! Better for the both of us.
- Happily.
- Yes, please! More money for us both!
- Good, better Christmas presents.
- At this point I'm used to it, but obviously I'd like to make more money so I can treat my girl right.
- More power to them, honestly.
- That'd be awesome, means we've got even more money together.
- Why would I care about that?

Let's Talk About Sex, Baby

Here's the deal: have lots of sex! Hook up! Have a hoement! Don't feel bad about it!

We think it's important to *not* keep track of how many people you sleep with. Whether you are a Jac, who lost her virginity at twenty-three and was so scarred from the experience that she didn't sleep with anyone for three years after that, or your number is higher than the digits in your bank account, the number of people you have slept with is no one's business but your own. Your number does not define you in any way whatsoever. We live in a progressive society, yet the double standard that still seems to exist between men and women regarding sex is unfair, damaging, and downright degrading. Why can men brag about "boning chicks" so freely and give each other gold stars when they get a new notch on their belt, but women are shamed for our hoetivities? You should never feel shame for having a fun drunken night with a guy. You should never feel shame for sleeping with someone on the first date. You should never feel shame for exploring your sexuality. Do you know what you should feel shame for? Judging other people based on what they do behind closed doors. It's absolutely ludicrous when someone asks you how many sexual partners you've had, as if the number says anything about your character. We talk about sex pretty openly because we feel like it's important. It's important to normalize an act that almost every single person on this earth does, yet one gender feels a lot more guilt for. Maybe by sharing our ridiculous and often embarrassing stories, it will make at least one lady feel less alone. At the end of the day, humans are sexual beings, and we should be proud of that. So go forth and fuck! And remember to use a condom!

Losing My Virginity

This is the story of how I lost my virginity. I guess I'll preface this with the fact that I lost my virginity at twenty-three years old. I was the last in my friend group, and pretty much of everyone I knew, to lose it. There wasn't really any profound meaning for why I waited so long to have sex. I never had boyfriends in high school, and I think I knew deep down I wasn't emotionally or mentally ready for it as a teenager.

Looking back, I do believe that I lost my virginity at the right point in my life. I was old enough to make rational decisions, but young enough to still have a stupid experience without too much pressure. I wasn't waiting for any religious reasons, but as I was getting older, I did find myself start identifying with my virginity a little too much. I grew up in a music-filled world where any girl hanging around bands was considered a "groupie," so I would end up using my virginity as a weapon to combat that stereotype. But it did come to a point where I felt I was ready, and I needed to take the power back and make it something for me instead of using it as a defense mechanism.

When I was twenty years old, I got a message on Myspace from this super-cute redhead. He had a ridiculous scene haircut, played guitar for an up-and-coming band in my music circle, and just seemed like an all-around fun guy. We started chatting online a bit, eventually ended up meeting and hanging out, and I totally fell for his awkward charm.

I was absolutely obsessed with this guy. He was engaging and charismatic and friendly and hilarious, super outgoing but socially awkward, which I found to be the most endearing thing about him. I was completely and hopelessly lost in the dicksand. But what my naïve eyes couldn't see was that he was also young and dumb and, at the end of the day, he was not the right person for me to be giving my heart to. He pulled me in with sweet words and promises, but those promises were as empty as the bottles of whiskey we went through every night together. I thought our connection was special, and maybe it was, but I bet I wasn't the only girl who thought she had met her quirky future boyfriend.

But when this all started, I was super green and I had my love goggles on. I wanted to believe in all of the good he had to offer, which was an ongoing mistake I made a few (dozen) times after that. But I was enamored by him, I was in teenage lust, and I just wanted someone to love me back *so bad*. He gave me enough attention over a few years, and I thought he really cared about me. So, he was the one I felt comfortable losing my virginity to.

At the time, I was working on a punk-rock traveling music tour called the Warped Tour. It was the middle of July, and I was on an off day in Billings, Montana. The tour would always route our off days in the most random, small towns with literally NOTHING to do, so I'd usually spend my days perusing an empty JCPenney and having a gourmet dinner at Applebee's. This day was no different, so I found the local mall, grabbed an Auntie Anne's pretzel, bought a pair of flip-flops from PacSun, and by 2:00 p.m. I was bored off my ass, and it was time to find somewhere to get drunk.

Coincidentally, the redhead texted me just as I was heading out of the hot spot of the Billings mall, asking if I wanted to meet him and his guitar tech for drinks at Buffalo Wild Wings. I immediately said "YES, PLEASE," because I loved any excuse to drink. When I arrived at B-Dubs, there were four empty shot glasses on the table, and the guys were already well on their way to blackout land. My veins were pretty much 90 percent whiskey at this point, so my body was begging for that liquid gold. I ordered the first round of Jameson for our group (which I can't even smell anymore without gagging), along with some boneless wings and a root beer. The rest of the afternoon turned into a total blur, and by the time we left, the entire table was filled with empty beer mugs and half-eaten platters of French fries. I'm pretty sure Redhead and I got into a fight, because I vaguely remember going outside and having a five-minute drunken cry while licking buffalo sauce off my fingers.

When it was finally time to leave, Redhead invited me back to his tour bus, which was parked outside a seedy motel on the side of the road outside of Billings. I obviously said yes, so we picked up a pack of Bud Light and made our way out. We spent the night playing beer pong and shotgunning beers. As I sunk a ball in the last cup of our game, he leaned over to me and

said "Do you think we should get a room here?" and I knew exactly what that meant. Maybe it was the eight shots of mid-tier whiskey, maybe it was the romance in the Billings air, but the timing just felt *right*.

When we checked into our room, Redhead said, "We only really need the room for an hour," with a wink, and I remember the look of horror on the attendant's face. We were two totally wasted dirty punk kids, checking into a $30 motel room for *an hour*.

The motel room was . . . interesting, to say the least. It reeked of stale cigarettes, paint was peeling off the wall in real time, and there was a damp brown spot next to the bed where someone must have recently spilled a cup of coffee . . . I hope. There was one of those weird quilted blankets on the bed that literally never gets washed, complete with bodily fluid stains, and the bedside light kept flickering on and off. I am almost positive that someone had been murdered in that room at some point and the ghost was definitely judging my questionable life decisions.

So first thing's first: your girl's gotta shower. Layers of dirt, sweat, and chicken-wing grease were built up all over my body, and the last thing that filthy room needed was anymore grime. After I washed the drunken day off of me, I stepped out of the shower, soaking wet and in my most vulnerable state, and looked over at him waiting on the bed, fully naked. Oh shit, here we go. I nervously sat on the edge of the mattress in my towel, not really knowing what to do with my hands, or my mind, or anything, really. Do I do a sexy hair flip? A strip tease? Give him a BJ? Even though I had a copious amount of liquid courage, I had zero idea of what comes next. He took the lead and placed a comforting hand on my thigh, pulled me in for a kiss, yada yada yada, ninety seconds later it was over. He immediately jumped out of bed, muttered something under his breath, and bolted out of the room. THAT WAS IT????? I waited twenty-three years for a pump and dump?? The whole thing felt like a fast-forward blur, and I was left there confused, distraught, and physically and emotionally naked. I curled into a ball in the corner of the room and cried for a good hour. Looking back on it, I'm most concerned with my bare butthole coming into contact with the damp brown spot on the carpet. But when I finally pulled myself together, I snuck out the back entrance and called a taxi without him seeing me.

I saw him the next day, and he acted like nothing had happened! Any time I'd try to bring it up, he pretended like he didn't know what I was talking about. Did I have an insane lucid dream? Was there a glitch in the Matrix? I literally had to check my texts and bank statements from the night before to make sure I wasn't making the whole thing up. And, I mean listen, I would also love to Eternal Sunshine that night out of my memory. But the aftermath was an absolute mindfuck, to say the least.

This particular summer on the road, I found myself in a very messy love hexagon. I was obsessed with the redhead, but I was also having a summer fling with a lead singer who had a girlfriend, and I was toeing the emotional line with my bestie, who ALSO had a girlfriend. I'd vent to my bestie about Redhead, and he would get *furious* trying to protect me without overstepping his boundaries. I'd have sleepovers on the lead singer's bus, and the redhead would send me texts threatening to kick his ass. It was a total disaster, but it was never boring. Because there was so much happening on the road that summer, the whole situation didn't seem to affect me much. But looking back, I was totally turned off by sex for *years* after that, so I think the whole situation just gave physical intimacy a really weird connotation for me for a while.

I was the "manic pixie dream girl" a lot in my youth. Most of it was my fault, because I was always chasing emotionally unavailable musicians or guys with girlfriends. I was the exciting, carefree "vacation girlfriend" who would make every dude I was involved with question everything he had with his current (seemingly boring) partner. I don't really know why I kept putting myself in those situations, because all they did was hurt me in the end. Maybe it was the chase, and wanting what I didn't have. Or maybe I knew subconsciously I wasn't ready for an actual relationship. Or maybe I was just masochistic (realistically, it's probably that one). Regardless of what it was, I have paid the price of my bad karma for a good decade of dating absolute douchebags after that!

In conclusion, I bet you never thought you'd hear about Buffalo Wild Wings and sex in the same story. And for that, you are welcome.

Bedroom Baptism

In my thirty-three years of life, I've dated many different kinds of men. I've never been the girl who had a "type." I always knew that I needed to go full on Baskin-Robbins while I was still young, because one day I would be having the same flavor EVERY. SINGLE. DAY for the rest of my life, and I wasn't planning on hitting my grave having only tried vanilla. This girl needed thirty-two flavors and then some!

Even when I was in middle school, I would bounce around from Peter, the towheaded–skateboarding–class clown to Blake, the star athlete. The world was my fashion pop-up and this totally sane pattern continued throughout my twenties. I once dated a forty-year-old nightclub owner because I wanted to see what it would be like to have daddy issues. (Turns out, you actually have to have daddy issues to be able to fuck a forty-year-old when you're twenty.) I dated musicians, actors, investment bankers, potheads, athletes, and basically any of my friends' hot roommates. I really loved how I could date a guy and be able to temporarily step into a new life. I took on their hobbies, their friends, their kinks, you name it. What can I say? I'm an actress and needed the research. I also think it's bullshit when girls are shamed for this behavior or accused of not having their own identity. (*In my opinion.*) So, sorry for your boring life, Stacey, I guess you should have asked for more samples.

The other very important reason for dating these different types was to audition different bedroom styles. How was I supposed to know what I liked if I didn't try them all?! My mom famously asked my sister and me one day, "Why would you buy a car before test-driving it?" Very valid point, Mom. Thank you for your indirect permission to be a skank.

Now, before I dive into my most memorable sexual experience (you're welcome), I'm going to throw out a little disclaimer here, in case there are impressionable young ladies reading this. First of all, why are you even here? And second, while I am a big advocate for "test-driving" men, please don't be a dumbass, and always wear your, ahem, driving gloves. Men are disgusting animals crawling with diseases, and the universe thought it would be nice to give them zero symptoms for most of these diseases and infections, while women's vaginas practically fall off the moment they come in contact with any of them. Not to mention that sex feels the fucking same for us whether there's rubber involved or not, so don't live dangerously, just use the fucking condom. And when the asshole complains that it doesn't feel the same for him, you tell him that you don't give one single fuck, point to the door and tell him to remember the sound it makes when its shuts behind him. (This also feels like the perfect opportunity to tell all you ladies to stop calling your friends in tears when you find out you have HPV. News flash: EVERYONE HAS HPV!!!!! Just stay up-to-date on those annual paps, and everyone should be okay . . . I think.)

With that being said, it's time to lube up your gears, check your engines, and get ready to rotate your tires, because this is the story of my most memorable "test drive."

The year was 2008. I was a twenty-two-year-old professional dancer in my motherfuckin' prime . . . no cellulite, the perkiest ass this side of the Mississippi, and the skin of an infant. My only maintenance included highlights every six weeks to brighten my naturally dishwater-brown hair and the occasional $20 manicure. (I was so naïve about the small fortune I would eventually have to spend on the upkeep of my appearance once I hit thirty, but I digress.) Things were good, and I knew it was never going to get better than being single and twenty-two in New York City. (Spoiler alert: In many ways, I was right.)

So I was sitting in a Midtown bistro with my friends, drinking mimosa after mimosa (because sugar wasn't the enemy yet), when a gorgeous guy breezed through the front door of the restaurant with movie-star looks, wearing a peacoat. To a girl in her twenties, a man in a peacoat represents adulthood and a guy who "has his shit together." It was a stark contrast to the broke-ass North Face–fleece-wearing man-children I had been dating. My vagina instantly quivered.

Over the next hour, my girlfriends and I acted like rabid, feral beasts. (For any *Real Housewives* fans, imagine Ramona Singer after six pinot grigios whenever a man with a pulse enters a bar.) We laughed a little too loud, we shouted across the restaurant, and we essentially heckled this handsome man until he relented and came over to our table.

His name was Steve. He was a twenty-eight-year-old actor visiting from Los Angeles. *How exotic,* I thought as I bit my lower lip. My inner monologue went something like this: *With that jawline and those bright blue eyes, he must be the next Brad Pitt. How lucky am i to have met him before his big break?!* (This was before I ever lived in Los Angeles or worked in Hollywood and realized that everyone in the whole fucking city looks like this.)

We proceeded to chat Steve up, and I became even more enchanted with him over the next hour or so. I'm not sure if it was his extreme arrogance or the way he used tactics that he must have learned from the infamous dating book *The Game.* In the book, the author essentially teaches men to give women backhanded compliments to break down their self-esteem *just* enough so that they eventually believe you're the only one who could possibly love them . . . which means they will never leave you. Before you get angry and start hating men even more for this piece of literature and go full Bobbitt, I'll point out that nowhere in the book does the author state that this technique is reserved for only men to use. I personally adopted this tactic years later, and that's basically how I bagged my husband. It works like a charm.

So, as Steve was sociopathically mocking my career as a dancer while complimenting my legs at the same time, I was slowly falling more and more in love. (And it's important to note that he hit on every girl at that table separately, but I was desperado and the one who took the bait.) He asked if I had plans to go out that night, and like any thirsty and horny girl in her twenties, I eagerly exclaimed, "Yes!" LIES! ALL LIES. I had no plans, but I wasn't going to let Steve know that. (Sidebar: It needs to be said that while I want to blame my extreme youth for this eagerness, that would also be a big fat lie. Up until I met my husband at almost thirty years old, I would have dropped every plan I had on a dime and coordinated an elaborate twenty-thousand-dollar party just on the off chance that my crush would meet up with me. Stop judging me. I never claimed to be a hero.)

So . . . yeah, we were going out! I rallied all my girlfriends to go out that night in the hopes that I could have a sexy New York City sidewalk make-out session with a strapping actor-stranger named Steve. By the way, women should receive participation trophies for putting on full clown makeup and straightening their hair to go out *just* to support another woman's dream of possibly dry humping some dude later to the sweet sounds of Nickelback.

That night, I put on an outfit more suited for a seventy-five-degree spring evening and not the current twenty-six-degree tundra, but I refused to blow it with Steve. This was before I learned the art of sexy subtlety when it came to dressing myself, but then again, who really cares when you're 105 pounds of lean muscle? I miss 2008.

Much to my delight, Steve showed up before midnight. (Sadly, this is a victory when you're a thirsty idiot who is used to waiting until 3:00 a.m. to finally bump into your crush.) And by "bump" into him, I mean texting every one of the friends you have in common, fishing for his location, or eventually drinking enough to simply text him for a booty call.

So I was pleasantly tipsy when Steve showed up, but PLOT TWIST: He told me he was sober, a recovering alcoholic. No disrespect, but today, that information would have sent me straight for the hills. At that time, I heard "possibly damaged," and I was practically salivating. How exotic, how exciting, how dramatic . . . an addict!

The stars aligned that night, and it ended with a steamy make-out session on the uber-romantic Ninth Avenue in Hell's Kitchen. I refused to take it any further, because I wanted to fool him into thinking I was a lady. (And also because at that point in my life, I had only had sex with three-ish people. I still believed that "my number" mattered, and I wanted to make absolutely sure this handsome, sober, devil stranger was worth the notch on the ol' belt.)

Over the course of a couple months, we went from talking on the phone to me buying a ticket to fly out to LA to see him. (Although he still doesn't know that's why I made the trip.) I told him I was coming out to visit my friend who was working out there. Lies. Important life lesson being taught here: never let a man know when you're making an effort to see him. Eagerness can often be a boner killer. I still lie to my husband and say I was already in the neighborhood if I meet him at his office for lunch. Never stop playing games. It's the key to a happy, sane adjacent relationship.

My first night in LA was dog farts. He showed up to my hotel room in a onesie . . . yes, a fucking onesie, like a child. Where was my inner ref to throw out the first red flag? Oh, I know, she was still off getting her butt-hole waxed in preparation for fucking a goddamn dreamboat! Anyway, this onesie ensemble was a stark contrast to the sophisticated peacoat. I was so confused. I was thinking, *Who the fuck is this guy? Does he even like me? Does he not? He's clearly not trying to impress me. Is this the friend zone? Is this real life?* It tortured me. It made me want to jump his sober bone even more.

We proceeded to have, from what I remember, pretty normal sex. Missionary, maybe a little oral, with the grand finale being a sensible doggy-style. (I miss the days of doing doggy-style and being so confident that even my butthole felt sexy and attractive to stare at. Now it looks like an abandoned haunted mine.)

I moved from the hotel to his apartment on the second night because I had already proven that I was a strong independent woman by booking and paying for my own hotel room for one whole night. However, I don't know what was worse, my shithole hotel room in Hollywood or his apartment. His apartment was exactly what you would expect of a twenty-eight-year-old bachelor in LA who's an actor (and by "actor," I mean, like, did one independent Western movie about snakes in a bar). It was a courtyard-type apartment building with a pool in the middle of it all. Just dirty water and dead leaves floating around, with even dirtier kids swimming in it. He had a two-bedroom, and his roommate was an amateur or aspiring bodybuilder. I can't remember which one, but both were roided and sad. The bathroom inside the apartment had that familiar chalky bachelor film all over it. It was bleak. But again, it didn't stop me. I wasn't going to let a cloudy shower door stand in the way of my weekend of sex with a solid ten.

The first couple of times we had sex that weekend were relatively normal. On the last night of my weekend, he was going down on me while I sat on a garage-sale desk in the corner of his bedroom when he offered me a cigarette . . . mid cunnilingus. He said something along the lines of, "It turns me on to watch you indulge while indulging me." This guy was good. It was the first time someone had really talked dirty to me, and I was suddenly a porn star with more confidence than Jenna Jameson. I was hooked. This was my sexual awakening, and I was READY.

That progressed into him taking photos of me during sex (which, praise the lord above, did not live on in my Cloud), then to lots and lots of costumes he would buy for me to wear. One of the most memorable ones was a white thigh-high tight and a white platform stripper shoe. Think "Leg Avenue Naughty Angel" Halloween costume. (Let's be honest, "Naughty Virgin" was probably more what he was aiming for because men are twisted.) Interesting choice, but I didn't care, I was a sexual beast. I would have worn a Time's Square SpongeBob costume if it meant steamy sex. We had sex EVERYWHERE: in the car, on a lookout on Mulholland, in a friend's backyard—you name it, we did it. The sex was constant and probably should have been an indicator that his addiction wasn't reserved for just substances. But guess what? My vagina was his kryptonite, and I was down for that. Our long-distance fuckfest continued, and I was blossoming into a full-blown sex expert.

How did I ever walk away from that, you ask? Let me explain. Steve was a full-blown (very proud) SEX ADDICT!!

More specifically, though, my "aha moment" came six months later. (No pun intended.) I was tied to his four-poster bed. (Yes, another red flag. Who has a four-poster bed in a six-hundred-square-foot apartment?? Not his first rodeo.) I was wearing a white ruffled thong with nothing else, and he was pouring red wine all over my naked body. It was like a scene out of a porn called *The Sexcorcist*. This was the closest I had ever been to being baptized, and suddenly the spirit moved me. In that moment, I also realized that I couldn't possibly keep up with the charade. I knew that I was probably days away from having to strap on a dildo or learn how to shoot ping-pong balls out of my vagina, and that just wasn't my journey. So I threw on my clothes and took my sticky ass to the airport.

It fully ended when he tried moving to New York for me, and I had the flashback from my baptism and gave him a firm no. I knew I didn't have the stamina to keep this up full-time. And I'm not even Catholic! I had things to do, goals to achieve. I had to stop starring in the filthy red room so I could start starring on Broadway, and our sex schedule was far too grueling for me to do both. And, if I'm being completely honest, I mostly said no because I had just met another guy in a strip club in New Orleans who seemed pretty promising. You heard me.

So there you have it. I had a magical, twisted tryst with a sex addict, and it was (mostly) glorious. My thoughts and prayers to the girls chained to his bed as we speak.

He was never going to be my forever person, but he taught me my own boundaries in the bedroom and (shout-out to Zach) I ultimately ended up with the perfect flavor for me . . . something between vanilla and Christ's blood.

LADY THOUGHTS

Sexpectations

JV: How much sex is enough sex when you're in a relationship?

KK: I think that you have to have a conversation with your person what their expectations are. I remember one time I had a boyfriend, and I was like, how many times a week do you want to have sex? He was like "every day," and I was like, it's never gonna work out, because I'm not a sex-every-day kind of person.

BT: Who has time for that?

If You Don't Fuck Your Partner . . . Someone Else Will

KK: I would say, if you go six weeks without sex or trying to have sex, start looking at his phone.

BT: Agreed. And if he's not complaining about it, be concerned.

JV: Or if they stop trying.

Fuck Buddies

KK: Should you have a fuck buddy?

JV: Yes, in between relationships a good fuck buddy is great.

BT: A good fuck buddy is hard to find, though.

JV: It's hard to find a fuck buddy because somebody always catches feelings. That was my problem. I could never have a fuck buddy because I'm an emotional person, and I always connect the two. I could never separate sex and feelings, but if you can, godspeed. I just don't want a fuck buddy who spends the night. Once we're done, they gotta leave.

Sex Tapes and Sexting

BT: Never ever ever ever ever make a sex tape.

JV: People will always use a sex tape as blackmail. Also, you don't want to always live in fear, thinking it's going to be leaked one day.

BT: That's the thing. Sometimes you're in the moment, and it's hot. Weird, gross things are hot. But it's like having a drunken night and having to watch it back the next day sober.

JV: And it's never flattering. It has to be light enough to see, which means it's too light.

BT: Which means I can see my butthole, and I don't want to.

One-Day Stand

My one-night stand was at 2:00 in the afternoon. Yup, you heard that right . . . I had a sexual tryst with a complete stranger in broad daylight and never talked to him again. And I was sober. SOBER!

It all started when I was watching a short-lived sitcom on TV about a group of single strangers who meet in a bar and how fate directs their destiny in a single night. How original! The show itself was subpar at best, and I think I mildly chuckled twice . . . thrice if I'm being generous. I was about to change the channel to *Arrested Development* when a burly redhead caught my eye.

I'm sure you can pick up on the fact by now that I have a very interesting attraction to redheads. I've been thinking long and hard about where this could possibly stem from, and I believe the inception of my redhead love goes back to Ron Weasley. There was something about his chubby cheeks, insanely pale freckled skin that would sizzle when exposed to five minutes of sunlight, and gorgeous sunburst locks parted ever so elegantly down the middle that really did it for me. And somehow, some way, that teenage crush really transferred its way into adulthood.

So, I saw this dude on the screen. He was rugged, a little out of shape but in a cute way, with bright fucking red hair. Like, I don't know if they did some weird color correction on the screen or if my TV was just malfunctioning, but his hair looked like a goddamn highlighter. I watched for a few more minutes, and he was the only one on the show who was even remotely funny, and he just seemed to have this *vibe*. And by "vibe," I mean he was probably a total douchebag, so HELLO THERE, COME TO MAMA! So I did what any normal millennial girl does when she sees a hot dude on her TV screen: I googled him immediately. This obviously led me straight to his Twitter and Instagram, which I stalked extensively to see if he had a girlfriend or not. After scrolling all the way back through some embarrassing audition clips and disgusting Vegas pool parties, all the way to his vacation to Barcelona in 2012, by deductive reasoning I decided that he was, in fact, single. SCORE.

So then I did what most millennial girls are too embarrassed to do . . . I slid into his DMs. And I'd like to make a note here: I was sliding into DMs before sliding into DMs was a thing. Back in my day, I called it "the Twitter Con," because Instagram and DMs hadn't even been invented yet, so for me it was just this fun game I'd play to date random D-list actors I would see on shitty TV shows. And for someone who had waxed off three-quarters of her eyebrows that never grew back, I was pretty damn confident when it came to digitally hitting on guys. I had literally zero shame, which you will understand in one second, when I tell you what the DM said:

> If you were president, you would be Baberham Lincoln.

Yeah, you're welcome. Keep that one in your back pocket, because *it worked*. He wrote back immediately, and after a few flirty messages, we moved our love affair to texting. I made sure to ask my preliminary questions: are you single, how tall are you, have you ever murdered someone, etc. He seemed to check out as a non-psychopath, but he was sort of boring, seemed kind of stupid, and constantly made grammatical errors. My twenty-six-year-old self was a professional at ignoring red flags, so I continued the flirtation because . . . why not? After a few weeks of late-night, slightly tipsy back-and-forth, we finally built up enough tension to bring this digital flirting into the real world.

It started one night when we were both in our respective households and the texting chemistry was off the charts. We were both semi-realistically considering peeling ourselves off the couch to meet for a nightcap, but I zonked before we could come up with a concrete plan. I never go out after the sun goes down, so good luck convincing me to put makeup on and leave the house at night. The vibe continued into the next morning, and he was leaving for work later that night for a few weeks, so I knew if I didn't want the chemistry to fizzle, I had to ACT NOW. That day happened to be a day I was on an insane deadline for work but also working from home. He kept tempting me with different situations where he could come over and "distract me from work," and I finally caved and said he could come over for forty-five minutes. Not a minute longer! I literally set a timer.

He told me to "leave the door unlocked and be waiting in bed naked." Ha, yeah right, buddy. I lived in Hollywood, and my neighbor's apartment got broken into literally yesterday. But after a few minutes of serious contemplation . . . I left the door unlocked and waited for him in bed naked. Because I'm a sucker.

I was restricted on time, so my hair was still wet, and I hadn't had time to put a stitch of makeup on by the time he got to my place. Again, I only had a quarter of my eyebrows, so this was especially frightening. He stayed at my apartment for a total of thirty-four minutes, which gave me eleven minutes of free time after. I'll spare you the details because they were so unmemorable that I couldn't recall them if you paid me. But I guess just picture what sober run-of-the-mill missionary sex with a stranger in broad daylight would be. I give it a good five out of ten, and honestly, I could have really used that half hour to get some more work done, but you know . . . had to do it for the story.

I started dating a new guy shortly after my less-than-enthralling one-day stand. The new guy was pretty rad and actually put some effort into planning some really fun unconventional dates. For our first date, he took me to an L. Ron Hubbard play. We got kicked out for smuggling in Jameson, and he still gets harassed by Scientologists to this day. For our second date, he took me to a comedy show. I didn't know who was performing, but I was obviously down because I love me some stand-up. I am almost legally blind and I forgot my glasses, so we got to the venue early to get a seat in the first few rows so I could actually see what was going on. After a few pre-show whiskeys on the rocks, I was ready to chuckle. The first act came on, cracked some jokes about traffic in LA, and on to the next. Then, to my utter surprise, who came strolling out on stage, an arm's length away from me? MR. ONE-DAY STAND HIMSELF. I immediately sunk in my seat, tried to cover my face with my hair, and downed the rest of my drink before he saw me. Well, that didn't work, because he noticed me within thirty seconds.

He obviously noticed that I was on a date, so he took it upon himself to make me super uncomfortable the entire show. At first he kept trying to wink at me, but he couldn't really wink that well, so it just looked like he had an eye twitch. After a few failed winks, he stepped his game up. Anytime he would talk about something sexual, he would come over to our side of the stage and lock eyes with me the entire joke. Like, so intensely, to the point where he wouldn't even blink the entire time. So he went from blinking TOO much to not blinking at all. One time he even licked his lips ever so slowly *while* staring into the depths of my embarrassed soul. My date was oblivious to the intent behind the embarrassment and just assumed he chose us as the couple to heckle the entire time.

The show ended, and I immediately bolted from the venue, because if he was savage enough to point me out in front of an entire crowd, he obviously would embarrass me if we ran into each other in public.

I never heard from him again, until one day, a few months after our fateful encounter, when I received this random text:

> Remember when I came over in the middle of the day and we boned? Lol

So what did I learn from my one-day stand experience? Never sit in the front row of a comedy show, don't trust a dude who says "lol," and sex with a stranger is always better with alcohol.

If You're Happy and You Know It, Thank Your Ex

We know, there is *literally* nothing worse than a broken heart. We laser our buttholes, birth children, and stomp through life in four-inch stilettos, but a breakup instantly trumps any other pain we will ever experience. Why can coconut oil heal our yeast infections, split ends, and sunburns, but it does nothing for our shattered hearts? That's because there is nothing you can do but bide your time until a week, a year, or a decade later, the ghost of relationships past magically lifts its dark curtain of love. Time is the coconut oil of life, which is annoying because it works so fucking slow sometimes. Your ex will eventually feel so yesterbae, but until then, the only thing you can do is look back and be grateful for the lessons you will ultimately learn from your crumbled relationship. You are going to feel lonely and sad and mad and pathetic, and you'll read poetry and cry at red lights when Adele comes on the radio, but that's just the way life is. Learn how to be okay on your own. Embrace the silence. Find out who you really are when everything else fades away. *That* is the most important thing you can ever do for your heart.

To pass the time until your heart feels better, we think that you could benefit from a sexorcism. (Don't tell your mom we gave you this advice!) Having physical intimacy with a stranger kind of slaps you in the face and rips the Band-Aid off. And make no mistake, you won't feel any better. But in some weird, ass-backward kind of way, it'll be an integral part of the healing process. And, at the very least, creating a new booty call keeps you from getting drunk and calling the ex. If you're not up for sex with a new person, get on a dating app and swipe your little heart out. Just having attention from a potential mate is exciting, even if you don't plan on acting on it. Sometimes you get so hyper focused on the specific way your partner treats you in a relationship and you've normalized shitty behavior for so long that exposing yourself to someone new and different opens your eyes to new possibilities. Dating a new person, even if they're a shithead, too, puts a Band-Aid on loneliness until time heals the little cracks in your heart.

Here's a life tip: Make a list of the qualities that you want in your next partner. Let's get woo-woo for a second and really garner the law of attraction. You get what you put out into the universe, so stop spending all

MAN MANIFEST LIST

THIS IS JAC'S ACTUAL MAN MANIFEST LIST. HONESTLY, THESE ARE QUALITIES ANY DECENT HUMAN SHOULD HAVE, BUT IT'S SHOCKING HOW HARD IT IS TO FIND A NON-DOUCHEBAG OUT THERE.

HE IS:

⬇ (FILL IN YOUR ANSWERS HERE) ⬇

TRUSTWORTHY

RELIABLE

EMPATHETIC

HIS ACTIONS ARE:

CONSISTENT

RESPECTFUL

THOUGHTFUL

HE MAKES ME FEEL:

ADORED

CALM

STABLE

HE ALWAYS:

IS CAREFUL WITH MY HEART

MAKES ME FEEL IMPORTANT

IS ON MY TEAM

HE NEVER:

LIES TO ME

MAKES ME WORRY

DISRESPECTS ME

of your energy wallowing in your breakup. It's time to put some positive vibes out there and dream up your next guy. What is he gonna be like? How is he gonna treat you?

Jac did this after her last breakup and came to the harsh realization that her ex possessed zero of the caring qualities she was looking for in a partner. Use her actual manifest list as a guide, and add your own personality traits at the end!

Remember, your last relationship is only a failure if you didn't grow as a person from the experience, so don't continue to make the same mistakes over and over again as you move on to the next guy. Think of your breakup as a blank slate. You get to start over, be extremely picky, and finally find the right guy for you with nothing holding you back. How dope is that?! This manifest list is your bible now, so always refer back to it when you date new people. Keep your head in the game when you start your new vajourney, and don't get distracted by sparkly things. Remember the qualities that matter: reliability, empathy, kindness, and stability. Qualities that don't matter: looks, height, charisma, and net worth (But who are we kidding? A high one *is* a bonus.) We don't care if a dude is the most charming guy in the world. You know who else was charming and handsome? Ted Bundy. Don't let your breakup be in vain and just keep dating douchebags. Elevate!

Ah yes, the age-old question: Can you stay friends with an ex? Fuck no. You have enough friends. You don't need any more. Especially not a friend who carelessly threw your heart in a blender. Post breakup, ask all your real friends to refrain from telling you any info about your ex. What they're doing, who they're dating, and what they're posting is irrelevant to you now. Don't post things hoping they'll see them. It's embarrassing, and everyone can see through it . . . especially them. In fact, it's time to block them so you don't obsess over them seeing your stuff. No matter how crushed you are, you just have to Joey Fatone your relationship and say "Bye, Bye, Bye."

Speaking of friends: Try to remember that we've all been that girl going through a breakup. As much as you feel *so alone* wallowing in your sadness, we actually *do* know what you're going through. And because of that, we will listen to you talk incessantly about your ex like a broken record. But there is an expiration date.

Yes, there is an acceptable frequency with which you can mumble on and on about the same shitty dude, and we took it upon ourselves to quantify that for you. For every month that you were dating, you get **one convo** to complain at brunch that lasts no more than twenty minutes. We really want to gossip about *The Bachelor* after you're done, so please don't ruin our bottomless mimosas by dragging it on any longer. If you were engaged, you get a bonus two months of endless heartspeak, and if you were married, you get an additional six months. If you have kids involved and there's a custody battle, then once a month you're allowed to ugly-cry on our shoulders for the rest of your life.

But here's the thing: If we're telling you the same advice over and over again and you're not changing what you're doing, you are officially an askhole, and it's time to figure your shit out on your own. Or it's time to seek the professional help of a therapist. If you're not being proactive in your healing process and consciously making good decisions to better yourself, we have nothing to offer you anymore. There is literally nothing more annoying than trying to be a good, understanding friend to someone who throws our thoughtful advice into an endless abyss.

SHOULD YOU DATE HIM?

BECCA

Bounce-House Breakup

I brag a lot on the podcast about how I've never been dumped. Well, confession: That is a dirty, filthy lie, and I'm here to come clean. Yes, I have, in fact, been dumped. His name is Sean McVay. Sean FUCKING McVay: the current head coach of the Los Angeles Rams football team, the youngest head coach in NFL history, and the man currently coaching MY local football team. But I'm fine, he's fine, EVERYONE IS FIIINE! His face is literally everywhere in Los Angeles, mocking me and reminding me of all my shortcomings and failures. However, I've decided to take it as a cue from the universe that it's time for me to stop running from my past and finally speak my truth.

Our steamy love affair started (and ended) in the fifth grade. He and I lived in the same suburban Atlanta subdivision, a relationship of convenience, if you will. Sean was a towhead with a perfectly round bowl cut, bright white arm hair, and tan calves. I was a calf girl back then. Isn't every ten-year-old? He was one of the school's best athletes and wore athletic shorts to school every day. PANTY. DROPPER. He was my perfect tweenage dream.

The way I bagged Sean isn't dissimilar from how I've always nabbed my men. On a hot summer day, I would go for a casual jog through our neighborhood. Yes, I was a ten-year-old girl who still hadn't gotten her period yet, and I was fucking *jogging* through the neighborhood like a thirty-seven-year-old suburban housewife determined to get her prebaby body back. Anyway, I would go on these Lolita jaunts so I could run past Sean's house six or seven times until he noticed me. I would wear only a sports bra and Soffe shorts, rolling the waistband at least six times to barely cover my birth canal. (Shit, this makes me think that I need to stop judging young girls for wearing janties—a cross between jeans and panties, for those of you adorably out of the loop).

Sean and I had a blissful first couple weeks as the power couple of Sope Creek Elementary School. I was loathed by most of the other girls in my grade, as I should've been, and it felt terrific. I'm pretty sure no physical contact was made during that time, and I doubt we even communicated on anything other than AOL Instant Messenger, but we were in love. Or so I thought . . .

One weekend, Sean invited some friends over to take advantage of the bounce house in his backyard that had been ordered for his younger brother's birthday party earlier that day. *Amazing*, I thought, *a bounce house is the absolute ideal location for my very first kiss.* (You can take the girl out of Georgia . . . amiright?) So, with my confidence sky-high, I threw on my brand new pair of white, skin-tight bell-bottoms. Let me remind you that it was summertime in Georgia—temps in the high nineties and humidity off the charts. Most girls were running around in jean shorts from Old Navy, but not me. I've always been a fashionista willing to sacrifice comfort and crotch rot in the name of style. I also knew that my ass looked great, and I couldn't wait to prance around in front of Sean in my sexy new Lycra/polyblend pants. It's disturbing that at that age, I already knew what white pants did to a man. It's also disturbing that, unlike other girls my age on the heels of puberty, no one had to tell me things like "Enjoy your body now, because it only gets worse." I got the memo. I lived the memo. I was the memo.

So I marched down the street with my supportive girlfriends/personal cheerleaders (who referred to Sean and me as Barbie and Ken), ready to receive my very first smooch.

I strutted over to the bounce house like a proud peacock, but before Sean could even catch a glimpse of my tight derriere, his friend Blake popped his head out of the bounce house and said, "Becca. Sean doesn't want to go out with you anymore." BOOM. Life-ruiner. It was over, and suddenly I hated Sean (and my stupid white bell-bottoms) more than life itself. With my tail between my (very sweaty) legs, I made the trek back to my house and spent the rest of the evening sobbing over the death of Barbie and Ken. The Dreamhouse/bounce house fantasy was officially crushed.

And you know what? The worst part is that Sean never even showed his fucking face. He just kept bouncing around that fucking trashy bounce house, letting his smug-ass henchman Blake do his dirty work. He was

THE DOS & DON'TS OF HEART BREAK

DO: INVEST IN A GOOD VIBRATOR. GIVE YOURSELF SOME ORGASMS. LET YOUR PHYSICAL SELF FEEL GOOD EVEN IF YOUR EMOTIONAL SELF DOESN'T.

DON'T: TOUCH YOUR HAIR. WAIT AT LEAST A MONTH AFTER YOUR BREAKUP BEFORE MAKING ANY DRASTIC CHANGES TO YOUR PRETTY MANE.

DO: WAKE UP EARLY AND GO FOR A WALK WITH YOUR COFFEE. STARTING YOUR DAY WITH FRESH AIR WILL MAKE ALL THE DIFFERENCE.

DO: GO SEE A THERAPIST. IT'S FINE TO VENT TO YOUR FRIENDS EVERY ONCE IN A WHILE, BUT NO ONE WANTS EVERY CONVERSATION TO REVOLVE AROUND YOUR SHITTY EX.

DON'T: EXPECT CLOSURE. IT DOESN'T HAPPEN LIKE IT DOES IN THE MOVIES. MOST OF THE TIME YOU'RE LEFT LIKE ?!?!?!?? AND YOU JUST HAVE TO ACCEPT THAT AND MOVE ON. PUT ON THE SADDEST PLAYLIST YOU CAN AND FEEL REALLY FUCKING SORRY FOR YOURSELF FOR 24 HOURS.

DO: ONLY LISTEN TO MUSIC THAT MAKES YOU FEEL HAPPY AND EMPOWERED. DON'T LET A SAPPY LOVE SONG SNEAK INTO YOUR BOSS BITCH PLAYLIST.

DO: UNFOLLOW THEM ON SOCIAL MEDIA. DO NOT LURK. THEY ARE DEAD TO YOU NOW.

DON'T: DWELL ON THE "WHAT IFS" AND TRY TO RATIONALIZE CHAOS. SOME THINGS JUST DON'T MAKE SENSE, AND THAT'S OKAY.

DO: BURN HIS SHIT. ALL OF IT. ROAST A MARSHMALLOW ON THE FIRE LIT BY THAT HALF-ASSED CARD HE GOT YOU FOR VALENTINE'S DAY.

DO: FIND A LARGE BODY OF WATER. THE OCEAN, A RIVER, A LAKE. PUT YOUR FEET IN IT AND CONNECT WITH NATURE.

DO: TRAVEL TO A NEW COUNTRY, A NEW CITY, OR A NEW NEIGHBORHOOD. NOTHING WILL MAKE YOU FEEL BETTER THAN A NEW EXPERIENCE.

DO: GET NEW BEDDING. YOU DON'T WANT HIS SHITTY PHEROMONES HAUNTING YOU WHILE YOU GET YOUR BEAUTY SLEEP.

DO: REARRANGE YOUR ROOM. ANY WAY TO DISTANCE YOURSELF FROM MEMORIES OF HIM WILL HELP YOU IN THE LONG RUN.

DO: TAKE UP AN AGGRESSIVE OR CHALLENGING WORKOUT. MAY WE SUGGEST BOXING? YOU CAN PRETEND HIS FACE IS THE BAG.

DON'T: REACH OUT. IF YOU FEEL LIKE YOU WANT TO WRITE YOUR EX, WRITE THEM AND SAVE IT IN YOUR NOTEPAD. DO NOT SEND.

REMEMBER: YOU WERE OKAY BEFORE HIM, AND YOU WILL BE OKAY AFTER HIM.

a goddamn coward. A ten-year-old coward. I mean, how is this same man a head coach in the National Football League?! He can scream at 250-pound linebackers all day, but he didn't have the courage to tell a seventy-five-pound girl dressed like John Travolta from *Saturday Night Fever* that he didn't want to go out with her anymore?

So, there you have it, the worst breakup of my life. And after the infamous breakup of 1996, I told myself that I would never let another man RAM my heart again. (See what I did there?) But no hard feelings, Coach! From the bottom of my cold, half-dead heart, thank you. You really did coach this girl to bounce back and never be dumped again.

Prince Charming
Is a Fraud

It started like a goddamn fairy tale. This charming, gorgeous, successful man popped into my life out of nowhere and swept me off my wobbly little feet. He was hilarious, charismatic, outgoing—a man I had always dreamed of—and he always knew exactly what to say to make me feel like the most important person in the world. I had never really believed in soul mates until I met him, but I couldn't deny the absolute euphoria this man made me feel. *This* was what it felt like when you met "the one." How was I so lucky to find the most incredible man in the world? And how was I so lucky that he chose *me*? It took less than forty-eight hours for him to tell me he loved me. I believed him, I said it back, and I meant it. Within a week, he was gushing about how he couldn't wait to marry me, how he couldn't wait to start a family with me, and how he couldn't believe his lucky stars that he finally met his twin flame. He wanted it all, and he wanted it all with me. I actually felt comfortable sharing the deepest parts of myself with someone for the first time in my adult life, and I was absolutely thrilled that we seemed to have the same morals, values, beliefs, goals, and dreams. I couldn't believe that someone seemed to mirror me so perfectly. I sat in awe, with my jaw on the floor, listening to this gorgeous man feed me fairy-tale promises of an undying love and a forever life together. He was my real-life Prince Charming.

He came on strong, but he was also walking the walk while talking the talk. He sent me a dozen roses on a Thursday "just because." He immediately plastered me all over his social media. He complimented me on the things I always wished someone would notice: my sensitive heart, my thoughtfulness, my attention to detail and "the little things." He was attentive and a great listener. Our first date was so extravagant, it felt like I was the fucking Bachelorette. He lavished me with expensive meals and designer clothes, which I never asked for but greatly appreciated, and it just made me feel so special. Sure, it was fast; sure, it was over the top, but

it just felt so *right*. Wasn't this what "love at first sight" was supposed to feel like? He was like a drug to me, and I just wanted more and more and more.

And, listen, I have always had a very naïve heart. I grew up with two parents who love each other unconditionally and who have showered me with nothing but unselfish love, and I didn't realize until I got older how rare this type of relationship is. I always just assumed that everyone had good intentions when it came to love, and that everyone meant what they said. I'm sensitive, empathetic, and I have always yearned for that big romantic love story and for someone to adore me back, so I tend to enter relationships with wide eyes and an eager heart. My vulnerability has always been one of my biggest strengths and one of my most destructive weaknesses. No matter how tough the exterior of my heart gets, it'll always be a big squishy mess inside. No matter how many times I'd get knocked down by love, I'd get right back up again (yup, I'm like the Chumbawamba song). When someone promises me something, I believe it. So I believed everything he said. He made me feel important, beautiful, valued, and admired. He understood and soothed my insecurities, and he sympathized with my sensitivities. He promised me the world. In return, I effortlessly gave him my trust, loyalty, and investment. I felt safe with someone for the first time in my adult life, so I let my guard down immediately and entirely. I was drowning in the type of love I always wished for, and I didn't want to come up for air. I pinched myself every morning, hoping it wasn't all a dream. It all felt too good to be true. And that's because it was.

It took a few months for things to start unraveling and for me to see the cracks that were forming, and it took a while longer for me to fully understand the depth of all the inconsistencies that were quickly becoming the norm. It crept in so slowly and quietly that I never even realized anything was really changing, until everything changed. It started small and insignificant. The texts slowed down, which I just chalked up to being normal for any relationship. Then the compliments dwindled and eventually stopped altogether. Then there were a few hurtful comments here and there. Then subtle little insults that turned into pretty obvious insults. First in private, then in public. Then a few negative comments about my body. Then some criticism about how I loaded the dishwasher, and then about how I made the bed or chewed my food, and finally about literally everything I did. Then the morals and values that seemed to mirror mine so perfectly started to shift. I began to notice how all of his relationships were being orchestrated and everyone in his life was being used as a pawn against one another. One by one, he started to take back every single promise he had made to me. And before I knew it, I was dating a complete stranger.

A man I thought was genuinely kind and happy-go-lucky started having outbursts that were heartless, spiteful, and straight-up cruel. The compliments and adoration soon turned to disrespect and belittlement, and my insecurities and vulnerabilities were used as a weapon against me. He knew exactly what buttons to push to hurt my heart the most, and he knew precisely how to tear me down in the most destructive and complete ways. All of the extremely intimate and incredibly important things I shared with him were now being used as tools to emotionally harm me.

At a strangely casual pace, I went from feeling like the most special person in the world to less than average and entirely replaceable. Nothing in my life had any significance anymore. He made condescending, misogynistic, and narcissistic comments at the drop of a hat. The focus was entirely on him, his work, his friends, and his life—and I was the bad partner if I didn't blindly support and agree with everything he did. He belittled my career, rarely acknowledged my accomplishments, and seemed to get some type of pleasure from destroying my happiness. I felt myself constantly trying to explain fundamental concepts of human emotion to him like empathy and compassion and loyalty and kindness, only to be met with dead eyes and a blank stare. He was dismissive anytime I tried to tell him how I felt, so I eventually just crawled into myself and kept silent for fear of being chastised for just being myself.

I constantly felt like I was on edge and walking on eggshells around him, worried to death that I might say or do something to make him leave me. Even though he was the one emotionally bulldozing me, somehow *everything* was always my fault. The problem wasn't his malicious actions, but my overly sensitive reactions. I was too delicate, too needy, too reactive. The lies and hypocrisy were constant. And because of this, I was anxious. All. The. Fucking. Time. I couldn't sleep or eat because the fear of losing him consumed my every waking moment. I felt myself constantly apologizing for *literally* everything, terrified that any argument could be our last. And this all deeply confused me, because I have always been a very level-headed person. I've never been emotionally erratic or volatile in my adult life, but during that relationship I was absolutely unhinged, and I was constantly questioning my own sanity and reality.

And while he was crushing me over and over again to my very core, the only thing I could think about was how I could win back the man I had instantly fallen in love with. I was addicted and desperate for anything to bring us back to where we started and give me that dreamy high again. I thought if I just agreed with everything he said and was the "easy cool girl," we could get back on track. I turned into a meek, insecure, submissive shell of who I used to be. But the more I folded for him, the worse it got.

He chased me, he caught me, he devalued me, and he discarded me.

I won't get into the specifics of the relationship or what ultimately led to the breakup, but everything eventually exploded. I was left hollow, shell-shocked, and broken to my core. I'm almost embarrassed to admit how fucked up I was, because the relationship wasn't that long in the grand scheme of life. But the moment it ended, a switch flipped, and I finally realized that I was being emotionally manipulated and gaslighted the entire time. I was allowing myself to be treated as lesser than because I was brainwashed to believe I was nothing without him. But once I was out, there wasn't a single cell in my body that wanted to get back together with him. All I knew was I wanted to get the hell out of that nightmare. The inevitable heartbreak I could handle. I wasn't a little kid anymore. I knew the world would keep on spinning and I could gather my pride, which I had carelessly spilled all over the floor, and move on with my life. I never thought I'd lost the love of my life, and he will never be the one I wistfully think about as the one who got away. The thing that really crushed me was that I couldn't trust my own instincts anymore. I felt totally conned, and I'd always thought I was too smart to ever be "that girl." I'd always thought I was a perceptive, rational, intelligent person with a healthy level of self-worth. But there I was, a tangled mess of confusion and shame because I'd gotten someone so fucking wrong.

I had pretty regular panic attacks for about a year after the breakup. Sometimes they would be triggered by a song or a guy putting his hand on my leg during a date. And sometimes they would happen out of nowhere. Everything would come and go in waves, and it truly was the most unstable I've ever felt (aside from being in my actual relationship). I took up hot yoga, I meditated, I went to therapy, I confided in my friends and family, I journaled a lot, I went on dates, I kept busy, I went to a million happy hours, I got under someone else, and I never ever once looked at his social media. I did all of the things you were supposed to do to try to heal a broken heart, and I was extremely proactive about feeling better. Yet while I kept it together on the outside, the anxiety of being completely deceived kept creeping into the recesses of my mind. I felt so alone. I felt so stupid. I felt like such a fool. I kept beating myself up because I wasn't getting better. I wasn't healing as fast as I thought I should be, and I was so mad at myself for being such an idiot.

It took me a good year to actually be okay again, and I mean *really* okay. And it took even longer for me to relearn how to properly love someone. I held it together on the outside, but looking back, I was such a damn mess for longer than I'd like to admit. It took time to rebuild my heart, to be able to trust myself and my instincts, and to be in a place where I could genuinely care for someone again without being so unstable. I have a new barrier around my heart that no one will be able to penetrate, and that's because nothing in this life is for certain. And at the end of the day, regardless of what happens, I have to be okay by myself. I'm in a healthier and stronger place than I ever have been in my entire life. I know what I deserve, and I will never settle for anyone less than someone who treats me like a goddamn queen.

I realize that my situation could be so much worse, and I feel fortunate that I got out when I did. But the more I talked about my disaster of a relationship, the more I realized that this type of toxic behavior is so textbook and these types of relationships are all the same. And sometimes you don't realize what's happening until someone hits you over the head with the truth. So if you're reading this and it sounds all too familiar to you, **this is your sign**.

Since my shitshow of a relationship, I have learned a lot of lessons along the way. I've learned that love should be earned, not given. It takes time to know someone, and even more time to love someone. I've learned that when something seems too good to be true, it usually is. I've learned that you shouldn't feel so damn lonely in a relationship. I've learned that it wasn't my fault, and there is not anything wrong with me. I've learned to protect my heart and be hyper-aware of red flags. I've learned that relationships shouldn't be so fucking hard all the time. I've learned that I don't believe in soul mates, but I do believe that you can choose to love someone with everything you've got. I've learned that a relationship should be balanced, with both people giving their all. I've learned that vulnerability is a strength, and that the right person will value and empower such a wonderful quality. I've learned what it feels like to thrive on my own. I've learned that time does heal all wounds. I've learned to trust my gut and my instincts again. And, most important, I've learned to love myself, and I wouldn't take that back for anything.

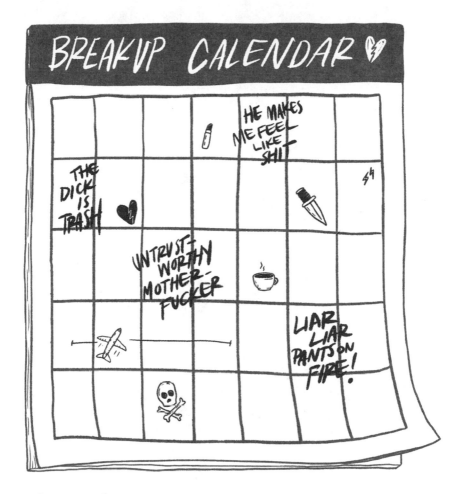

HOW TO MAKE YOUR OWN BREAKUP CALENDAR:

1. PRINT OUT A ONE-MONTH CALENDAR & FILL IN SOMETHING YOU HATE ABOUT YOUR EX IN EACH SQUARE.

2. HANG IT UP WHERE YOU CAN SEE IT ALL DAY LONG.

3. EVERY DAY THAT YOU GET THROUGH WITHOUT TEXTING YOUR EX, CROSS IT OUT.

4. AT THE END OF THE MONTH GIVE YOURSELF A HUG, YOU MADE IT!

Same Penis (or Vagina) Forever

"Marry a man who loves you more."
—all of our moms

Newsflash: When you pick your forever person, you're never going to feel like you 100-percent made the right choice. You are going to have to *tell yourself* over and over and over again that you made the right choice. If you told us that we could have our *dream* handbag, it would be a Hermès bag. It's the most expensive, luxurious item we've lusted after our entire lady lives. But, if you tell us that's the *only* bag we can carry for the rest of our goddamn lives, no matter what the occasion is, we're going to question our decision constantly. What if we're going to a funeral? Or a mud race?! We'd need a CamelBak for that! Finding your lifelong partner is kind of like finding your Hermès bag. Do you want to carry him around every day into every adventure? Not really, but guess what? That's the trade-off.

Say it after us: You cannot change a person.

You
Cannot
Change
A
Person.

The person you're sitting across from on your first date is going to be innately the same person sitting across from you on your twentieth wedding anniversary. You can change his shoes and make him grow his hair out, and you can change the way he goes down on you in Sexico, but you're never going to change the fact that he has a wandering eye, or has no ambition, or lashes out at you for no reason. You're never going to change the fact that he never learned how to do laundry or that his mom enabled him to be a lazy slob, or that he's not adventurous and outgoing, or that he doesn't want to take responsibility for his actions.

So, if you are a Jac and you are an experience-driven person, you want to be out and about doing all the Jactivities and seeing the world. If you choose to be with an antisocial partner who wants to be inside his little cocoon all the time, at home playing video games, you can't expect him to change what fuels his soul to accommodate you.

So, what's our advice? When you pick your forever person, don't look at them and imagine what your life will look like in five or ten years. Look at what your life will look like in forty years, when he's old and bald and wrinkly and his balls are sagging to his knees. Look at what your life will look like in sixty years, when you're wiping his ass because he can't go to the bathroom on his own. Will he still make you laugh? Will you take care of each other when life gets hard? Will his hand on your knee still make your heart happy? There are a number of people who could be a good match for you, but you choose your forever person because *you want them around*, not because fate brought them to you, and definitely not because you "can't live without them." Barf. We think the idea of soul mates is bullshit. You have to be realistic. You *choose* your partner, so choose wisely. And the truth is that you will choose the right person at the right time, and it's never going to be how you thought it would be.

And we don't care how old you are or how many of your friends are married with kids. Do. Not. Settle. We would rather die alone than end up with someone who doesn't deserve our greatness. If you have to spend every day for the rest of your life with one person, make sure they're worthy and that you're not with them because you're scared to be alone or you feel like time is running out. There's a lot of pressure from society to be on the correct timeline of life. High school, check! College, check! Then you get your internship, get engaged, married, and then it's time to have a baby. Life ends up feeling like this daunting to-do list, and before you can come up for air, you're spending all your free time at Chuck E. Cheese's, wondering where you lost control of the steering wheel. Don't let yourself get desperate and make sloppy choices just because your life doesn't seem to match up with society's plan for women as a whole. And guess what? Technology is pretty great these days. So if you feel your biological clock ticking, but you haven't met your partner or aren't ready to have kids just yet, freeze those eggs, girl (if you can afford it)! Never marry someone because you feel like your eggs are dying. Take the power back and rewrite your own timeline.

Also, don't marry the best sex of your life. This is the guy who will literally rock your socks off in the bedroom, who you will think about when you masturbate years later, and who is probably having sex with someone else while you're reading this right now. You don't want to marry that guy. You want to marry the guy who you have **great** sex with, but who (more importantly) treats you nicely. Because even the craziest, most passionate, kinky sex eventually turns into married sex at some point. There's not one single person, unless you marry a sex addict, who's gonna stay as hot in the bedroom with you as he started. Even Kanye probably gets sick of sleeping with Kim, you know?

Marriage Material

I'll never forget what my mom said the day after my first date with my future husband.

She said, "Wow, he sounds amazing, you better not screw this up!"

She was right. Chris is the opposite of the kind of guy I've always gone for. I had spent all my life cradling injured birdies and trying to fix them. I always went for the artistic guy who wrote poems and songs and who texted prose at 3:00 a.m. I think in my twenties I pretty much exclusively dated some sort of musician. I *loved* a guy who didn't have his life together. It took years of therapy for me to realize that I acted this way for two reasons.

First, musicians are hot. Talent is hot. Dark rooms and tour buses and tight jeans are all super hot. But what makes a great front man isn't usually what makes a great human being. Second, I was hard-core codependent and I had such low self-esteem that I handpicked men who really needed me and my killer organizational and life skills, because somewhere deep down inside me, I didn't feel like I actually deserved to be loved just for me. I have a long list of red flags that have made me swoon, including but not limited to: drinking problems, always being late, forgetting I exist for days at a time, drug problems, and lack of knowledge of how to do laundry and pay bills. It was a real bonus if they were ousted from their families, didn't have families, or had bad blood with their families. I loved a man who had been arrested, asked to borrow money, then disappeared. Get me a guy who lived with his mom, didn't have a real job, made jewelry part-time, or was a "DJ." It was a bonus if we could fit in the same size pants.

My mom's advice to me was always "Marry someone who loves you more than you love him." It's harsh, but it's actually true. I have obsessed and watched enough of my friends obsess over impossible loves. There is nothing more thrilling on earth than the person you can't fully have. It's hard to break the cycle of how addictive and fun it is being with a bad boy.

It's a thrilling ride to never know where you stand with someone and to live your life on the edge. It feels good to be needed by a lover, and for it to be an all-encompassing, addictive, can't-get-enough rom-com.

But I know for sure that I wouldn't have the life I have if I hadn't married the good guy who wanted me in return.

I met Chris three times before I remembered him. He was persistent, to say the least. I went to his birthday party with the full intention of trying to hook up with a different guy I thought was on the guest list. That guy never came, but a slightly tipsy Chris walked across the room with his arms flung over two girls and said hello (it is pathetic that he had to act like a douchebag for me to take notice, but it worked). The next day he asked for my phone number and then, get this, he CALLED ME ON THE PHONE to ask me out. He picked me up for our date in a nice shirt and a clean car, and he had made a proper reservation for dinner. He didn't kiss me until our third date.

When I first met Chris, I had some major trust issues, so he would let me look through his phone whenever I wanted for the entire first year we dated. He was a former musician with tight jeans and good hair who had switched over to managing the next round of superstars.

On our first trip together, the water in the shower was so salty that my hair wouldn't untangle, and he washed my hair for me every night with bottled water. I once got stuck in a landslide on a work trip, and I called him crying, and he got in his car at 1:00 a.m. and drove north for five hours to come save me on the roadside. He has never called me "Keltie." He just says "my love." My parents love him, and he texts them by himself to check in. When I can't go to birthday dinners or events with my friend group, he goes alone and hangs out with all my girlfriends. He gives me tons of space to be a crazy workaholic, and when I'm in work mode, he makes me tea and kisses my forehead and then leaves me alone. He has a file on his phone of all the details about me, including my shoe size, ring size, social security number, parents' birthdays, etc. When I say I like something, he will take notes and then, months later, surprise me with that exact thing. He goes on the dance floor with me at weddings and holds his own.

How to Get the Ring You Want

Show him the ring that you want. Don't let him get creative. **NEWS FLASH:** Men are stupid. If you are picky and you want a specific type of ring, then you should tell him *exactly* what you want. Men are morons, and the chance of them getting it right on their own is slim to none. Also, don't copy your friend's ring. It's tacky and very *Single White Female*. If your guy presents you with Grandma's family heirloom ring, you have to accept it. Turn it into a necklace pendant and then get a new ring on your ten-year anniversary. **DON'T FUCK WITH GRANDMA.** She'll start haunting you from her grave.

He hates drama and noise, like me, so we rarely fight. When we do, it's a grown-up discussion about why we are fighting. One time, I was mad at him and he made a poster-board presentation of his love for me to make up for it. He knows how to cook, clean, and do laundry. He can figure out the hard and confusing things about taxes, paperwork, and mortgages. He has the appropriate grown-up clothes to wear to any event, and a section of his closet is grown-man suits with proper shirts, ties, and dress shoes. He is my biggest fan, and although he is very private in his own life, I will often come home to find him watching my TV show. He will always turn to me and say, "good one tonight." He's just really great to me.

I owe a lot to Chris because he gave me room to grow into this version of myself. He's let me change and has never held me to being one woman. I have hundreds of different sides to me, and he's been along for the ride.

When I stopped being busy trying to save someone else, and I got to focus on my own life, really amazing things started happening to me. My advice is to choose the good guy. The guy who calls you back and wants to spend time with you. The guy who makes things like grocery shopping fun.

Our marriage is simple. We love each other and make the mundane days of working adult life fun. We choose each other as often as we can, and we don't make it a big deal when we can't. I let him do his thing, and he lets me do mine. We trust each other. We are nice to each other. We have a similar set of goals for the things we would like to see and do in our lives. We have similar outlooks on the way the world should work. We have the same values at our core. We both love our work, we love music, we love our little life together, and we also love to get completely wasted and make out like we are in high school.

Mr. Snack Martin

I DEFINITELY didn't grow up dreaming about my wedding day, and only occasionally did I think about having a forever husband. Husband, yes. Forever? I doubted it. One of my biggest role models was my Granny June, and she was married four times (twice to the same man).

Quite frankly, I think I was a little intimidated by marriage (and at times grossed out) because of my parents' obsession with each other. They met when my mom was fifteen, and they have been happily (and sexually) together ever since. Yes, my parents are still boning after forty-one eight years of marriage. How do I know this, you ask? My father alludes to it regularly. Thanks for the night terrors, Dad!

Growing up, I would go out to dinner with other families and notice that the other dads weren't very shy about hitting on the perky-boobed waitress at the local LongHorn Steakhouse, and it was always so shocking to me. In my thirty-four years of life, I've heard my dad say that only *one* other woman besides my mother was "attractive," and that was Teri Hatcher (obviously, in her *Lois & Clark* days). We have spent the last two decades roasting him for it because it was incredibly out of character. Tom Tobin set a high motherfuckin' bar. That asshole . . .

My dad instilled a very impactful lesson in me with his deep devotion/sick obsession with my mother. The lesson was that you should choose a man who not only respects you but WORSHIPS you from damn near the beginning. Because of this, I have never really chased men. Don't get me wrong, I would get pretty bummed out if the hot guy in the bar showed zero interest in me, but that's usually where it stopped. I very rarely put myself in the position of impressing some uninterested guy or "getting him to fall in love with me," like so many of my girlfriends who would lust after men who were simply not into them and were never going to be. I would always think, *Why play a game you can't win?!*

Of course, there was a downside to this mentality because, in my twenties, it meant that I ended up with guys who adored me but who I didn't necessarily adore back. And, if I'm being completely honest, I loved the way that made me feel. I always felt like I had the upper hand in the relationship AND was constantly (usually subconsciously) putting out the vibe that I could live without them . . . and nothing keeps a man loving you more than aloofness (I'm dead serious).

However, after about a year of being with that kind of guy, I would get to a place where I would rather rip off his head and shit down his neck than actually sit across from him at a dinner table and watch him chew. This sort of solidified the idea that I would never meet a man I wanted to spend more than a year with, let alone the rest of my life. I was certain my life was headed toward Granny June status.

In recent years, I started to observe my parents a little more closely, because I was stumped. I didn't understand how my mother stuck around through all this smothering!!! And not only did it appear that she was sticking around, but she was still putting out (like I mentioned earlier), and that was a sign that she still held a candle for good ol' Tom Tobin. How was this possible?!

Well, just like Jane Goodall, after years and years of observation of these two primates, I realized that I was missing something all along! I noticed that while my dad worshipped my mother and thought she was the most beautiful human on planet Earth, he still challenged her. And she him. It wasn't the same kind of crazy sick love like I had for my Maltese, Sophie, which I had always mistaken it for. It was sort of conditional. There was balance. And over the years, I have realized that unconditional love and adoration are reserved for your kids and your pets, not for your spouse.

When Zach and I started dating, I still sort of expected him to think every little thing I did was spectacular, even when I was on my worst behavior, but that was certainly NOT the case. He challenged me, and this was something new and (kind of) exciting for this self-obsessed actress. Don't get me wrong, there was still a very healthy amount of adoration there. (He will kill me for writing this, but before we started dating, anytime he would see our mutual friend, he would ask where I was and if I was single. This went on for a DECADE.)

Here's the thing: Zach Martin really adores me at my best and accepts me at my worst . . . but he doesn't let me stay there too long without showing me he's slightly disappointed, and I think that's a great thing (especially for a monster like me). It sounds cheesy, but his expectations of me are what keep me constantly working on being a better person and a better spouse. He can only get away with this bullshit because, deep down, I truly believe that he is a fantastic fucking human, and I respect the shit out of him, even when I want to suffocate him in his sleep.

Let's try a little exercise. I want you to think of a super strong woman in your life (possibly a little narcissistic and extremely opinionated). Does she primarily date men who are doormats? Did said woman end up marrying a doormat? She probably did, right? She's with a man who worships her and lets her get away with murder, correct? Now, if she's been in this relationship a while, has she gradually become even more self-centered, less self-aware, and pretty much horrible to be around? That's because she didn't marry someone who would check her ass when she was being a pig. And, by the way, this is not me being judgmental. I'm fully aware that in the wrong relationship, I am capable of becoming this woman.

Before all the feminists come after me, I married someone who puts my ass in check *only when necessary*. I still act out, I still say inappropriate things at parties, I still share way too much information about my bodily functions at the dinner table, and he simply shakes his head (mostly) lovingly. I still Dutch-oven him almost every night, and only once in our five years together has he ever suggested we stop farting in front of each other. After all, he knows who he married, and he never wanted to change me. In fact, a lot of things about me that most men couldn't handle, he takes in stride, and he may never admit it, but I believe they are some of the reasons he married me.

Here are a few other important reasons why I will be with Zach for as long as he can put up with me—and ladies, if you're smart, you'll find someone similar.

I married the man who will show up for anyone in his life when they need help, whether it's for a flat tire or life advice. I married the man who loves his family more than anyone else I know and genuinely enjoys being around them. I married the man who knows how to grill and lets me sit around and drink when we have people over instead of helping him in the kitchen. I married the man whose heart explodes every time he sees our goddaughter, Frankie. I married the man who plans the greatest vacations and knows how to make a plan in general. I married the man who laughs at me when I'm silly and who makes me laugh when he is. I married the man who doesn't seek out the spotlight (thank God . . . there can only be one star in the family), but when he's in the spotlight, he is a bonafide leading man. I married the man who supports my dreams and thinks I'm hot when I'm naked no matter what. And, most important, I married the man who is VERY discreet when he finds another female attractive, and for that I love his dumb ass.

I'M NOT WITH STUPID ANYMORE

The world has made divorce seem like the ultimate failure. But the truth is, statistically, most of us are going to have a happily-ever-after that involves at least one, or possibly two, divorces in our lifetimes. There can be a ton of shame in going to Splitsville. But the truth is that most people's heads are so far up their asses dealing with their own drama that they will barely even notice your divorce. We barely cared about your significant other, and we're certainly not judging you for your divorce.

Are your parents going to be disappointed that they spent all that money on your fancy wedding? Sure. Is sadsturbation going to be the only thing in your bed for a few months or years? Most likely. Do you change your name back? If you want—we don't care. Are your long-lost friends from high school gonna see you change your relationship status on Facebook? Maybe. But, again, they're more interested in who commented on the video of their kid eating lemons to notice. All of it is slightly cringey, and of course it all comes with a mini backpack full of humiliation, but the bottom line is that you don't have to live your life in a relationship that doesn't serve you.

You can split up the plates, you can split up the furniture, and you can make a clean break and not have a trashback haunt you for the rest of your life. You can co-parent your kids and roll your eyes in secret at husband number one. But after the dust settles, you can and you will have a second (or third or fourth) marriage that is happy, fulfilling, and everything you'd wished the first had been.

Divorce is like a paper cut. It's annoying and it hurts like hell. You can't really see it, but it bothers you so much and it stays with you, until one day it magically feels a little better. And the next day, even better than the last. Hang in there and look on the bright side: divorce is *very* "in" these days. Half of the population (and one-third of the LadyGang) has tried it at least once.

Captain Keltie and the Tale of Her Divor-sea

As the sole divorcée of the LadyGang, I've been asked many times to talk about my first marriage, how it started, how it ended, and why.

The truth is that it feels like an entirely different life.

I met my first husband shortly after I accepted my first adult job as a "showgirl" aboard a world traveling cruise ship somewhere between Cancún, Mexico, and Juneau, Alaska. I was a fresh-faced and very over-whelmed eighteen-year-old who had somehow convinced herself and her parents that she was ready to go off into the world all alone. I was being paid $1,842 in American cash dollars every month to sing and dance my heart out, in a blue sequined thong, while singing "Sea Legs Circus at Sea . . . Tonight!" three times a week.

As far as love went, I didn't know myself at all, but I did understand that my self-esteem could be directly reflected by the interest I was re-ceiving from the opposite sex, and it had been that way my entire life.

It started in the first grade when a boy named Darren threw up on me in reading circle, then left me handmade crayon hearts in my pencil box the next day. Swoon.

When I was in fifth grade, I spotted a boy from my class walking down my street. I promptly ran to my bedroom, pulled my last-place dancing trophy from my shelf, and brought it outside to yell aggressively across the street, "Look what I got!"

I was now eighteen years old, and I had never been the first choice for anything or anyone. I had grown up throwing myself into a "dance ca-reer" that consisted of 2 percent natural God-given talent and 98 percent grit and "make-it-work" mentality. I had also grown up throwing myself at boys who ignored me. I wore outlandish clothing and put on shows to draw attention to what was clearly the raw sexually attractive quali-ties of my killer dance moves to anyone who would watch. I've always been the type of person who believed and lived inside the belief that my achievements made me desirable. That if I was "famous," "the winner," and "a star," somehow that meant people would love and adore me.

When I completely surprised everyone in my small Canadian home-town, as well as myself, by booking a big fancy *American* dance job, something in me changed. All of a sudden my very secret, almost impos-sible lifelong dream of moving to New York City to become a Radio City Rockette and dance on Broadway seemed somehow . . . possible.

So there I was out in the world, with my guts, my courage, and a passport. When you come from a town like mine, and you've lived in the same house since you were born, where your dad only let the entire fam-ily drive used cars, where you had the same best friend since first grade, where you could get anywhere in the town without using a map, where you could go out for dinner and order without even looking at the menu, being launched into a rocket ship of newness and change was almost de-bilitating. I consider myself a pretty brave person, but I forced myself to become an adult overnight, while all of my friends were still picking up their yearbooks from graduation.

Living on the cruise ship, I was all alone for the first time in my life, completely cut off from the world. This was all happening to me in a time before cell phones. I would have to stand in line at a port to buy a long-distance calling card once a week, and then wait in line again to get to an available pay phone. Each time, I would enter my parents' or friends' home phone numbers in the hopes that, through the time differences and lack of caller IDs, they would know it was me and answer the phone. If they didn't answer, it would be another week before I could talk to them. This was a time when the internet was something very new and barely understood, when you could go online with a dial-up connection for only ten minutes at a time. I was someone who deeply needed the validation of people around me telling me it was going to be okay, and there was no one around me that I even knew.

But this is an essay about divorce—so let me introduce you to First Husband, a man who shall remain nameless.

First Husband and I met while I was doing my fancy American dance job on a cruise ship, where it was really, really normal for complete

strangers from completely different countries to "couple up." Relationships usually lasted as long as a ship's contract did. Some couples followed each other from ship to ship, some broke up when one half left for another ship, some left the ship but left behind herpes as a parting gift to a final one-night stand. The fun, passion, and adventures that the passengers on board were having on their dream vacations was absolutely nothing compared to the real-life soap opera that was going on below deck. Beer and wine were $1 at the crew bar. Loneliness was free. The whole bottom two decks of the boat reeked of desperation.

His six-by-eight bunk-bed room, complete with a stranger roommate, was just two doors down from mine. It was normal for everyone in our hallway to leave our doors open as we got ready for work. For the dancer cast, this meant gluing giant eyelashes to our eyes and pinning in big chunks of fake hair for our nightly shows. The others would be having a fresh shower and shave after a long day on the beach before putting on their suits to head to deck to help the passengers.

That was one of the things that I remember falling in love with about First Husband. He wore a suit, every single night. I had just graduated from high school a few months before and had gone to a prom where all the scrawny boys in my class, who I had known since they were little turds in first grade, rented oversize suits from the suit store at the mall. They looked like pseudo-men, all standing in a line with us girls in our gowns.

First Husband was different—he was a MAN. He wore a suit (that he owned) with dress socks and dress shoes! He listened to Frank Sinatra as he shaved! He owned fancy store cologne, not drugstore body spray! First Husband also hailed from New York City, the city that had been my obsession since my aunt had taken me to see the touring company of *Cats* in my hometown. Broadway: the magical, mystical place where theater nerds like me went to sing and dance and jump on tables à la "La Vie Bohème" in *Rent*.

Not only that, but First Husband was Italian. He was strong in his conviction that Italians were the best people on the planet and that New York City was the best city in the world. He swore that baseball was the only sport that mattered, Sinatra was the only music worth listening to, and chicken breast was the only acceptable healthy food available on the ship. He was so sure of himself, so unbelievably confident. First Husband was also my height (5'6"—not his fault), balding (also not his fault), and someone who generally thought he was better than everyone else, including me (definitely his fault).

As for me, I was so completely afraid and unsure of myself that it was the easiest thing in the world to slip into believing everything he liked was what I liked. I had been ripped away from my home and had made him my new traveling "home base." I quickly began turning my back on everything that made me myself. I was suddenly embarrassed to be from Canada, and that I had a funny accent that made me sound "dumb." I was embarrassed that I liked hockey, and even though I hadn't eaten meat since the eighth grade, I started eating giant chicken breasts at dinner beside him. I wanted to be perfect for him. I wanted to not be alone.

Falling in love with First Husband looked a lot like this: sneaking away to see each other during our work hours (his at the diving shop and sports adventure desk on Deck Five), and then him sitting with the other show boyfriends (see? everyone was doing it) in the second level of the theater for the second show of the night in that damn suit, drinking a grown-up cocktail, and clapping for me. All it would have taken for me to become obsessed was the clapping, but the fact that he liked me back was awesome, too.

On days we were not working, we would sneak away to the most beautiful beaches in the world and swim, sit out on the rocks, and tell what little life stories we had to each other. We would spend time in line for pay phones to call our families and watch coveted VHS tapes of *Friends* reruns in one of our tiny cabins.

We had actually worked out a pretty good deal for a while. First Husband's roommate was knocking boots with MY ship roommate, so we split rooms, and First Husband and I shared one while the roommates took the other. It was like being an adult and living together, without any of the actual grown-up responsibilities. We didn't pay rent. We didn't have bills. We didn't pay for food. We didn't have car payments. We were literally being paid to travel around the world and work for maybe three hours a day. It didn't matter that we were the same height because we barely wore shoes!

In the middle of all this—losing myself and pretending to everyone back home that I was living the life of my dreams—I got "fat." I was always the tallest and thinnest dancer in class—the girl who always got chosen to be lifted in a pas de deux and who constantly reveled in people grabbing her shoulders as a kid and saying, "Oh, you are so thin, my dear." The combination of living on a floating hotel and never having to walk anywhere, the change from dancing four to five hours per day in high school to dancing three to four hours per week on the ship, becoming a chicken-breast devotee, and spending all my free time either lying in the sun, on a bunk, or on a beach and drinking meant that I gained twenty-five pounds. This sent me into a disastrous spiral.

My dance contract had weekly weigh-ins as part of our job. Every Thursday morning, the female dancers would be lined up in their pajamas and have to step on the scale to record their "show weight"; each week mine got higher and higher and sent me into a tailspin of depression and obsession. I would do what any dancer girl would do: I would stop eating for two days, go to the gym for three hours a day, and then, on day three, secretly run down to the crew shop to buy three candy bars and run to my room and devour all three in one sitting before First Husband got back from work. Then I would hide the wrappers in the garbage cans away from our room so that I could act confused about why I wasn't losing the weight.

After a while, I got into the messy stuff when my roommate and I discovered Diet Fuel and diuretics. Diet Fuel was actually so bad for you that I think it's now illegal, but we would pop two pills before each of our shows every night and be completely wired on caffeine in the hopes of burning "extra calories." Then, on Wednesday, before weigh-in day, we would stop drinking water, take handfuls of Ex-Lax and diuretics, and hope that we could somehow shit out twenty-five pounds before the morning. It never worked.

The clincher in all of this, and the reason for what happened next in our relationship, was that First Husband loved me anyway. I was unlovable, miserable, a complete psycho, and I hated myself. I was full of doubt, fear, confusion, and dread. But he loved me in spite of it all, and that's all I needed. That was the only question that mattered. We never talked about our hopes, dreams, or future. He just loved me. I was at my lowest, full of hatred for myself, and he still wrote me cute cards and called me "principessa." I was so immature that I didn't understand the importance of self-love or of being okay with myself. I couldn't stand myself, but he wouldn't leave me.

It makes sense to me now, why I woke up one freezing Alaska morning and said yes to his proposal. I remember it so perfectly. As I got out of bed, I found a note card on our tiny room desk with clues for a treasure hunt. This treasure hunt would take me all over the city of Ketchikan, Alaska, in a helicopter and lead me to the edge of a mountain cliff. There he was, waiting just for me. As he got down on one knee and asked me to marry him in that irresistible New York accent, I meekly answered, "YES!"

However, I also remember one incredibly heartbreaking detail of that day that I am beyond embarrassed to admit. As we walked down the mountain a now newly engaged couple, I thought to myself, "Well, it's just an engagement, I can always call it off."

But I didn't call it off. Instead, I moved our relationship ahead at lightning speed. I made scrapbooks, and plans, and bought wedding magazines, and called my parents. I made lists and I checked off the lists. I made my parents take out an ad in my hometown paper congratulating me on my engagement with the words "New York Wedding Summer" underneath. I'm not sure what I was trying to prove, to others or to myself, but it was all one big farce. I had no idea what I was doing. I guess in some weird way I felt like I was proving myself to everyone who ever doubted me.

Eventually, First Husband and I left the ship and moved to New York to set up our big fancy NYC life together. Actually, it was a city called East Meadow, which was technically in New York State and on Long Island, but impossibly far out from both Broadway and the big city. We rented an attic in a totally average suburban house. First Husband's stepdad bought us a car that I couldn't drive (I didn't drive stick). I was too far away from the train to Manhattan to walk to it myself, so I had to ask First Husband to drive me anytime I wanted to go anywhere. I was teaching dance at some local dance studios, and every week, when I got paid in cash, I handed the wad over to First Husband. In order to go into the city to take a ballet class or audition, I would need to ride one hour on the rail and then walk thirty-three blocks to the dance studio on Fifty-seventh Street, because I was a tiny little human in NYC for the first time and I couldn't for the life of me figure out the difference between uptown and downtown trains. Every time I would ride the subway in Manhattan, I would, without a doubt, end up going in the wrong direction and missing my class.

In addition to feeling completely stuck in my own life, I was also attempting to morph into the "wifely" version of myself that my soon-to-be husband wanted me to be. I was constantly at family events with his oversize Italian family, and I quickly learned that a woman who didn't know how to cook, didn't go to college, and ate pasta sauce out of a can had a long way to go before being accepted. It's crazy to think now, but at no point in this process did I stop to wonder if the life that I was building was the life I actually wanted. I felt so much pressure to succeed in this new world that I ignored every single little rumbling in my gut that said everything about my world felt wrong.

I remember one night when I invited the huge Italian family over to our one-bedroom attic for dinner, a dinner that I was going to cook. I walked myself to the store, lugged the groceries back, and began the process of burning everything and having all my dishes come out at completely different times. When we finally sat down at our tiny table, the family began giving me feedback on my cooking: "It's cold," and "You should make sure the dishes all come out at the same time." It was a complete disaster. It seemed that my soon-to-be in-laws, my soon-to-be husband, and our soon-to-be city all had it in for me. I was failing miserably at trying to prove to all of them that this is where I was supposed to be.

Over and over again, the universe sent me messages that I completely ignored. I ordered a wedding dress from my hometown bridal store. When it arrived, I took my future mother-in-law for my fitting, and the look of disappointment on her face when I walked out of the dressing room wearing my gown choice was palpable. Making matters even worse, the hometown bridal mart had hemmed and cut the dress four inches too short, and there was no way to fix it.

When my mom arrived in New York City ahead of our wedding, she slept on the couch in the attic for a week to help me with final preparations. One night, I found her hiding alone in the closet, crying. My future in-laws had made her feel completely inferior, too.

The day of our wedding, more red flags appeared. First of all, I knew maybe seven people at our wedding, and not by choice. I was just twenty years old, and this was years before any of my friends had their lives figured out enough to purchase flights from western Canada to New York City.

It was an aggressive wedding from the start. We married in a huge church in Queens, with a full Italian church service to appease First Husband. I remember standing outside the gates of the church and getting ready to walk down the aisle with my dad and crying my eyes out. I had dug the hole so deep that it was now a $20,000 hole, complete with a white dress and a father who, as we stepped around the corner to start the service, said to me, "Here we go." Now I am convinced that he meant "You don't have to do this."

We had a big, tux-wearing, four-course-meal reception. I danced with the uncles who hated my cooking. Those same uncles got in a fistfight in the lobby during the speeches. I was married in a too-short dress, wearing a pair of flat shoes from the little girl section of Payless ShoeSource and a tiara. I was exactly what everyone wanted me to be, and I have probably never felt less like myself. I don't know why I did this. I guess I was afraid to be alone? Or I thought I somehow owed it to First Husband after spending those years with me during my terrible weigh-ins and the tear-filled days after. Maybe my entire life had become another one of my giant checklists. Now that getting married and moving to New York City were checked off, I could continue to race against the imaginary clock already haunting my heart daily, setting unrealistic goals that no one, besides myself, had asked me to make.

To be honest, our relationship wasn't all bad. I knew in my gut it wasn't exactly right, but I was determined not to fail. We ate Italian food. I taught dance classes. We did the big Italian family thing. I eventually learned the difference between uptown and downtown and took the subway to dance class. I started working as a dancer more and more. A commercial here. A music video there. Shockingly, just six weeks after I became a Mrs., I was asked to become a Radio City Rockette at Radio City Music Hall. When I got that magical call, I was so excited because this had been a lifelong dream for me, and in addition to that, the Rockettes were a New York institution. So what if I couldn't cook? I was going to be a "World-Famous Radio City Rockette," and I imagined my new NYC family and First Husband radiating with pride.

But there was a problem. I learned that as a first-year Rockette, I wouldn't be dancing in Manhattan. Instead, I was being placed in the touring company of the Rockettes on a four-month out-of-town deal. When I walked proudly into the kitchen and told First Husband the big news, I expected that this person who was my ride or die, till death do us part, good times and bad would be happy for me. A hug? A tear? Even a happy dance or words of pride? Nope. Instead, First Husband looked at me with evil in his eyes and said, "So you're just going to leave me here all alone then?"

My heart broke. It was crushed into a million little pieces. My failure flashed in front of my eyes and ripped through my veins. I knew in that moment that I had picked the wrong person, picked the wrong life, and that it didn't matter how many meatballs I learned how to make—I was never going to be what he wanted. More important, I realized that I was never going to be what I wanted, with him in my life trying to control me and fit me into the perfect housewife mold that I was clearly never going to fit into. But I held on.

We traveled to Canada to visit my family, and it became clear that First Husband suffered openly from something he could not control. He thought he was better than everyone else. He thought Canada was stupid. The money was colored? Dumb. Everyone drank beer? Fattening. Our accents? Dumb. The airport didn't have moving walkways? Dark ages. We ate at restaurants that weren't organic? Criminal. In fact, while out for dinner one night with my friends, First Husband ordered a salad without dressing because he was sooo healthy, and our "stupid" Canadian eateries didn't have healthy options. So there I am with my closest friends, trying to act like I was happy, while my holier-than-thou husband was munching down on a giant bowl of lettuce. Lettuce. Nothing else.

So it all fell apart. It fell apart so quickly and so dramatically. My dad came to NYC to help us fix up our place, and First Husband yelled at me one night in front of my father. Honestly, I was lucky my hot-blooded dad didn't punch him in the face right then and there. I could see it in my dad's eyes while he shrugged his shoulders, and I tried to stay busy in the kitchen in order not to cry, but the jig was up. The facade I was showing everyone in my life, that I was happy and that everything was working out, was deeply flawed.

I wasn't perfect either. I was selfish in the pursuit of my dreams. I left and went on tour, and then I left again and moved across the country for another gig. I stayed out late in the city go-go dancing for money to pay rent, and I hid my wedding ring when I found myself sitting next to cute New York stockbrokers on the train. I was hungry for any kind of positive attention and a glimpse at what my life could look like if I had made a different choice. I daydreamed about my next life, in which I would be living alone in my dream city, a girl doing it for herself, without the constant guilt of having to explain myself to this militant fun-sucker of a man. I turned twenty-one and I drank like a fish. My eyebrows were thin, and my liver was fat with vodka. I was broke, afraid, and miserable.

So now to the actual divorce. At some point, around eleven months in, I decided that I was done. I came home. I sat on the end of our bed and I said straight up, "I am not in love with you, and I am leaving you." Next I called my parents, who I had mostly avoided for those eleven months, and I told them. Then I took off my engagement ring and I left it on our tiny kitchen table. I slept at a girlfriend's place nearby, and since this was in a time before Instagram, cell phones, and being able to track anything and everything a significant other was doing, I didn't really think about him. I listened to sad music, drank a bottle of wine, and smoked a pack of cigarettes, even though I was never a smoker.

But I was not sad. I did not feel lonely. I did not feel alone. In reality, I had been alone the entire time. I had been weak, scared, and codependent. I had married the first guy I met out in the big real world because on paper he seemed like a good idea. When we split and I left, what I felt was an overwhelming sense of sweet relief. I knew that I was unhappy, and that he was unhappy, too. I had been trapped inside a hell of my own making, and I had spent so many hours trying to figure out my escape plan. Once I actually told the truth and ripped the Band-Aid off, it was liberating.

To this day, I have never missed First Husband. I have never once since that day regretted that decision or wondered about him or his life. I simply wished him happiness and silently thanked him for what I had learned. (Still, I made an entire decade of mistakes following the breakup.) I think it was shocking and weird, but there was never an opportunity for our divorce to get really ugly. I ghosted this man before ghosting was even a thing. I was just gone. Poof! I can't imagine what I put him through, how hard it was on his side. What he felt or what it was like for the perfect son to tell his perfect family that his choice of wife had been imperfect. I don't know what it was like to go back to our house and see half the plates missing, and (weirdly—not sure why this was the thing I took) my side of the IKEA nightstand set gone.

He called me a week later and asked if I wanted to go to therapy. I didn't.

I called him months later to let him know I had filed for a $35 divorce online. We signed the divorce paperwork.

A few years later, he called me asking for a copy of the papers. I assumed it was because he had located a perfect Italian wife who would love to live in his trap of perfection, so I happily sent them along. I never heard from him again.

On what would have been our ten-year anniversary, I wrote him a big apology letter and sent it to the only address I knew, his perfect parents' house. I admitted to being messy, and drunk, and hurtful, and not the right person for him. I never heard from him after that, and I do not know if he ever received my letter.

I realize that divorces are messy. That feelings are messy. That when kids, and houses, and twenty years or more are involved, it adds to the level of drama and mess. I know that things like cheating, new girlfriends, stepmoms, abuse, and money (or lack of money) all make divorce a very horrible thing to go through. I know that not everyone can walk away so easily.

But what I also know is this: You don't have to be unhappy. You don't have to stay in a relationship that doesn't serve you. You can make a really important life decision about someone and then change your mind. You can fall in and fall out of love. You can also love someone and hang on to them far longer than you should. That deep truth that sits in your gut is your compass! You can spend a ton of money on a big fancy wedding and a year later call it off without being a terrible person. You can disappoint your family, and they will still love you. People will talk about you, hate you, judge you, and misunderstand you, and it will have nothing to do with you. You can say vows to someone and then take back your vows, and then years later make vows to someone else and really mean them. I learned that marriage and partnership exist to make your life better, not whole. You have to be a whole person before you can possibly figure out how to be a duo. Getting engaged, or wearing a ring, or being married, or moving in together don't mean that it's your forever love. Just because someone swears they will love you forever doesn't mean that they will.

Was I pissed that I had invested all my saved cruise-ship money into our life together and didn't get any of it back? Sure. Did I hate him a little bit? Absolutely. But I knew that being righteous in our goodbye would just make it harder, and I just wanted to wipe my hands of the entire thing.

My biggest mistake was dragging out the whole thing so much longer than I needed to because I didn't want to be the bad guy or let other people down. I didn't want to be not perfect. I didn't want to have this history against me. I had to walk through life as a failure, a "divorcée," and that stung. I was paralyzed by what everyone was thinking and saying about me. I spent many evenings imagining the dinner table conversations First Husband was having with his family and what a horrible person they would all be agreeing I was. Of course, people talked about me and made up lies about me somehow tricking First Husband into marrying me so I could live in New York City, as if I was smart enough to hatch such a plan at twenty years old. I learned to drown out their whispers.

But the truth was that no one who actually mattered to me even cared. Not one person. My real friends hugged me. My realest friends laughed at me, because all along they knew I was an idiot. My family, though confused by my soap opera of a life, supported me. I knew in my heart that never once had First Husband and I discussed getting married before he surprised me by asking. I should have been brave enough to say my truth that very first day, but I wasn't. I was immature. I was a people pleaser. I now had an ex–First Husband. I wished him well. I continued to pursue my dreams. I put myself first. And, eventually, my cold, black, disappointed heart came to life once again. Fun fact: I ended up doing all the things he never believed I could do and more—but by the time I did, I had someone in my life who would run into a room with balloons and hugs to celebrate even my smallest victories.

Treat Yo'Self, 'Cause No One Else Will

Investing in your mental health takes a lot of courage and often gets overlooked, but at the end of the day, it is the best thing you can do for yourself. We've regretted outfits, and we've regretted most of the dudes we've dated, but we've never regretted any of the time or money we've spent trying to be better human beings. Self-love can be a face mask and a bubble bath, blasting heavy metal in your car, mastering Kundalini yoga, or years and years of intensive therapy.

We all suffer from something, yet everyone is so scared to talk about their head and their heart. Mental breakdowns are not just for the rich and powerful, nor are they only for those with massive trauma. Just like you can pull a muscle after a strenuous workout, you can hurt your brain after a period of prolonged stress or a big life change. You are not alone in your struggle, and there is nothing too small to be worthy of your feelings. You can still suffer from anxiety even if you had a happy childhood, and you can still suffer from depression even if you have "nothing to worry about." We hereby give you permission to give the finger to anyone who tells you to "smile," to "get over it," or who labels you "crazy" for *just having feelings*. We've all got emotions, insecurities, and hormones, and we know how hard it is to balance even the normal stresses of life. You can get all the Botox and a whole collection of expensive shoes, but at the end of the day, that won't fix you. It really doesn't matter what you look like on the outside if your insides are all fucked up.

LADY THOUGHTS

Everyone Is a Mess

JV: I think the older I get, the more normal I feel, because I've realized how bonkers everyone else is, too.

BT: Ditto.

KK: When you're young, you're so self-involved that the whole world is spinning, and it seems like everyone else has it together. It feels like everyone else has it together except me. And the older you get, you realize you're a mess, she's a mess, he's a mess.

JV: Yes! You start to see all of the cracks in everyone else's "perfect" lives. We're all just fucking messes.

BT: I had the opposite trajectory.

KK: You did?

BT: Yep, in my twenties, I was carefree and cool as a cucumber. The older I got, the worse my anxiety got. No one is immune to life's anxieties. You either start off with them, or you get them as you get older. Ain't life grand?

The Keltdown

I tried to drive my car into a wall once. On purpose.

I wouldn't have considered myself suicidal, but at the time, I was constantly overbooked and completely drained. I felt like my life was just me running on a treadmill nonstop. All I needed was to get off and catch my breath. I needed a break. The guilt of getting everything I wanted and hating it was isolating. I know I'm not alone in having felt this. There were so many moments during this period where I can fully admit that I wished I would catch mono, or the flu, or some sort of horrible illness where I had to lie in bed for a month. If I got sick, no one could blame me for somehow being weak or being a "quitter." I needed someone to make me a meal, run me a bath, and tell me it was all going to be okay. I needed to be ten years old again. I needed my mom to make me a cup of tea with a side of warm, buttered toast.

For the first time, I really understand why people went to rehab for "exhaustion." I had always thought this was silly and such a champagne problem. But it had become real for me. Rehab sounded like a fucking dream.

It all started when I was late to a shoot for my TV reporting job. I was at the end of my rope, hysterical, exhausted, feeling like I just needed it all to stop. I was trying, unsuccessfully, to find a parking spot in a six-story parking structure. My phone was going crazy with calls and "where are you" texts. The time on my dashboard was haunting me with every passing minute that I was not exactly where I was supposed to be. At every corner of the structure, when I would be stuck behind some tourists moving at a snail's pace, I would slam on the horn. Every time I drove to a new level to park, with growing frustration, I would rev my engine, push the gas pedal to the max, and speed down the corridor, just to slam on the brakes only seconds before hitting the wall at the end. I had near miss after near miss. My car started to smell like burnt rubber, and this act did nothing to calm me down. I was having a full-blown panic attack, meltdown, breakdown, whatever you want to call it. I realize this was insane. It almost seems silly now.

It's important to note that this all happened in the middle of a very bad year. My work schedule was nutty: I got up at 3:45 a.m. to go to work, and I was working at least twelve to sixteen hours a day, plus weekends. At the same time, my hair started falling out, I was gaining weight, I lost sight in my left eye, and I was randomly covered in hives for no reason. I was constantly irritable and exhausted. If I wasn't standing up straight in a tight dress, dazzling TV audiences with my bubbly personality, I was alone, in a black room, either asleep or staring at the ceiling without the energy to even turn the lights on.

I had worked so hard to get this fancy dream job that I didn't want to disappoint anyone or lose my coveted spot. So I said yes to every opportunity. I became the yes woman, and I was rewarded for it. Constantly, I heard things like "You are such a trouper," "You have such an amazing work ethic," and "You are so dependable." This adoration fueled me, but eventually I had nothing left. While I was saying yes to everything work-related, I was saying no to my self-care. For more than three years, I was saying no to resting and eating properly.

What's crazy is that the act of trying to drive my car into the wall of the parking structure while weeping, screaming, and honking was not my rock bottom. After that moment in the parking garage, I eventually found a parking spot. I dried my tears, put on my lipstick, and went on with my day. No one would have even noticed anything was wrong with me.

Later that week, still teetering on the edge of whatever bout of depression had hit me, I flew to Las Vegas to be a judge at the Miss USA competition. I was in my hotel, in a spiral of tears, when I decided to call my husband, not exactly sure how to describe my continued descent into this dark place. I remember saying to him, "I feel weird and, I dunno, babe, I tried to run my car into a wall." It came out of my mouth like I was saying, "I took a shower today." My husband was stunned and immediately sprang into action. Full of concern, he said, "That's not normal, Keltie." But this just made my cry more. I got more frustrated by the fact that he was pointing out my flaws instead of just listening to me. I hung up in a fit of fury.

The next thing I knew, my doctor was calling my cell at 9:00 p.m. My husband had called him in a panic. Everyone was worried about me, and

I felt like I was in the middle of an intervention. This is when I officially hit rock bottom, because my secret was out. I wasn't strong. I wasn't a "trouper." I was a straight-up mess of a human, and I felt like a stupid child. I was so embarrassed. Just hours away from being seen as a "stand-up and successful human" about to pick the next Miss USA, I was basically on psychiatric hold in the middle of a Las Vegas hotel room.

Later, a doctor would discover that my new job was causing my body to revolt, leaving me with adrenal blowout and, eventually, an autoimmune disease. Apparently, one of the side effects of having thyroid issues can be depression. It all makes sense now, but at the time, I just thought I was "tired." As a woman, you spend so much of your life rising above the cramps and bleeding of the red tide that just being tired can sometimes seem like a good day. We're like little machines, nothing stops us.

The shitty thing about rock bottom is that it hurts like hell. The great thing is that when you are down, down, down, and even when you fall down one more notch after that . . . you can only go up. As a grown-up, you are kind of on your own. I woke up the next day with the same job, the same pressure, the same brain, and it was up to me to look at my life and make the necessary changes. The kicker is that when I am the worst version of myself, I can easily spiral and make laughable decisions. Feeling low? Definitely eat an entire ice cream cake. Wait, what? Now you feel worse? Good, now look for whatever "fix" is next. It's a vicious cycle. It's a pathetic feeling when you can't even trust yourself to be on your own side, right?

Eventually, for me, what helped was an honest conversation with a psychiatrist, monthly professional help, some new boundaries (I still struggle with saying no), a cocktail of medications, and many, many nights of sleeping with a deep conditioner on my head. Though it was not easy, my sight came back, my hair grew back, and, eventually, my smile came back, too.

I've hit various versions of rock bottom at different times in my life. We all have. For me, they happened during my first heartbreak, my first big career disappointment, my tenth heartbreak, the first time I attended a funeral for a friend, the first animal I ever had to euthanize, having a car accident, and spending six months having to learn how to write again with my newly useless hand.

Our rock bottoms are our own, and no one has the same story. Our human struggle is deeply personal, and I don't believe in comparing to find out which one of us has had it worse. Life is hard for all of us. Things that broke me might not break you, and vice versa.

I once had a friend named Rachel. When we were living away from home, Rachel's mom sent her a flashlight in the mail with a Post-it attached that said, "Use when you find yourself in the dark place." Whenever one of our friends would be having a hard time, Rachel would pull that flashlight out of her bag and let one of us hold it. It's been years, but I always think about that flashlight. It's a great reminder that when life gets hard and dark, we have to find the light. I find the light by sitting where the sun hits my face, taking a walk even though I'm busy (specifically without a phone or other distractions), calling a friend who wants nothing from me and can do nothing for me, making a hot bath and filling it with good-smelling bubbles, organizing my closet or kitchen, and listening to music. Listening to music reminds me of when I was a teenager and thought the world was ending . . . only it never did.

The catch, of course, is that the only person who can actually find the good days in your life is you. I don't know how to fix us so that none of us ever suffer. But I do know that it's okay to be gentle with yourself and to acknowledge that you are low. There is no shame in being a perfectly flawed human who feels things deeply. Depression isn't something we have to fix. It's not a broken bone. We all have a part of us that we walk beside every day that has the ability to take us down. I've learned to love the rock bottoms of my life. Sometimes I welcome that feeling in. I just listen to Coldplay as I eat fried food, candy, and then cake with some more fried food. Cry. Journal. Complain. Cry. Sulk.

But I've learned to see the warning signs that I'm not taking care of myself and that I'm heading in the wrong direction. Mostly, I've learned to say hi to that dark part of myself and then kindly give it the middle finger.

Spiritual Therapy

I grew up in a household where the only coping mechanism I learned when something shitty happened was to pick myself up, dust myself off, and move on. Now, don't get me wrong, I'm not completely knocking this technique. It's definitely how I am able to repeatedly walk into hundreds of audition rooms and face the dead eyes looking back at me without having my spirit completely crushed when I don't get the job. I have never been the type to wallow in anything for too long, and up until the age of twenty-seven, I never had anything happen to me that didn't warrant a good old-fashioned "Tobin shake-off."

But in July of 2014, while packing for an upcoming vacation that I was going on with my boyfriend of a year and a half, I received a phone call that changed my life forever. My boyfriend, Matt, whom I lived with, whom I had been trying on engagement rings with the week before, had died in a hotel room in Philadelphia on a business trip. He was thirty-one, and he died from a valve detaching from his heart. I was suddenly a girl with a dead boyfriend. Talk about something you can't shake off. Instead, it shook me to my core and nearly killed me.

Until that summer, I had never understood depression. I was sympathetic to anyone dealing with it, but I couldn't fully grasp what it meant to be depressed. Needless to say, I was immediately thrust into the crippling depression and anxiety that comes from losing the love of your life. I won't share the details of that time now, and I'm not sure I ever will, but I want to share how I eventually coped.

Since no one in my family had ever talked to a therapist, the idea seemed very foreign to me, but I knew I needed to talk to someone or I would never be able to remove the dark veil that was covering my entire world. One of my best friends had a therapist she loved, so she asked for a recommendation for a grief counselor. She warned me that this type of counseling had a spiritual element to it, and that it might not be a good fit for me. I had nothing to lose and everything to gain at this point, so I made my appointment.

Before my session, I couldn't get the "spiritual element" out of my head. Was I going to walk into a smoky, incensed-filled room to find a woman with cult-length hair telling me to wait for the comet? Or even worse, would I have to CHANT? I was the girl who refused to "om" in a yoga class, for fuck's sake. How had I agreed to see a spiritual grief counselor?! Thank god I was too desperate to let any of those fears stop me.

I was pleasantly surprised when I arrived at the very standard office building in Westlake Village and walked into the suite. My counselor, Amyra, came out to greet me. Much to my delight, Amyra looked pretty normal. She was a middle-aged woman with a short curly bob and very kind eyes. *Phew,* I thought, *I might make it through this session without having to chant or throw chicken bones.*

I spent the hour telling Amyra my story. She sat there with a loving look on her face, and she made me feel safe to say and do whatever the fuck I needed. It was liberating. I felt a little lighter after the first session.

God bless my friends and family during this time, but my old habits of not wanting to show vulnerability made it impossible for me to really open up to anyone I knew. I went through the first year or so after Matt died clenching through all these encounters with them, because I refused to show anyone that I wasn't resilient and strong. I also hated feeling pitied, and so I never wanted to give anyone the opportunity to pity me.

That one hour a week with Amyra was the place I could lose total control and say things without being judged. There was the safety of knowing that I could completely break down in front of this person and not have to worry that she was going to tell our mutual friends the details, or to worry that I would have to be socializing with her later and pretend I didn't share such intimate thoughts.

Now, I'm sure you're wondering at what point the spiritual stuff snuck in, so here it is. I have never been a religious person, and I was raised with zero religious education, which were elements that made dealing with death a little more challenging for me. I didn't have a visual image of a place filled with clouds and rainbows and pearly gates where Matt was dancing around with other friends and family members who had passed. I had the fuzzy memory of a plot of dirt and a casket, and that didn't exactly comfort me. However, I had always felt that there was more to life than what we were experiencing, and I had faith that things were bigger than us—I just didn't know how to really practice that, and I had doubts that there even *was* a practice for it that I would be able to subscribe to. But Amyra helped me harness what that was and focus my energy on the bigger picture, the stuff beyond us. And it seems weird to say, but in the five years of working with her, I have not only felt more comforted when thinking about death, but I have learned to operate from a more empathetic, elevated, and conscientious place.

I have learned that sometimes I need to do things like write people letters I never intend to send in order to release resentment. I have had assignments where, every day for thirty-three days, I have had to look at myself in the mirror and repeat an affirmation that could help me shift a false belief I had about myself. I have had to do adult coloring books to learn to "play" again. I have been assigned countless books to read and have written things called "ideal scenes" in which you essentially manifest your future. I have literally set something on fire in the exact spot in our bedroom where I was standing when I received the news that Matt had died, so that I could release the bad energy and memories from that place. And you know what? It worked. I no longer gasped for air when I found myself standing in that spot. As someone who had the habit of going to worst-case scenarios in my fantasies, Amyra taught me to ask, "Why not win in your own fantasies?" She taught me to give people the benefit of the doubt, and the most valuable thing I've learned in five years—and the thing that has forever changed my life for the better—is that "everyone is just doing the best they can with what they've got." As soon as I was able to accept that as truth, I released so much anger. I no longer resented people who weren't handling life the same way I was. I no longer judged anyone for not doing things exactly the way I thought they should. Most important, I am able to forgive people who have hurt me.

So if you're a shake-it-off kind of gal who hates vulnerability (we can't all be Brené Fucking Brown), find yourself a good therapist. You might be pleasantly surprised by how vulnerable you're capable of being with a stranger who you don't have to see at brunch every weekend.

A Lady in the Streets, But an Anxious, Insecure Shell of a Human Being in the Sheets

Why am I my own worst enemy? I am a fierce, intelligent, badass bitch, but I constantly find myself fighting a battle inside my own head over the dumbest shit sometimes. When I open up any social media app, I immediately get bombarded with insane bodies, outrageous vacations, and happy couples. Perfection in all facets of life is literally getting shoved down my throat everywhere I look, and the more everyone else is #blessed, the more I feel #stressed.

I'll go ahead and say it: Social media is fucking toxic. Apps that were originally supposed to connect people have turned into massive sources of anxiety and self-esteem crushers for so many people, including myself. We're now in a constant downward spiral in the competition for followers, likes, comments, and external praise. We just want more, more, more in an effort to feel validated in our lives. It's narcissism at its finest, and it's addicting as hell. What a great cocktail for healthy self-worth, right? Ugh.

I'll rewind a bit. I was never super confident in my looks growing up, but I never really obsessed about them either. And I hid my typical teenage insecurity under ten pounds of black eyeliner and overly contrasted pictures from the "Myspace angle" (if you know, you know). Sure, as a teen I'd look at Britney Spears on the cover of *CosmoGirl* and wish I had her abs, but she was an untouchable angel to me. There was this sense of disconnect from the perfection I saw in magazines because I knew the polished bodies and faces were perfected by professional hair and makeup artists, studio lighting, photographers, and artistic airbrushing. Plus, they were celebrities. It was like comparing dollar store apples to Whole Foods oranges.

And then social media came around. It was a gradual process; I followed a few beauty bloggers here and a few fashion influencers there. Slowly but surely, my feed started filling up with *only* beautiful people living extravagant dreamy lives. And I found myself getting super self-conscious about things I had never even noticed about myself before. Like the size of my nose, or the gobble under my chin, or (and I'm not kidding) the skin on my eyelids. I went from seeing perfection only on billboards to seeing perfection in "normal girls" in every single photo on my social media feeds.

Like any other moderately insecure young adult, I started comparing myself and obsessively picking apart my flaws. I found myself glued to my bathroom mirror, hyper-analyzing my face far more often than I would like to admit. I would spend hours lifting my eyebrows and pursing my lips and squishing my nose to see what I could change that would make me look like all of the pretty girls I saw on my phone. But what I wasn't taking into consideration was the tens of thousands of dollars spent on rhinoplasties, breast implants, liposuction, lip filler, and lasers it took to get there. Oh, and Photoshop, of course.

I'm self-aware enough to realize that I'm scrolling through avatars and fairy tales of people's cracked lives, but I'm not self-aware enough to not let it get under my skin. It's like a head-versus-heart thing. But it's *way too easy* to alter a photo, and I felt this subconscious pressure to keep up. If you can't beat 'em, join 'em, right? So I started altering my pics, too. Nothing huge. Tiny tweaks. I'd make my waist a little smaller or my lips a little bigger. And then I'd get comments complimenting my tiny waist and my pretty lips. People were praising the very things I was altering in my photos! So now, not only was I comparing myself to other people, but I was comparing myself to this enhanced version of myself. What an ugly vicious cycle, dude.

And it wasn't just my physical appearance. I was fabricating this bogus life of happiness in my relationship at the time on social media, too. From the outside, it looked like I was *living the liiiiiiiife*. From the outside, I was super in love, traveling the world with a mega hot dude, without a care in the world. From the outside, I was always happy. But on the inside,

I was miserable. And ironically, the sadder I was, the more perfect our relationship appeared on my feed. When I was hurting the most, I would overcompensate with a super sappy post to justify staying in my crumbling relationship. But in reality, "the luckiest girl in the world" had just gotten into her fiftieth screaming match over fucking pancakes.

Once I began to realize the disconnect between my real life and my online life, the more I began to realize that everything I was seeing on social media was total bullshit. And it's not like everyone is just posting their happy days. Everyone is just posting what they *want everyone else to see*, even if it's a lie. No one posts about real-life shit like heartbreak, loneliness, financial problems, mental health issues, or insecurity. No one talks about the flawed stuff, because the flawed stuff won't get you likes.

I've always been pretty outspoken about how social media grinds my gears. One day, I was venting about how I unfollowed all of the perfect "Instagram girls" on social media because they made me feel bad about myself. And that's when Becca hit me over the head with the truth bomb (she's really good at that, by the way). She said, "Jac, *you* are that annoying bikini-wearing, globe-trotting Instagram girl to some people, you know." And I realized that I was so far up my own ass on one end of the spectrum that I didn't even realize that I was *literally* part of the problem for others.

From that day on, I made a pact with myself to be a little bit more honest on social media. To show my cellulite sometimes. To post my unattractive outtakes along with my best photos. To refrain from smoothing out a pimple. To be more honest when I'm not feeling my best. To post not only when I'm feeling real pretty, but also when I'm feeling pretty real. It's ridiculous that it takes courage to post an imperfect photo, but it does. And guess what? The flawed stuff *does* get you likes. Because our flaws make us human, and in reality, everyone is actually craving a true connection and something to relate to. We're at a point in society where everyone is sick of seeing the facade of curated bullshit on our feeds—and now it's actually *refreshing* to see some vulnerability and reality on social media.

So now, for me, it's all about balance. I'm still going to post pretty photos in my bikinis on vacation. Because I like to, and because it's part of my job. But now I realize that posting a shitty fire selfie doesn't make me feel any happier, and posting a lovey picture with my boyfriend won't save a failing relationship. The more real I am on social media, the more confidence I am finding in accepting and even embracing my imperfections. I'm finding myself wasting less and less time in front of the mirror. And it's way more fun being myself than being a fraud. Trust me, you should try it.

Through this I've learned that insecurity and self-worth don't discriminate. Human beings are flawed and envious by nature, no matter what deck of cards you're dealt in life. Supermodels are still photoshopping their own pictures, and they are *supermodels*. How fucked up is that?! At the end of the day, everything is relative, and I don't think it's fair to judge anyone for their relationship with their own body. But to anyone who wanted to unfollow me because I was "one of those Instagram girls," I hope my dimply legs can shed some light on the fact that I'm just a normal gal with normal-gal problems.

And listen, I know my rant sounds trivial and unimportant in the grand scheme of our issues on this planet (like, literally—we need to save our planet). But at the very core, self-worth directly affects everything you do. From how well you perform in your job to how long you can hold on to friendships to how deeply you can love another person. It all comes back to your relationship with yourself.

So, if you're 100 percent secure in the meat suit you live in, I applaud you. My ramblings won't apply to you, and I'm trying to get there at some point, too. But for any ladies out there who feel lesser-than when they're mindlessly scrolling through their social media feeds, just remember that the perfect girl you see on your screen is probably just as insecure as you are.

Maybe She's Born with It, Maybe It's Photoshop

Experts say that comparison is the thief of joy, and this makes lady life extra hard since comparison is inescapable these days. But the truth is, 99.9999999 percent of these "perfect" girls you see on social media get shit done to their faces and bodies. Don't believe us? Try this little exercise: Google "[insert celebrity's name] before and after."

If they don't have a new nose, a brow lift, butt implants, or lip injections, we'll pay you $100 (that'll get you about ten units of Botox, FYI). The most fucked-up thing about this "social media culture" is that everyone is pretending like their new face and bod are God-given. And listen, we are in favor of anything that makes you feel happy and confident. But it's extremely misleading when people straight up lie and claim things are natural when they aren't, and it makes the rest of us feel like trolls.

It's easy to fall down the rabbit hole of huge lips, hourglass figures, no cellulite, and perfect little noses all over social media. But no one, and we mean no one, is born with a sixteen-inch waist and a forty-five-inch ass. Everyone is editing their pictures, and even the people you assume don't edit their pictures ARE EDITING THEIR PICTURES. Supermodels, movie stars, bloggers, and even the girl in your book club are all tweaking their photos in some way or other.

Because the three of us live in Hollywood, we get to see these girls in real life and witness the Instagram vs. reality part of it all. Sometimes we're pleased to see a few wrinkles and a little bit of acne on someone we thought was unattainably flawless, but other times these women are simply unrecognizable in person compared to the perfectly curated photos we see on their feeds. There are a bunch of celebrities who notoriously alter their photos to look like a totally different person, and all the comments are about how hot they are. They're *celebrities*, so everyone knows what they look like in real life. And even though it's an inaccurate representation of them, no one seems to care.

We know this is depressing, so it's time for a little self-esteem boost! Imagine your favorite celebrity or influencer, and now realize that they're about three notches less hot than what you see on your feed. (Us inclued.) But we actually have an easy fix: STOP FOLLOWING ANYONE WHO MAKES YOU FEEL BAD ABOUT YOURSELF.

Instead of following supermodels or your frenemy from college who became an Instagram influencer, what we suggest is following ladies who look like you and accounts that make you happy. Becca follows girls with short legs. Keltie stopped following anyone under thirty-five. Jac mostly follows French bulldogs. You gotta know thyself to feel good about thyself!

WHO YOU SHOULD FOLLOW ON INSTAGRAM:

FUNNY OLD PEOPLE

YES!

DROOL-WORTHY FOOD

DEFINITELY!

CUTE DOGS

OMG DUH!

NOPE!

SUPER HOT CHICKS WHO MAKE YOU FEEL BAD ABOUT YOURSELF

No!

Nooo!

"Stars, They (Hate Themselves) Just Like Us!"

This is the part where I am supposed to make you feel better about yourself by telling you that all of the many, many, many celebrities I've met during my ten-plus years covering the red carpets of Hollywood are totally photoshopped and that they don't look anywhere near as perfect in real life as they do in their movies and commercials.

I can't do that because there are, in fact, two celebrities who are as perfect in person as they are in their magazine ads, commercials, and movies.

Charlize Theron and Jared Leto.

Charlize looks like human Photoshop. Her skin is so perfect, so poreless. Her high cheekbones and big eyes rest dramatically atop her supermodel-long body. Even her nail beds are long, with a luscious cuticle surrounding them. She's the kind of woman who doesn't have her nails painted, because her nails are naturally shiny and she's so magical that she would never have even a little bit of dirt under them. The whites of her eyes are whiter than white, and she is so pretty that you don't even notice what she is wearing, or what her hair is doing. Everything falls away in the presence of that *FACE*. How is her hair THAT blonde but also that shiny and seemingly healthy? What is this tan? She's perfectly sun-kissed yet ageless, freckle-less, and shows not a single age spot on her neck. Her neck is an entire other chapter. She's also cool and seems to have no idea that she is a perfect specimen of a human! She's Oscar-winning talented. On top of all that, the lady wanted kids and didn't have a love of her life around to procreate with, so she just did the damn thing and built her dream family, sans man, and adopted—twice. *Plus, that face!*

Then there's Jared Leto. I want to point out that, yes, I am incredibly biased based on the 1990s mega cult hit *My So-Called Life* and Jared's role in that TV series as Jordan Catalano. Jordan's moody, shearling-coat-wearing, brooding half smiles were my first celebrity crush and, to be honest, the only fictional character that I've ever written about in my journal. Jared has skin that looks like he was born yesterday. At the same time, his face is masculine and rugged, like he loves to drink tequila on the beach and stay up all night. His eyes are the bluest of blue, and he's so handsome in real life that it's almost difficult to look directly at him. His eyes send mixed messages of "I want to get to know you" and "You will never be as smart and worldly as I am, you fool." His hair, oh, the hair! It's so shiny and brilliant, and its natural ombré is so perfect that even the most skilled hairstylists could never re-create it. I would pay money to have Jared sit at the end of my bed and let me brush his hair for an hour. He is also a poreless wonder, which would make you believe that he spends millions of dollars a year on the top skin care and laser treatments, but he has an air about him that implies he washes his face with a bar of soap and has never even applied moisturizer. Jared has sold a bazillion records, also has an Oscar for acting, and on top of that, he loves to take his mom as his date to big events. Le sigh. Jared is perfect.

Both of these stars seem completely bulletproof. They truly find whatever life force they need inside of themselves, and they are totally secure. They are the only two celebrities I've ever met that give off this vibe. They really do not need your approval.

Everyone else—every single other superstar I've met up close—is much like you and me. Little insecure human beings full of the emotional residue of the times they got picked last for the team in school. Sometimes I think people from show business can be even MORE insecure because they have been tortured by years of rejection and comparison in Hollywood. These stars, whose pictures we bring into the salon when we want a haircut, all live somewhere on the sliding scale of "has way more wrinkles IRL" to "looks nothing like themselves IRL." Personalities range anywhere from "Do you like my thing?" to "Please like my thing" to "I have no idea what I am doing" and then all the way to "I know my thing is terrible and I am crushed by the weight of that, so I'm going to act extra difficult so that everyone thinks I'm important."

Here's what I know. I hope this brings you some comfort when you look in the mirror or think about your life. The men and ladies of Hollywood have wrinkles, stretch marks, acne scars, gray hair, badly tweezed eyebrows (that won't ever grow back), period panties, zits, bad breath, dry cuticles, chin hairs, family drama, times they cried at work, times they acted insane after a bad breakup and wished they could have taken it back, yeast infections, food in their teeth, and, much like all of us, they are truly just waiting for someone to say "Good job!" Ninety-nine percent of their hair is fake (yes, even in the commercials), as are their eyelashes, lips, cheekbones, and bodies. Pieces of them have been lifted and tightened and filled and pulled. Ribs have been removed, earlobes have been shortened, and fat has been sucked. These people are constantly seen in front of beautiful, high-powered lighting, after teams of professionals put them together, and then, after all of that, they are photoshopped within an inch of their pores. They have billboards in Times Square, shelves full of awards, and purse and shoe collections that would make anyone feel like an "it girl."

Even after all of this, many of them still walk into a room unsure of themselves.

I'm not saying any of this to be mean. I'm the most insecure person I know! But I am so often bombarded with images of perfection and confidence, and inspirational quotes telling me to "Be myself," that it's hard to feel remotely close to the level of woman the world tells me I should be. Especially after waking up in the morning after a few days of junk food and not enough sleep to see fried hair, under-eye bags, and uneven skin. Every day, all day, I am bombarded by people constantly yelling their achievements at me on social media and at dinner parties. Gouging my eyeballs with their bikini shots and their "candids." On a good day, I can handle it all. But it's really hard to feel okay during my bad days—and I'm sure it's the same for you.

Even after all these years, and all these wins, a fantastic career, a great marriage, and the amount of straight-up privilege I've had, I still don't feel like I did a good job unless someone says to me, "Good job." (Bonus points if that "Good job" comes from Jared Leto.)

I'm a Monster!

I was fortunate to have a really great childhood, raised by two incredibly kind and supportive parents who sacrificed everything for my happiness. Despite that, I struggled with something that almost every single girl on this planet has struggled with, and that is a battle with body image and body dysmorphia. My confidence as a child was embarrassingly high. I thought I was the coolest and the funniest and the prettiest (even with my thick-ass glasses) and the best piano player (I sucked). But once I went through puberty and the pressures of society came crashing down on me (as they do on everyone), things started to shift.

I was a tiny little thing my entire childhood. When I was fifteen years old, I was 5'6" and eighty-five pounds. People would stop my mom in the mall and accuse her of starving me because I was so thin, but in reality it was just the skinny prepubescent genetics. I got my period shortly after that and actually developed an appetite for the first time in my life. Jack in the Box breakfast Jacks and venti Frappuccinos were my go-to breakfast every morning, and because of this (along with getting six . . . yes, SIX cookies with my Subway sandwich every day), I gained forty-five pounds in a year. The weight came on super unevenly to my lower stomach, outer thighs, and face, and my skin stretched so much that I had stretch marks and cellulite all over my legs. Oh, and a brand-new double chin! Lucky me. I wasn't overweight by any means, but it was a dramatic change to what I was used to my whole life, and I literally looked like a different, puffy-faced person post puberty. It actually didn't bother me too much in high school because I was too concerned with what Taking Back Sunday lyric I should instant message my crush, but once I hit my twenties, my confidence in my body image, and myself in general, really started to plummet.

As I got older, I started obsessively searching for a magical cure for my mental, emotional, and physical instability. I have been prescribed Wellbutrin, Adderall, Xanax, Ambien . . . you name it, I've taken it. I had regular panic attacks, I wasn't sleeping, and I felt generally emotionally unstable and constantly on the verge of a breakdown, usually triggered by my relationship with my body. After none of the pharmaceuticals worked their magic on me, I got swindled into the "healthy lifestyle" cult mentality, and I thought that food allergies could be the problem. I went to a "holistic allergist" and took an offensively expensive blood allergy test. (Like . . . do those even work?) At the time I saw the allergist, I was already vegetarian, but my test came back telling me I was *severely* allergic to literally everything, from dairy to eggs to fish to gluten to soy to nuts to all meats. My stomach felt fine after eating all these things. But, aha! This must be what's making me feel like balls all the time.

So I cut everything out of my diet and went vegan, gluten-free, soy-free, and nut-free, and I lived on "air and sadness" for a little over a year. I purchased all of her "recommended vitamins," which cost me a chill few hundred dollars a month. I was on my way to my best new healthy life, so I decided to see a "health coach" I fell for through an online ad, who charged $200 per weekly session and who also forced me to buy his bullshit supplements for the "best results." Thinking back on it, he was *for sure* part of a pyramid scheme. Because I was so hopelessly far down the healthy "woke" rabbit hole, I was the perfect candidate to be swindled into buying any essential oil, detox juice, healing crystal, magic pill, group meditation, vaginal steam, or kundalini yoga class thrown my way. I met with naturopaths in basements, Reiki masters in parks, and psychics over the phone on a regular basis. Every "specialist" I met with was *positive* they knew the cure to my struggling body and mind. And I was desperate and naïve, so I believed them. I was spending an exorbitant amount of money that I *didn't have*, in hopes that something would hit. In addition to all that garbage, I weighed myself three times a day, obsessively tracking the slightest gain or loss. During this time, I was also working out two hours a day, so it was safe to say that literally everything in my life revolved around food and exercise. I was a nightmare to date or even be around, because I couldn't eat or drink anything anywhere. And it wasn't in the holier-than-thou kind of way; it was in the "I'm miserable and missing out on life" kind of way. All my friends would be slamming BBQ chicken wings and fries at happy hour, and I'd be sitting in the corner, quietly asking the waiter if there was gluten in the salad dressing. I had to research any food or drink outing days in advance to try to figure out what and if I could actually eat. Not only was I limiting my food intake, what I *did* eat had to be organic, non-GMO, blah blah blah. I was reading labels and ingredients with a magnifying glass like a vegan Sherlock Holmes, googling any unfamiliar words. This "healthy lifestyle" was taking over my life in the worst way possible. Not only was I mildly anorexic, but I was also developing an obsessive case of orthorexia. I was literally making myself sick if I consumed something "wrong." I remember eating one (ONE!!!) bite of a Del Taco quesadilla and three (THREE!!!) French fries after a night out drinking, and I made myself sick to my stomach for *days*. If I pound some late-night fast food now, all I have is a bad case of the toots and some mild constipation. But back then, I felt so guilty that I dared eat a few French fries that I went on a week-long juice cleanse to even out my food sins. I did these dangerous juice cleanses at least once a month, and I think it messed up my metabolism rather than doing me any good. I would deprive myself so severely that I'd end up bingeing on things like a jar of almond butter and five avocados in the middle of the night.

The entire time, I felt like a huge bloated mess, even though I was a size six. I nervously avoided the mirror at all costs, and when I did catch a glimpse of my body, I saw a hideous whale. Rolls and dimples and loose skin and cellulite and my repulsive face overwhelmed my vision, and I could barely make out the sad but wonderful human standing behind all the noise. And what did I have to show for all of this food sacrifice? A twenty-pound weight gain, cystic acne, an empty wallet, and a generally looming sense of anxiety and defeat. Even though my entire life revolved around being healthy, I still hid behind my clothes. Baggy band tees and boyfriend jeans were my go-to because I was too scared to show my body at all. I was so mad at myself, and I just felt gross all the time.

This was obviously not a sustainable way to live, and it finally came to a breaking point when I was at South by Southwest later that year, drunk at 1 a.m. and starving, and the only thing to eat was a Jersey Mike's turkey sandwich. It's kind of ironic, but one bite of that delicious $5 all-American sammie with extra mayo changed everything for me. I realized that *tasty food brings me happiness.* It finally hit me that food is such an important and rewarding part of life. Food brings us together, it teaches us about people, and it gives us human expression and a general sense of community. I *love* going out to eat. It's one of my favorite activities, and one of my favorite ways to experience the world while traveling to new countries. Eating brings me a very simple sense of joy. I love trying new cuisines and experiencing the ambience and interacting with people. I love the experience as a whole. I finally realized that I was depriving myself not only of delicious treats, but of all the important underlying meaning that came along with food. And, ironically, all it took was a chain-restaurant sandwich.

I decided that day to stop living a life fueled by guilt. I stopped looking at food as the enemy. I stopped counting calories and obsessing over every little thing I put in my mouth. I stopped dreading looking at my naked body in the mirror. I stopped depriving myself of the basic things that bring me joy. I stopped picking apart every little flaw and started viewing my body from a place of gratitude. I haven't weighed myself in more than five years. I started eating whatever I want, but I've learned portion control and balance. I went from gluten-free to gluten-weeeeee. I love hamburgers and chicken nuggets and ice cream, but I eat all of my favorite foods in moderation. (And I know that there are millions of people with real, detrimental food allergies out there, and I can't even imagine how difficult that is for you.) I work out when I can, but I don't feel guilty when I can't. I've figured out what works for my own body. And I'm self-aware enough to know what triggers me when it comes to my body image, which means I don't want to hear about your keto diet or your workout plan, Karen.

But, most important, I've learned to accept my flaws and embrace my body. The girls always make fun of me because I "never wear any clothes," but this is honestly a relatively new confidence I have in my body, and it feels *good* for the first time in my life. I'll always have cellulite no matter how skinny I am, I'll always have small, floppy boobs, and I'll always have hyper-extended knees and elbows that look wonky in photos. But I also have a lot of great physical qualities and a healthy body that deserves to be celebrated.

Ever since I had this realization, I dropped the extra weight without effort, my skin cleared up, and I generally feel healthier mentally, physically, and emotionally. And I'm not a total pain in the ass to be around anymore! Listen, as much as I feel like I've come a long way from eating air and sadness, and my body dysmorphia has calmed down a lot in the last few years, I'd be lying to you if I said I have been magically cured. I still get down on myself every single day, because the path of acceptance with body image is a never-ending journey. But I stopped letting my negative thoughts get the best of me twenty-four hours a day. Some days I feel pretty, and some days I feel like Shrek. And I'm okay with that.

It Costs a Lot of Money to Look This Mediocre

By the time I was in third grade, I could already pick out who was the prettiest at my school and what that meant. In class, the girls with the pretty hair and pretty dresses were always favored over the girls with tragic bowl cuts and mud-stained sweatpants. Life started to be all about outward appearance: who had the Guess jeans, the good hair, the fancy sneakers, and whose moms let them wear colored lip gloss to school. I look at my niece, who is around the same age right now, and I cannot fathom that she's at all interested or aware of these things, but if she is anything like I was—she has already begun to think that people's opinion of her matters. A lot.

I remember the first time I was aware that body shape was going to impact my life, and it's all thanks to Dolly Parton. For Halloween, my mom had allowed me to wear her old vintage ice skating dress. It was made of green velvet and had little white pom-poms around the edge of the skirt with a matching vest. I was beyond proud. When I left for school that morning, it was like I was on the catwalk of Paris Fashion Week. I loved my look. Later in class, when we had the Halloween parade, I started looking around and realized that all the other princesses and superwomen (even the zombies) had better costumes than me and were getting more attention. Then, for whatever reason, I grabbed two of the balloons floating in the middle of the class party, stuffed them down my shirt, and when people asked me who I was, I replied, "I'm Dolly Parton!" I was a hit. My classmates couldn't get enough of me. I was the talk of the third grade. It was then that I realized that even though I knew almost nothing about Dolly Parton, I knew enough. I knew that boobs mattered. Boobs made you popular.

But my boobs never came. As I got older and older, everyone around me was developing, and I remained flat as a board. I experimented with stuffing my bra and wearing my brother's massive oversize T-shirts (so that no one would notice) while explaining loudly, to nobody in particular, that I was a ballerina and that it was important for me to not have boobs.

Life went on, and when I left home to become a professional dancer in New York at eighteen, I learned the showbiz secret of wearing a bra where the cup was completely filled with foam. This allowed for my tiny titties to swish up perfectly, forming a faux cleavage (I think they make these officially now and they're called "add two cups," but at the time, we made our own). I faked it till I was naked, and I saw a cool twelve-year-old boy's body staring back at me in the mirror.

Itty-bitty-titty committee aside, the most hilarious thing about my twenties is that I legitimately thought I was HOT SHIT. I learned to do a black smoky eye, I bleached my hair blonde, and I got a "dark" weekly spray tan. I had freckles and age spots, horribly overplucked eyebrows, and blue nail polish. But I felt like I was a goddamn supermodel. I even coined a term for my hot twenty-something self, "braless and flawless!"

It wasn't until I moved to Los Angeles and started working in TV that I realized I was a hideous beast who needed to change almost everything about myself.

Back I went to the "add two cups" bras. I learned about the lasers that can take away sun spots, the creams that take away zits, hair extensions, lash extensions, nail extensions, and eyebrow rehab (yes, I went). Los Angeles is a place where the two prettiest girls from every small town in the world gather to realize that their towns had very low bars for looks. We now have a term for this called the "glow up." But for me, as all my parts started to glow up, one thing started to sag down.

My chin.

Call it DNA. Aging. Gravity.

Maybe it was because social media starting ruling my life. It seemed like the more time I spent on TV, the more unkind messages I would receive from the viewers. Everything from my "saggy knees," to my "horse face," to "piss ants for eyes." People would say to me, "Oh! Just forget it, they're just jealous." But just as I was brushing off their comments, I would catch a look at myself in the mirror, and for the first time, I would notice the flaws that the viewers were pointing out. I actually called my mom one night and asked her why she never told me that I had a massive forehead. She laughed and said, "Oh, honey, I never wanted you to feel bad about it," confirming that I had been blind to it all along. I was not hot shit. I was a hometown ten, a New York seven, and a Los Angeles four.

As my career on TV began to heat up, I would run home after work and watch my show and segments with excitement. I was beyond proud. I was thrilled. I was lucky. I was working my ass off, and my star was rising! I was also really good at completely tearing myself apart. My voice, my cadence, but mostly MY NECK. While interviewing celebrities, I spent most of my time on camera being shot in profile. In my eyes, that profile perfectly showed my double chin! A wattle!

Living in Los Angeles, I started to look at all the things I could do to fix this problem with my face. At first, a dermatologist suggested that I fill the muscles in my neck with Botox so that I would release some of the tension pulling down on my jaw. Hundreds of dollars later, I was frozen. It didn't do much. Next, at a facial place, a lady convinced me that what I really needed was an at-home laser machine. She wanted me to use it every morning and night for skin tightening. I kept the machine charged up in my car, and every day on my way to and from work, I lubed up my neck and drove while lasering my neck over and over. This tiny bit of equipment cost me an entire two-week paycheck. I bought the masks, the sleeping creams, and the tightening rubs. When the fad was to "freeze the fat," I connected my neck to a giant vacuum, let it suck up my chin fat for forty minutes, and froze it. It hurt like a bitch! For the low cost of hundreds of dollars, it actually made it worse. I used contour makeup and stopped letting people photograph me from the side. Next, I was talked into injecting my neck with fat-eating enzymes. It was beyond painful and crazy expensive. The first week, my neck swelled up to the size of a tennis ball, and I had to sleep sitting up, in pain, with a tensor band around my head.

My husband was thrilled. Although I do believe that some of the fat was removed, it did nothing for my saggy skin, and so I was left with even saggier skin, with nothing to support it. I gave up. I promised myself that I would stop messing with my face and that I was just going to have to deal with this new look. I would ask friends and family if it was noticeable, and I began to get the "Well, I never would have noticed if you hadn't pointed it out, but now that you have . . ."

Naturally, I started researching chin liposuction, and I was convinced that was what I needed. All these stars in Hollywood had twenty-year-old necks but were closer to fifty. I began to ask around in the Hollywood circles, "Who is doing this miracle work?" I got some recommendations and paid hefty "consultation fees" to meet with a few of them. Everyone said it would be easy to fix me, and that they would do this and that in one day, no problem. Finally, I was talking about it with a friend who happened to be an A-list celeb's personal assistant, and she suggested that I go to Dr. Diamond.

I went in for my consultation, and after taking horrendous side-angle photos of me, Dr. Diamond came into the room less than confident. I immediately thought, *Why did I mess so much with my face? Who had done all this to me? I was a thin girl and the problem was never fat!* He circled me in the chair over and over, said I had the neck of a sixty-year-old woman and that I had really done damage to my skin. He explained that you need the muscle and the fat under your chin to hold the skin nice and tight. Through my self-prescribed concoction of fat removers, I had removed all the fat from my chin. Now, there was nothing holding it up, hence the saggy skin.

I came back weeks later. This time, he called some colleagues into the room to discuss deep lasers that go inside the muscle to see if those might work. He then came up with a game plan! If they used the lasers, some chin filler, and his signature "minimally invasive neck lift," there might be a 10 percent improvement. He couldn't make any promises. I was hoping for more like 90 percent improvement, but I wouldn't admit it to him. I begged him to fix me 25 percent!

It turns out that minimally invasive surgery isn't really the correct title for what I had done. I suppose they call it minimally invasive because I have no big scars on my face. Instead, I had three little tiny holes made, one below my chin and two behind the ears. I was put under full anesthesia and, after the surgery, I was wheeled out in a wheelchair in a full head wrap. I had to sleep sitting up and alternated every twenty minutes from ice on to ice off for weeks. Dr. Diamond suggested that I spend an hour inside a hyperbaric chamber to help with healing. I was on serious drugs. I wasn't allowed to eat any solid food for two weeks, and I wasn't even allowed to suck through a straw, since they didn't want my chin muscles working at all. My face was swollen and bruised, and I didn't leave the house because I was wrapped up in a head wrap to help keep the chin healing correctly. I wanted this to work, so I followed the post-surgery rules perfectly.

Over time, the swelling went away, and my beautiful new chiseled chin began to make its debut! Ten percent? Heck no! I felt like a million bucks. Everywhere I went, people would say to me, "You're looking incredible! Have you lost weight? Did you get your eyebrows done?" I was thrilled with the results and, unlike my intentions for sticking those balloons down my shirt in the third grade, the outward attention was meaningless to me. My favorite part of my transformation was that when I looked in the mirror, I no longer looked straight at my neck. Instead, I began to look at the parts of my face that I love; my full cheeks, my cute ears, my freckled nose, my pretty, vibrant skin. I felt a confidence I simply hadn't felt in years. I know I'm supposed to have a different answer, about how beauty comes from the inside, but hell, my outside was cute again!

I used to think that people who had plastic surgery were vapid, with low self-esteem or daddy issues. I would question how a woman could ever put implants in her chest or suck out fat from her thighs. I blamed girls for taking the easy way out instead of learning to love themselves or heading to the gym. What this journey has taught me is that, in an effort to not be one of those "plastic" girls, I did all of the non-invasive treatments on top of each other, without ever really seeking the advice of a professional. What probably could have been fixed with a professional laser in an hour became an almost unfixable issue because I got sucked into believing that none of these treatments had any downsides.

While admitting this surgery publicly, and sharing it on our Lady-Gang TV show, I felt a lot of different emotions. I felt brave, because when I was researching the surgery there were so few women admitting they had done it. I felt scared that my coworkers, bosses, or followers would think less of me. I felt proud that I was changing the conversation in Hollywood! Instead of being like 99 percent of the women who just share that they are "drinking water and getting sleep," I was able to say, "Ladies in your thirties, forties, and fifties, your neck is normal, these women are having neck lifts and they're not telling you!" I felt a bit embarrassed and self-absorbed to admit that something as dumb as what my neck looked like would matter to me. But mostly, I felt really happy. When I looked in the mirror, or looked at pictures of myself, I felt pretty. I know that's beyond stupid. I can almost hear everyone saying, "But you were pretty before." Much like everything else in life, though, someone can tell you something a million times. Unless you really feel it for yourself, it doesn't matter much.

I feel pretty. In a world that makes me feel like a hideous beast all the time, it's nice to have one less thing to hate about myself.

My neck lift was selfish.

It was expensive and completely indulgent.

It was exactly what I wanted.

A COMPREHENSIVE GUIDE TO EVERYTHING KELTIE HAS DONE TO HER FACE

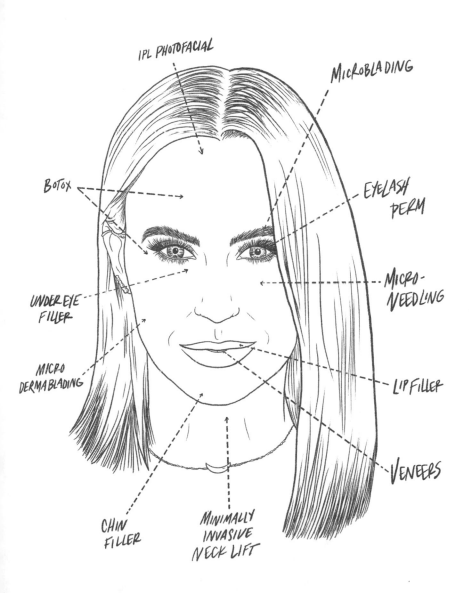

IPL PHOTOFACIAL

MICROBLADING

BOTOX

EYELASH PERM

UNDER EYE FILLER

MICRO-NEEDLING

MICRO DERMABLADING

LIP FILLER

CHIN FILLER

MINIMALLY INVASIVE NECK LIFT

VENEERS

SINCE KELTIE CAME CLEAN . . .

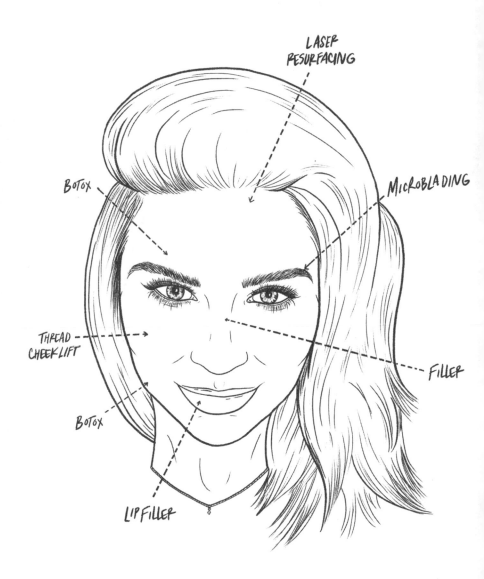

LASER
RESURFACING

MICROBLADING

BOTOX

THREAD
CHEEK LIFT

FILLER

BOTOX

LIP FILLER

JAC

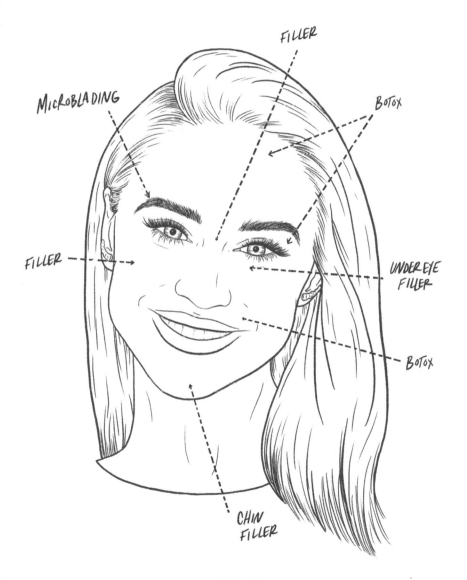

FILLER

MICROBLADING

BOTOX

FILLER

UNDER EYE FILLER

BOTOX

CHIN FILLER

BECCA

Stumbling Through Ladyhood

If you feel like your life is a disaster and you have no idea what you're doing, congrats! *That* is what makes you a lady! Women are complicated, intricate, messy, beautiful creatures, and it's about time we start embracing our imperfections. There's no handbook telling us how to be a modern lady, and we're all just trying our best to figure out this "life" thing as we go. When we think of a lady, we think of her as a perfect Audrey Hepburn, with her dress pressed, a fresh blowout, the doting husband, and everything on point. But even Audrey Hepburn was probably crying in the bathroom over her cheating man. Yes, even Audrey was (allegedly) cheated on.

Every woman wants the same things. We want security. We want to feel appreciated. We want to have a purpose. We want to feel confident. We want to have a full heart. We want to be successful. We want to feel wanted. It's easy to look around you and feel like every other lady has all these things figured out except you, but the truth is that we are all struggling and crumbling behind our smiling profile pictures. So that's why it is important to try (even though it's challenging) and celebrate the little victories without constantly seeing how you measure up to other people. Forgive yourself, and learn from your mistakes. Society makes it really hard to be a woman without feeling bad about ourselves all the time for simply existing. We are constantly being bombarded with so many unsolicited opinions about everything, from our choice of bathing suit to our choice of men, and the best thing we can do is to just be kind to ourselves.

So stop faking it until you make it. It's totally okay to ask for help. And that help can come in the form of family, friends, professionals, yoga, rom-coms, books, or weed. The truth is that you are the only one who really notices when your nails are chipping. Everyone else's heads are way too far up their own asses to care about your manicure schedule, we promise. And bikini waxes? Hate 'em. Sometimes we're gonna have some rogue hairs on our vaginas, and that's okay! In the same way you can let go of manicures, you can also let go of your inbox, saying yes when you want to say no, and overexerting yourself every damn day. Don't let the weight of being everything to everyone crush your soul, because ladyhood is a never-ending journey.

There are always going to be more emails. There are always going to be more family events. There's always going to be another birthday card to send. There's always going to be another hair to pluck on your body. It's time to let go of perfection, because something is always going to be falling apart in some aspect of your life. You should always *try* to be your best self, but being your 80 percent self is great, too.

We get it. As ladies, we're constantly being pulled in a million different directions, but we have to be selfish every once in a while to be the most capable version of ourselves. Let's apply the advice about "putting on your own oxygen mask before assisting others" to our lives. If you're not okay, you won't be able to attack life coming from a place of calmness and confidence. And then you're screwed, no matter how many squats you do at the gym or how many Gucci bags you have.

Remember, a lady is defined by her confidence. In a world where everybody is homogenized, you have to embrace the things that make you a unique, bad bitch. When everyone is trying to look the same and dress the same, your quirks are going to make you stand out in a room full of clones. No one notices your stretch marks, so don't let them stop you from feeling like Beyoncé in your new bikini. Embrace your strengths, but also embrace your flaws, because the combination of all these qualities is what makes you a rare, beautiful lady.

And while you're feeling confident in your own skin, remember that there is room for all of us at the table, and you don't have to sabotage the girl next to you to get ahead. True beauty comes from lifting up the women around you. Helping the women around you. Celebrating the women around you. Life is hard enough as it is, so having your own little LadyGang makes it a little bit more bearable.

Last, your gut is your guide. Before every huge mistake we've made in our lives, our gut was telling us "DON'T FUCKING DO THIS," and we did it anyway.

Things Every Woman Needs to Know

- How to give yourself an orgasm
- To wear SPF every day (your skin will thank you in thirty years)
- To wipe front to back
- How to properly pay your taxes
- How to give yourself a breast exam
- To always pee after sex
- Your happiest friend on Instagram is your saddest friend in real life
- To make sure your face doesn't show in the nudes you send
- To fuck the bad boy and marry the nice guy
- Nipple hair is totally normal
- Your eyebrows can make or break your face
- How to give a hand job
- Your wedding day is the most important day to you . . . and only you
- To pack extra tampons
- If you're not doing anything about your mustache, you have one
- The difference between a yeast infection and BV
- How to nail a job interview
- Always tip at least 20 percent
- Therapy is always the answer
- No one deserves a "birthday month" and a "birthday week" is bullshit
- Your ex is your ex for a reason—stop checking his Instagram
- To always sleep on your back, because side sleeping gives you wrinkles
- The wrong undergarments can ruin an outfit
- No one else is noticing your five-pound weight loss or weight gain
- How to properly apologize
- How to describe your strengths in one sentence
- How credit card interest works
- To never stand on the end in group photos
- No one cares how many likes your last Instagram post got
- To stop hating your body—chances are it will only get worse anyway

I Don't Want to Go to Your Birthday Party (How to Say No)

Rule number one: You can't be everything to everyone. If you think you can, you are gonna burn out fast. When you're saying yes to someone else, you might actually be saying no to yourself. This is not us telling you it's okay to be a selfish asshole all the time! There's a balance between only doing things that make you happy and being a doormat that spends every waking moment making everyone else happy.

You have to find the in-between. It has taken us a lot of trial and error, and what feels like a lifetime, to figure out how to say no with grace, but once we did, it was euphoric. When you get an invitation, it might feel like you need to RSVP immediately and stand by that decision like your life depends on it. But you have to learn to receive the invitation and really take inventory of how important your presence is. What does the day look like for you? Do you have a ton of work to do, and can you afford the **hangxiety** it may bring? Are there going to be energy vampires there that will suck you emotionally dry? Is your ex going to show up and ruin everyone's time? Would you rather sit on your couch in your sweatpants and watch reruns of *Seinfeld*? Take a breather, have a glass of wine, and then make a decision. Think about these important questions, and don't jump to saying yes just because you're feeling ambitious and want to please people. If your answer is no, that's okay. We're all adults, and most of us don't have time to go to Natalie's third birthday party of the month. And by the way, most of the time nobody actually cares if you show up or not. Don't use that fake pressure and made-up guilt in your own head to make a decision.

Most important, weigh how necessary that event is. Don't RSVP to your best friend's wedding and bail the night before because you're "burnt out" from too many happy hours. Don't say yes to fifteen birthday parties and then say no to your friend's mother's funeral because "Funerals make you uncomfortable." Guess what? They make everyone uncomfortable, especially the person who died (Becca only agreed to write this book to make this specific point).

Leaked Nudes:
No Regrets

Picture this: a warm summer day in August 2014. I was in Atlanta visiting my family and getting some quality time with my nephew, Jack. I was sitting next to my dad on the couch, watching sweet little Jack tinker with his toys. Since watching children "play" bores the fuck out of me, I decided to take a stroll on social media, Twitter to be specific—it was 2014, so Twitter was my lifeline. I clicked on the mentions tab, the place that was usually filled with *Glee* fans throwing compliments my way and telling me how amazing I am (yes, this is why actors are horribly conceited people). But that day was different. Instead of my usual accolades, a slew of nude photos of *myself* from many years before started traveling down my feed. My stomach dropped out of my butthole like I had just eaten gas station sushi. I quickly tilted my phone away from my dad, trying to convince myself that it had to have been a glitch in the app. Maybe those photos weren't sent to me from strangers across the ocean. Maybe my "cloud" (still unsure of how it even works) just happened to open up to my personal device and no one else's. But as I scrolled and scrolled and saw usernames like "dirtygurlz" and "supersluttychicks" with my nude photos next to their tweets, I quickly realized that a breach in security had definitely happened and that was indeed my bare beaver on the internet superhighway. (To get a little more specific, the photos were Christmas-themed: Santa hat, fur boots, full frontal, ho, ho, ho—you get the picture.)

My phone rang immediately, and it was my manager, Ricky. He informed me that there was a whole group of women in Hollywood who were part of the hacking, one of whom was Jennifer Lawrence. After hearing that I wasn't the only one, I was comforted—and it's probably because I knew that Katniss Everdeen was the only nude body anyone would care to see or go searching for. Phew! I got off the phone, took a deep breath, and wondered how long it would be until I heard from J. Law herself. I mean, at that point, wasn't it like we were both members of the same sorority?!

The next, and possibly biggest hurdle in all of this, would be breaking the news to my amazing, supportive, esteemed attorney father that he raised a daughter who not only decided to do a cheesy Christmas-themed nude photo shoot for her boyfriend five years ago, but also that by some crazy act of Satan, those photos had ended up on a public website called TheFappening. This was no doubt a stark contrast from my older sister Jessica's picture-perfect life as an attorney with a loving husband and a bouncing baby boy. So, in true Becca Tobin fashion, I decided it was best to just be blunt and rip off the Band-Aid.

I walked back inside the house, looked Tom Tobin in the eye, and said, "Dad, I'm gonna need you to stay off the internet for a while. Someone hacked into my photos, and my naked body is strewn across the internet." He looked at me calmly and answered, "Okay, no problem. I'm so sorry, sweetie." (And that's reason 6,897 why my dad is the greatest human on Earth.)

It was pretty much the same, non-judgmental, empathetic response I received from the rest of my family, and that reaction did something truly extraordinary for me. Since my family didn't react in a way that made me feel stupid or ashamed or gross or slutty, I decided that I wasn't going to allow this experience or other people to make me feel that way either. I mean, don't get me wrong, it was still a giant shit sandwich I was having to snack on, but it was going to take a lot more than this to kick my gorgeous Christmas ass.

The hours passed, and the calls came rolling in from friends, family, ex-boyfriends, etc. I realized that I needed to somehow acknowledge this event to the rest of the world (or, like, my five fans who cared). My response? A simple tweet saying "Merry XXXmas!" (Let me remind you that it was August.) And you know something? The tweet was a fucking HIT. I got responses from girls all over the world about how much my ability to make light of a shitty situation inspired them to do the same. I'm not saying we should all just sweep shit under the rug, especially when you're violated like that, but I am saying that there is a sense of freedom in being able to take back control.

After I was able to get over the initial shock and disgusting feeling of being violated, I took a step back and saw what those photos actually represented: a young woman feeling confident enough to take sexy photos for her boyfriend. Those photos represented something I was and still am fucking proud of: a positive body image and enough confidence to have fun with it. It meant that I was comfortable with my sexuality, and I feel grateful that I was able to express that in a healthy (and, in this case, very festive) way.

As women, we are often told to hide those parts of us, to keep them behind closed doors, and that if we don't, it somehow makes us slutty. Well, I'm here to tell you that "slutty" wasn't the worst feeling I could have felt during that time. The worst thing I could have felt was that the disgusting, sick, fucked-up man who hacked into my iCloud had somehow brought me down, defeated me, or made me feel ashamed.

I knew that my public reaction to these photos would impact other people, and I wanted the impression to not be about me somehow feeling sorry or ashamed of my naked photos. I wanted my reaction to be the thing I have carried with me for my entire life: We're all human. Shit happens; let's laugh about it so that we don't cry.

So the moral of this story is a couple things:

1. Just because people try to make you feel ashamed of something doesn't mean you have to feel the shame they clearly feel about themselves.

2. Jennifer Lawrence still hasn't called. It's fine, I've moved on. Have I though?

3. If you're gonna take nude photos of yourself, make sure you either leave your face out or love them enough to be proud of them if they land on TheFappening.com one day.

My Eggs Are Cooked

"Oh god, don't have kids, child-rearing is way overrated."

—my mom

As women, we spend what seems like our entire lives trying NOT to get pregnant. I estimated that I've experienced more than three hundred periods since I became sexually active. Three hundred weeks where my cravings went crazy, my boobs got sore, and I felt insane . . . at some point, a day or two before my crimson wave would actually greet me, I would say to a friend, "I better not be pregnant!" And then I would spend the next forty-eight hours worried sick that I was knocked up, and wonder what I was going to do, what the baby would look like, and if I was going to go to hell if I terminated the pregnancy because I was unemployed, living in a bunk bed in a closet (with twelve roommates) on the Upper West Side.

But then my vagina got old.

It started simply enough. I experienced a bout of tampnesia and made my way to the gyno. I prepared to see my doctor like I was going to be starring in an HD porn. Wax, shave, exfoliate, lotion, nice underwear . . . a refreshing wipe in the bathroom right before my appointment, in case any vagina sweat happened to congregate in my pristine vag pre-inspection.

I checked in. The waiting room was filled with baby bumps, and the walls were filled with baby announcements that all had weird ass spellings for normal names—which people don't realize is going to totally mess with these children when they can't find the keychain at Disneyland with CCAYRAH on it, just Sara (take it from a Keltie).

Next, we arrived in the room, where the paper "dress" was waiting for me. At this point, I knew I had an additional fifteen minutes of sitting on the bench, wearing the paper, with my socks on, feeling cold and alone, and looking at the plastic diorama of the uterus. I am in my thirties, and I still have some really big questions about all the body parts and how they work.

The doctor arrived. My legs were lifted up up into the awkward stirrups, and the cold duck machine was inserted inside of me. The doc instructed me to take a deep breath but never made eye contact with me for the next ten minutes . . . just my nether regions. It was terrible. After I sat up, some vagina juice slipped out and created a wet spot on the paper covering the table. I know that if I ever saw my doctor out in the real world, I would have to run in the other direction if my vagina leaked out onto a piece of office furniture.

What made this particular trip even more awkward is that, even though I had spent a decade using sunscreen, getting Botox, and yearly lasers treatments for "age spots"—even though I worked out, kept up with the trends, and plucked any gray hairs that sprouted from my head—my vagina didn't lie.

My lack of emotion from the Botox was evident when the lady doc said to me, "Listen, if you want to have kids, you should probably start trying."

And there it was . . . my vagina was officially past due.

It felt unfair. I still felt twelve inside. People constantly guessed that I was twenty-nine! I even still got carded at bars! Blood tests then confirmed that my eggs were almost gone, the chances of getting pregnant naturally got smaller every single day, and I was at the point in my life where any pregnancy would be referred to as geriatric. Here's a big fuck-you to whoever came up with this term for pregnancies over thirty-five. I can almost guarantee it was a man. Side note: Since my gyno exam, the phrase "geriatric pregnancy" was changed to "advanced maternal age" because of how upset women were getting about the term.

I felt weird. I felt conflicted. My answer to any of the people who asked me ten to forty-five times a day, "Omg! When are you having kids?" or commented, "Looks like a bun in the oven" after I ate a sandwich was always, "We're not trying, but we're not *not* trying." I wasn't on birth control.

But I didn't want a baby right now. I didn't know if I wanted a baby ever. I didn't even like babies. I refused to hold my friends' babies until they were toddlers because I was so afraid of breaking them. What I did love was that after spending a decade hustling for the dollars, we got our dream home and could lazily spend Saturday afternoons doing renovation projects and strolling the aisles of Home Depot with nowhere else to be. I loved that, after a decade of getting up before 5:00 a.m. to drive to work in the dark, I had been promoted to a job that allowed me (on most days) to drive to work with the rest of the morning commuters when the sun was already up. I loved being an entrepreneur for a buzzy company, and I loved having a little extra money each year to travel, spoil my family, and get a new bag.

On top of that (and I can see everyone judging me for saying this), when you wait until you are geriatric to start thinking about having a family, you have already seen all of your friends' marriages that have crumbled post-baby. Some of the most solid couple friends I've known fell into affairs, bankruptcy, divorce, all-around misery after having their dream baby. You have to admit, the odds are not great. I've also been around these friends long enough to see the absolute disaster that is co-parenting with someone you now hate (for everyone except the "consciously uncoupled" Gwyneth Paltrow and Chris Martin). The parents of the world don't really sell the dream to the non-babied. My thirties Facebook page is one big complaint forum for my mom friends, and my catch-up visits with them always include the words "it's a lot," "these fucking kids," "exhausted," "overwhelmed," "no time for myself," "I have no money now," and "this kid sucked out my beauty. . ." They always quickly follow it up with "but it's the best thing I ever did!" That being said, I have some mommy friends who have relished being a mom, and it's easy to see that they were born to momma.

I had a Cabbage Patch Kid growing up, but I was never into dolls. I was the kid who played "let's make my own magazine" and then spent hours cutting up old magazines and writing new copy for my "articles." I didn't have babies around me in my family, so the first diaper I changed was at twenty-seven while babysitting a friend's kid, and I had to watch a YouTube video explaining how to do it. My best friend once described me as someone who is "very hard on her stuff." I drop phones, and I scuff designer shoes the first day I wear them. As I write this, I have a cut on my nose that I got from trying to open a jar and then basically punching myself in the face. I would need to wrap my baby in bubble wrap 24-7 in order to keep it alive. On top of that, I'm selfish, impulsive, and a neat freak, and all my furniture is white. When (surprise!) my geriatric womb managed to get pregnant, and before I had a chance to even revel in my "Oh shit, this is happening" mind-set, I suffered a miscarriage. I could barely find the time to *lose* a baby. I was at the doctor's on a Wednesday afternoon and back to work in my adult diaper, shedding plum-size blood clots, on Thursday morning. A few weeks later I was told that some TV viewers didn't find me relatable because I'm not a mother. (I swear this is real, womanhood is a nasty beast, y'all!) The women I wanted to be growing up—Oprah, Dolly Parton, Liza Minnelli, Jennifer Aniston—never had children either. Oprah has her girls' school, and Dolly has her children's libraries, and even though sometimes these ladies get shit for not using the real estate of their wombs, I appreciate that there are unapologetic women out there who didn't have children and didn't get ousted from society.

It's messed up that vaginas have a past-due date anyway, when sperm works forever. The bottom line is that we all need to stop asking women when they are going to have babies. It's incredibly painful on every single side. It's not a cute joke or a conversation starter. It's a stick of dynamite that blows up our lady worlds every time someone asks. It's a constant reminder that we are getting older and less fertile every moment, that our bodies are revolting against us by either not getting pregnant or not staying pregnant, that we've spent hundreds of thousands of dollars to become a human science experiment to no avail, or that we are one of those "cold, hard career" bitches who is too selfish to change her life for another human. It all feels bad, and on a daily basis I have enough to feel bad about already. So please, stop asking me when I'm going to have a baby. When and if it happens, I'll let you know. Until then, it's just my lunch.

EER

How to Set Goals & Be Your Own Sugar Daddy

"Take what is yours. Do it nicely. Look people in the eye. Don't be shady. Don't be cunty."
—Alexis Martin Woodall, president, Ryan Murphy Productions

Wouldn't it be nice if we could just chill on our couch in a robe with cucumbers on our eyes and wait for the life of our dreams to magically fall into our lap? Unfortunately, a marvelous existence is not handed to you on a silver platter, unless you've got famous parents or you're the heir to Heinz Ketchup. The rest of us commoners have to put our heads down and work hard, diligently plan, and throw money into our savings accounts like our life depends on it. But the very first step to achieving greatness is visualizing your super dope successful future. "Ask and you shall receive" is real, bitches! Whether you're someone who writes a to-do list, goes and sees a psychic, or has a life coach like Tony Robbins, *you* get to decide what you want to achieve in your personal and professional life.

Want to start your own business? Move to the big city? Get that promotion? Have eight kids and be like Octomom? Have sex with Chris Pine? Skip town, change your name, and fall off the grid forever? No goal is too big or too lofty! We know that actually sitting down with yourself and enumerating your goals is an intimidating process, but writing down some attainable ambitions is the first step in your journey toward your one big dreamy life!

Look, we don't live in the clouds over here at the LadyGang. Goal setting isn't like having a genie in a bottle. Manifesting and vision boarding are great tools for motivation, but it'll come as no surprise that you need to put in the effort to turn these goals into reality. You can yearn after that diamond necklace at the jewelry store every day until you die, but unless you're Criss Angel or Winona Ryder, it's not gonna miraculously show up on your neck one morning.

You can't wait around for things to happen to you. Manifesting is all about focusing on what you have to do to get out there and get shit done. Hell, even if your goal is to marry a rich man, do your research. Look up the Forbes 30 Under 30, go to vacation destinations rich men frequent, and find your billionaire boyfriend. (But don't be surprised if he asks you to poop on his chest. There ain't no such thing as a free lunch, babe.)

Award-winning, TV show–creating, and overall genius Ryan Murphy was a guest on our podcast, and he told us, "It only takes one yes to change your life. It only takes one yes to rewire your brain. And no matter how many noes you get, if you just keep going, the odds are that you will get a yes." Take it from a guy who has won more Emmy Awards than we can count on one hand. Everyone gets shot down over and over again. Keep going!

And while you're out there kicking ass, it's important to learn how to celebrate your wins, no matter how small. Sometimes life is happening so fast around us that we never allow ourselves to take a second to appreciate all of the amazing shit we're capable of as women. Feel free to hug yourself every now and then, and recognize that you are a bad bitch who is killing it at life. You deserve all the drinks, a round of applause, and a new purse! Revel in the highs because, on the flip side, you have to learn how to deal with . . . *dun dun dunnnnnn* . . . rejection.

But the good news is that all of the successful people who seem to have a dream life probably have experienced far more rejections than wins and far more noes than yeses. Hell, the three of us have gotten rejected professionally more times than we can even count. Remember: you're only seeing what people want you to see, whether that be through social media or in the news or through a conversation over cocktails. This is real, grueling adult life, and you're not always going to get a gold star—and you most certainly won't always get a participation trophy. The secret to all of the ups and downs is allowing rejection to inspire you instead of letting it derail you. If you get knocked down, or get laid off, or didn't book your dream gig, instead of throwing in the towel or melting down . . . try to relax. A wise pussycat (Nicole Scherzinger), once told us, "What will break you will make you." Life *never* happens the way we think it will, so you have to be able to go with the flow to a certain extent and let it lead you in the direction of your destiny. The key to becoming the boss of your life is perseverance and the ability to (in the words of Taylor Swift) shake it off.

WOMANifest Your Destiny

I've always known my mind had crazy powers. When I was young, I didn't really understand what was happening, but I would go to sleep after lying in bed, visualizing something that was going to happen in my life the next day. Without fail, the next day would be exactly as I had planned.

I have been manifesting in some way or other since then. I was obsessed with the big city of New York, and there was something inside of me that knew I did not belong in my little town. I would have conversations in my head on my walk to school in the morning, and later in the day, I would be having those same conversations out loud. I would run around telling everyone who would listen that I was going to do this and that, and then somehow, I'd be that person, without even trying *too* hard. I don't know who the hell I thought I was!

My first official magical manifestation happened in 2010. I had recently completed almost two years of living on the road as a professional dancer as I toured with the Rockettes and then started a new show in Las Vegas. Once that ended, I went back to New York to be a backup dancer for Taylor Swift at the MTV Video Music Awards, and then I was back on the road kicking for Santa on tour . . . again. I had lived out of some version of a suitcase, away from my home base of New York, that entire time—almost two years.

I was burned-out and brokenhearted, and I'd met a guy online who lived in LA. I was convinced he was going to be the love of my life (yes, the same guy you heard about earlier). So, at a time in my life when I was making horrendous life choices, I decided I should move to LA for a guy I had never met.

I moved down the street from one of my best friends, Christina Perri. At that point, she hadn't morphed into a platinum-selling singer-songwriter, with her hit songs "Jar of Hearts" and "A Thousand Years," yet. She was simply a struggling waitress who wrote songs, who didn't dump me five years prior when I very briefly dated her brother (although he did). She helped me find a place to live, and I signed the lease without even seeing it. The next thing I needed in LA was a car. It's worth noting that I hadn't owned a car in over a decade and, being on a budget, I decided to buy one on Craigslist for $2,500, complete with blood splatters on the roof from what I can only imagine was some sort of prior accident. In other words, my life was a bit of a disaster.

Shortly after the move, and after two dates, it became very clear I was not the love of this man's life, and he ghosted me. I called Christina and asked her if she would come over with her guitar and play some tunes for me, so that I could do some "dancing" and make some videos for YouTube. At the time, I had a pretty popular blog that I shared my life on and a little baby following. She sat in the corner and played as I flailed around on low-res video. When we finished messing around, we stood outside my front door on the third floor of the building's terrace and looked over Los Angeles, staring in awe at the Capitol Records Building. Both of us were unhappy, frustrated with our lives, alone, and full of doubt. As we tried to pull each other out of the dark with an inspirational chat about following our dreams, we came up with the idea to write letters to the universe and ask for what we wanted. We figured that the world couldn't give those things to us if we weren't clear about what they were, so we wrote out our lists and shared them with each other. I wish I still had copies of those first lists, but I had no idea they would become so meaningful.

I do remember parts of hers and parts of mine. Mine was pretty pathetic, especially the expectations that I had for myself. I wanted to "quit Diet Coke," "get bangs," "stop dating assholes," and a few other things. Hers was more detailed: "get a record deal," "play three shows," and "meet Jason Mraz." On a whim, I decided to tape my list to the mirror in my bathroom.

This is where our story gets crazy, and it starts to seem like something out of a rom-com or a storybook. Within just a few months, almost *all* of the things on both of our lists had come true—or were getting close to coming true. Christina got a manager, played way more than three shows, met Jason Mraz, wrote a song with him, and got a record deal. I got bangs and my future husband. That year, it seemed like the secret to life was asking the universe for what we wanted. For the past decade, to this day, my friend and I have followed this annual tradition. I swear, I didn't make this up.

Since that first list, I've gotten more pointed and specific in my asks from the universe, but some of the things I've requested have included: "get engaged," "get a national hosting job," "work on *Entertainment To-night*," "get a LadyGang TV show," "buy a house," "go camping," and "see three concerts." All of which became reality.

I've never been into the fluffy shit in life. I've tried to meditate, and I find it useless. I only do the types of yoga where you sweat at a hundred degrees because it's actually an insane workout. I don't have time for that slow-brain stuff. I lie to my therapist almost monthly, and I've never completely finished a self-help book before skimming to the end so that I can get the ten lessons from it quickly. I have bought and not finished more than ten different "life workbooks," and I've started and quit at least fifteen "better your life" podcasts. I am such a realist. I am absolutely certain, however, that creating my manifesting lists and looking at them every day for a decade has contributed to my success and the overall happiness of my life. I know that my brain is the most powerful wish-granting tool I have. I know that if I think about something long enough, or visualize it enough times (some would call this a daydream) that it will eventually rise up to meet me in my life.

Make no mistake, there are years I haven't crossed off all the things on my list. But without a doubt, the universe will make it clear to me why it didn't work out, or, looking back over my lists, I can see that it was some sort of divine timing issue. The next year, that item will come into my life. For example, I once wrote that I wanted to be a host on *Good Morning America*. Through the power of manifesting, I met with the *GMA* team in New York City and screen-tested for the job (waaaahoooo!). I also asked "to move to a job where I didn't have to get up at 3:45 a.m., like *Entertainment Tonight*." Funny enough, writing a LadyGang book was on my 2019 manifest list and you are reading it now. A couple years ago, after working really hard on our podcast for many years and reinvest-ing every single dollar we made back into the business, I put on my manifest list that I wanted to pay each LadyGang member a certain, still small, salary. Not even four months later, our TV show was greenlit, and when the contracts came in, the fee for us to star in the show was the

_____ MANIFEST

YEAR: _____

PERSONAL

- ☐ _____
- ☐ _____
- ☐ _____
- ☐ _____

CAREER & $$$

- ☐ _____
- ☐ _____
- ☐ _____
- ☐ _____

FUN

- ☐ _____
- ☐ _____
- ☐ _____
- ☐ _____

HOME

- ☐ _____
- ☐ _____
- ☐ _____
- ☐ _____

HOME IS WHERE THE WIFI IS

EXACT amount I had manifested we would pay ourselves. That cannot be a coincidence!

Not all my asks have to do with business and being a LadyBoss. I often ask for personal and physical things. On one of my lists, I manifested that I would have my best body at age thirty-four. It was the best I've ever looked as an adult. I've since fallen off the train, but I did it! I manifested "growing mermaid-long hair for my wedding." I have manifested vacations, quality time with friends, saving money, and buying my first home. I manifested getting a dog! There isn't a one-size-fits-all rule for what a successful, happy life looks like for each of us. I wish for fame, fortune, and puppy kisses, and someone else might wish for babies and wide-open spaces. That's what makes the list so personal and, in my opinion, so powerful.

So how do I make my lists? In the fall, I start thinking about what I might put on my list for the next year. I keep an ongoing list in my phone, and whenever something comes to mind that I want, I write it down without any judgment. No dream is too big or too small. In December, I start to really look over the items and decide what sections of my life I need to add to. I like to do around six to ten asks per year, and I like a third of the list to be "adult stuff," like job, salary, and success. Another third is for personal development, like quitting soda and sugar while working out more. The last third I consider my "relationships," things related to friends, quality time, love, and family.

On New Year's Eve, I always find some quiet time to make my official list. This is where it gets a little tricky. I have found out that I need to be incredibly detailed in my asks. I never include anything vague like "fall in love," "be happy," or "lose weight." I always ask the universe for EXACTLY what I want. One year, I wanted to improve my health and bad eating habits, so I manifested that I would "eat something green every day." I am very clear and concise in what I ask. I make my asks lofty but realistic. "Becoming a billionaire" might be in the cards for Kylie Jenner, but it's not something I could actually accomplish within a year. I try to limit my asks to things that could be accomplished in that year. If becoming a billionaire was my goal, I would break that down to the yearly steps it would take to get there. I find the future and big goals really overwhelming, and it's hard to be motivated when your dream is so far away. Just like Christina did when she asked the universe to "play three shows"—she ended up playing way more, but three was her goal because it seemed like something she could accomplish.

Once I get my list together, I still share it with Christina, who inspired that very first list. Then I make a few copies of the list and hang them up where I will see them every single day. Right now, I have one list hanging in my closet above my underwear drawer and another in my office at work. Is it embarrassing when someone comes into these spaces and sees my stupid list? Sure. Especially when it's personal, like this year, when I manifested "have sex three times a week." But I believe the secret sauce in all of this is seeing the list and having it seep into your brain every single day.

As I accomplish things, I check off the boxes on my list, and there is honestly no better feeling in the world. I am not someone who has ever been able to keep myself on any sort of diet or workout plan for more than two weeks before I give it up, so trust me, I do not have some super ability or dedication to life that you don't have. I just stay committed to these very specific things for that entire year, and when I forget or lose focus, I see the list and get refocused.

As the year passes, even though my life changes and new goals pop into my mind, I never change the list. It stays up all year long. I file away those new goals for the next year. Once an ask is completed, I move on to something else on the list. I don't slow down my growth in any way, but if I happen to have a big career goal crossed off at the beginning of the year, then I'll focus on my personal goals. If the by-product is that more career stuff keeps happening, that's fine. But I don't adjust the list until the next New Year's Eve.

I honestly don't know why manifesting works. I am a normal person who comes from a normal family with normal circumstances. I struggle with insecurity. I'd rather shop online than work. I'm not a superwoman by any means, but here is what I know: You deserve it. You deserve the life of your dreams. You are the only person who knows those wildest dreams and wishes that your gut asks you for. They may seem so far away, or completely impossible, but admitting that you deserve them is the first step in them coming true. I believe writing them out and showing the universe that you believe you deserve these things is the first step.

Sometimes, it's embarrassing to give a voice to our dreams. But those are the exact same things that bring us the most joy. Life happens in tiny little increments of days that add up to years that add up to exactly what it is you do with your one magical lifetime. I hate the idea that any of us could be on our deathbed and have regrets about not doing the things we've wanted to do. It's completely okay to be selfish with your dreams and goals. It's okay to want the biggest, grandest things for your life. It's okay to want a great love, a great job, and a great life. **You do not have to settle for a little life.** I strongly believe that you cannot help yourself if you cannot define what it is that you want. On top of that, you have to dig really deep into your soul and believe that you deserve good things. This is some real hippie-dippie shit, and it works.

My Big Break and the Universal Energy Bank

In the entertainment industry, a common question I'm asked when talking about *Glee* is "How did it feel to get your big break?" It's such a weird concept to me, because it makes it sound like my success was a fluke or has to do with some sort of luck that's similar to winning the lottery. Every time it comes up, I give a polite response and acknowledge how "crazy lucky" I was to get that call from my agent, but I'm always thinking of the decades of blood, sweat, tears, and sacrifice I've put into my career, and that it was about damn time! Kidding—sort of. In reality, I had so many little breaks along the way that this "big" one sort of seemed on schedule because of my (slightly delusional) genius theory of the Universal Energy Bank.

I came up with this concept when I was living in my shoebox-size apartment in New York City, chasing my lifelong dream of performing on Broadway and feeling like I was never going to make it. I'll explain the backstory of my insane theory, and you can call me Tony Robbins afterward if you feel so inclined.

I fell in love with singing and dancing at a very young age (I believe I was four). I used to watch the original *Annie* on VHS over and over again, for hours on end, learning every song and every dance move. One day, my mom was on the phone with her friend, and out of nowhere I walked over to her, looked her dead in the eyes, and stomped on her foot. I was a pretty wretched child, but this move seemed especially satanic even for me. She was very confused. But, days later, we were watching *Annie* for the 876th time, and my mom realized that I was acting out the scene in which Annie stomps on Miss Hannigan's foot. (That wasn't the last time I used my art as an excuse to be a dick.) So, let's just say I had a flair for the dramatic and a dream to sing and dance for the rest of my life.

It was the end of middle school when I had to make the ultimate decision. Would I attend my normal public high school, continue to be popular as fuck, join the cheerleading squad, and get fingered by boys after school—or would I attend the performing arts high school, where I would be starting all over with a bunch of theater nerds and hard-pressed to find a boy who even liked vaginas? The only thing that kept me from deciding on the former was that I had a desire inside of me that was so strong I couldn't deny it. I knew that I would have to sacrifice getting frisky after the Friday night football games for tap dancing all night long at *Music Man* rehearsals—and that was okay because, deep down, I believed that someday the sacrifice would pay off. I didn't know it at the time, but that was my first deposit into the Universal Energy Bank.

After four years of singing and dancing through high school like a major dork, it was time to make another tough decision: Where I would attend college? I was at a crossroads. I could choose a school in the South that had a "great dance program" and ultimately get the best of both worlds (sororities *and* ballet class), or I could go all in and head to a theater conservatory in New York City. Again, I had to decide between the typical college experience that my sister and every human on the planet raved about or continuing my (sometimes painfully lonely) journey to Broadway. Even though I wanted to experience life as a "normal" person, I knew that I could never live with myself or be truly happy if I didn't fully commit to my dream. So I packed my shit and headed for the Great White Way, which was another major (subconscious) deposit into the Universal Energy Bank.

Although those "deposits" into the bank were challenging, nothing could prepare me for the years of heartache and sacrifice that came with being an aspiring musical theatre actor. Each day, I would have to wake up at 6 a.m. to get to ballet class after partying my ass off the night before. I would have to use my money to take voice lessons instead of buying concert tickets or new clothes. I would walk into hundreds of audition rooms, stand in front of strangers, and bare my soul just to be told "no, thank you" over and over again. The entire time, it felt like all this effort and sacrifice (and sometimes money) was simply falling into the abyss. I had been auditioning for every single regional theater job or shitty summer stock job that came my way, but I still had nothing to show for it on my sad, blank résumé.

Now, I'm not saying that I was doing something truly incredible or admirable, and I'm aware that there are people out there who don't have the luxury of being an "aspiring theater actor," so I don't deserve a goddamn medal, but I definitely made sacrifices that I doubted would ever truly pay off, and I know that no matter what dream you're chasing . . . you've been there.

It wasn't until I booked my very first professional job that something clicked. I realized that all those "failed" auditions and all that "wasted" money weren't a waste at all. They were simply deposits that I made into this Universal Energy Bank, and I was finally getting my payout. As soon as I started looking at my career like this, it was so much easier to make the effort and exert the energy, because I truly believed (and still do) that even if there is no immediate result or positive feedback from something, it doesn't mean that it doesn't hold value and that all the energy won't add up to some "big break" in the future.

This theory hasn't just helped me with career stuff; it's helped with my relationships, too. I recently heard a Hunter Hayes song, and the lyric was "I'm one heartbreak closer to you," and it reminded me of the Universal Energy Bank. If your heart is in it—your intentions are in the right place, you put forth the effort, you make the sacrifices—the Bank will fill up, and you'll get your breaks, big and small. Thank you for coming to my TED Talk. You can purchase my supplements and sweatshirts out in the lobby.

Let the Haters Be Your Motivators

"If you don't have haters, you ain't shit!"
–Keltie's mom, and everyone else, ever

Once you start putting in the work, you will feel yourself rising both professionally and mentally. Everyone will start to notice, and it might even piss some people off along the way. Your peers will see you being a boss bitch, and they might freak out because they are intimidated by your professional progress. But remember that they are just seeing the highs of your success, skipping over all the sleepless nights and hard work you put in to slowly climb the daunting stairs to your dream life. Any negativity thrown in your direction stems directly from jealousy. RuPaul once spoke these wise words to us: "If those bitches ain't paying your paycheck, then pay those Bs no mind." Surround yourself with people who will rise with you and cheer for your successes. And we give you permission to give the middle finger to anyone who drags you down.

Keep your blinders on, follow your path, and don't worry about what any of those bitches think.

Virgin Groupie

When I was in high school, I had a countdown on my desk until summer break—and not because I was excited to sleep in till 11:00 a.m. and sneak vodka from my parents' liquor cabinet. My countdown was for the Vans Warped Tour. For those of you who didn't rock studded belts and green hair in high school, the Warped Tour was a traveling punk rock music festival that had about forty stops and traversed the United States and Canada every summer between 1995 and 2018. My girlfriends and I would go to the Southern California tour stop to rock out to bands like Blink-182 and New Found Glory while discovering my next new favorite artists before anyone else. And, of course, it also meant that we would always meet some cute guitarists. It was an experience unlike anything else in this world. It was my favorite day of the year.

My musician friends nicknamed Warped Tour the "Punk Rock Summer Camp." They described it to me as a tight family of about five hundred people, traveling around the country from parking lot to parking lot, living a kind of carnie rock-and-roll fantasy life for two months straight. During the day, everyone was busting their ass in hundred-degree weather and living solely on whiskey and Hot Pockets. You were lucky if you showered more than once a week. Have to take a shit? There's a boiling hot porta potty over there (and cross your fingers that there's toilet paper). Everyone was working miserable fourteen-hour days in the sweltering heat and 90 percent humidity. Traveling in a cramped tour bus, you were stacked in small bunks with eleven other drunk idiots, and ten of them will definitely steal your beer. Everyone was literally ALWAYS hungover. The tour lived like millennial pirates, using Adderall as a form of currency and wearing dirty underwear at least once a week. And because of this wacky, unconventional lifestyle, you would create the most incredible, unique bonds with people you would otherwise never cross paths with in real life. But to me, this traveling circus of creative misfits represented something much more. It meant taking the road less traveled. It meant paving the way for my own destiny.

I had been to the Warped Tour during my high school years when it came through Los Angeles, and I spent all the rest of my free time attending concerts all over Southern California. This little music scene was the world I immersed myself in, and the band dudes and crew roadies I met along the way became my new dysfunctional family. When I became a legal adult, I didn't want to just go to one or two dates of the Warped Tour in my state. I wanted to travel on the entire tour over the summer and live my dream, just like the rest of my new best friends were doing. And, lucky for me, there were a ton of jobs available that were outside of being a performing musician, because the Vanek vocal chords could really give William Hung a run for his money. There were production jobs, roadie jobs, and sponsorship jobs. Working a sponsorship job meant that you would essentially represent a company for in-person marketing or sell their products. Sounds fun—I'm in!

Before we jump into punk rock summer camp, here's a little bit of my backstory. I was a straight-A student throughout high school and college, with a 4.4 GPA, a scholarship to UCLA, the whole thing. But I always knew deep down I wasn't going the traditional professional route after graduation to work for someone else. I was way too ambitious and spontaneous and adventure-driven. I knew I was going to build something for myself. I wasn't exactly sure what that was yet, but I knew it would be fueled by and involve the music scene. So I stuck it out at UCLA and graduated, but then it was Warped Tour on my mind. I applied for a job working for a sponsor of the tour and sent in my résumé, with a ton of experience and great work recommendations. During my high school years, I had interned at record labels and radio stations, and I was the youngest employee of the most popular alternative music website ever, absolutepunk .net (it's like the TMZ of punk rock). I was photographing some of the biggest bands in our scene for a couple of years, and I had my photos on numerous record covers before I even turned eighteen. Sure, I liked to party, but I took this shit seriously.

So I wasn't surprised when I was hired for a position (duh) doing in-person marketing for an organization on the tour. I was beyond excited and told all of my friends I had finally gotten my dream job! But I didn't even have enough time to have a celebratory Vodka Red Bull before I got a phone call from a woman telling me they were retracting the offer.

She told me, "We can't offer you the job anymore because there are rumors circulating that you have slept with multiple band members on the tour."

As we previously established, I was a virgin until I was twenty-three years old. And I stayed a virgin for a year after the initial conversation when she rescinded the offer to work on the tour. At the time, the naïve part of me thought there must have been a misunderstanding, and the conspiracy theorist in me thought maybe someone was trying to sabotage me. I had an acquaintance who knew a couple of employees of the company that had offered me the job, so I hit them up and asked if they had heard anything about my situation. "Oh, yeah, everyone thinks you're a slut and that the only reason you want to be on the tour is to hook up with band dudes. There's no way any of these companies are gonna take you seriously."

So here I am, a virgin being labeled as a groupie.

"Crushed" is an understatement. I was used to dealing with bullying and rumors circulating online. According to the internet, I had been pregnant about ten times before I was eighteen, and had had multiple STDs and multiple abortions from every band dude imaginable. There wouldn't be anything wrong with those things if they were true, but these were flat-out lies being spread to slander my name. My skin was so thick from dealing with daily lies that it never really bothered me before, but this was different. I didn't give a shit if Sally from Idaho thought I was a "groupie," but this was messing with my livelihood and my potential future career. I didn't even have the chance to defend or explain myself before the phone call was over and my punk-rock dreams flew right out the window. And the absolute worst part of it was that the woman breaking the bad news sounded . . . satisfied? Like she took some sick pleasure from ripping an ambitious young girl's dreams right from her fingertips. That's the one thing that still sticks with me today.

Listen, I'm not saying I was an angel either. There probably wasn't a lead singer I HADN'T made out with. This was the world where I spent all of my time, and these were the people I surrounded myself with, so it was only natural that I'd have a few too many shots of Jameson and make out with Pete Wentz every once in a while. SUE ME. We all drunkenly make out with our friends sometimes—mine just happened to be in bands. Whoops. But the thing that majorly bothered me was . . . not one single guy was asked if he had slept with girls who were on the tour. Not one single guy was being labeled "easy." No men on the tour had their work ethic questioned because of their sex life. The guys got high fives but the girls got shunned for the same exact act? That never made sense to me, and I'd be damned if I succumbed to society's bullshit double standards about hooking up. As long as I was kicking ass professionally, why couldn't I enjoy a good make-out? Double standards turn band dudes into rock stars and girls into disposable sex objects, and that fucking pissed me off.

The music industry, especially on the road, is a guy's world. Women are rarely hired for crew, and if they are, they have to have a super hard-ass persona to be taken seriously (as in, act like a dude). Band guys hooking up with multiple girls in a single night is the norm, and cheating on significant others is so common that no one even bats an eye. In general, girls who are seen backstage are often looked at as pieces of meat. I had experienced this kind of disrespect personally, and I had seen it happen to other girls more times than I could count. Obviously, this is a generalized statement that doesn't apply to all musicians, and I was lucky to befriend a lot of very respectful dudes in an often sexist world.

After all of the dust settled from my heartbreak over the summer that could-have-been, it turned out that not getting a job because of untrue rumors was a blessing in disguise. After that phone call, I was determined to stick it to all these judgmental assholes. So that's when I started the Jac Vanek brand. I went to the Warped Tour that summer in California and sold bracelets out of my backpack. I made more in that one weekend than I would have made during the entire tour, working fourteen hours a day for the very job I was denied. For the next year, I busted my ass with the goal of going on the Warped Tour, having my own tent, and working for MY OWN brand the next summer.

Wouldn't you know? The Jac Vanek brand blew up. But when it came time to apply to be on the tour the following year as a vendor selling my own merch, I was again met with double standards and hesitation, for the same reasons as before. I had to speak up for myself and refuse to take no for an answer, and I had to prove to the powers that be how determined I was and how seriously I took my business. Ultimately, they let me on.

That summer, I had a lot to live up to, and I was ready to carpe diem. I still partied and woke up every morning with a wicked hangover, but I was buzzing because I was finally given the opportunity to live out my punk-rock dream. I met thousands of kids, constantly sold out of merch, and made some of the best memories of my life. I was among the top ten vendors almost every day, beating out most of the headliners in merchandise sales. Veterans of the tour would walk past my tent with their jaws on the floor, not understanding why there were hundreds of kids lined up to get a silly rubber Jac Vanek bracelet. I was finally doing it! And I didn't stop making out with band dudes in the process. I found myself in overlapping love triangles, and I got my heart broken way too many times, but I wouldn't have had it any other way. The funny thing is, all the dudes I was smooching and anyone who actually knew me respected the hell out of me. They all rocked my Jac Vanek bracelets, and they even collaborated with me for exclusive products on the tour. I was being taken seriously without ever having to compromise anything about myself. And that was the first time I felt truly successful.

My first summer on Warped Tour was the launching pad for my professional career, as unconventional as it may seem. After kissing dozens of musicians, traveling thousands of miles back and forth across the country, and making a killing selling T-shirts at music festivals, I learned a few things. First of all, some people are dicks. You can't change what anyone thinks about you, and people only have as much power over you as you let them have. Second, there is nothing more valuable than doubling down on who you are at your very core. I was a boy-crazy, wildly determined kid who thought I could take over the world—and I still am. But, most important, I learned that the only way double standards can be eliminated is to fight back against them.

Started from the Bottom, Now We Are Slightly Above the Bottom

"The biggest mistake employees make is not understanding the true nature of the relationship. If you focus on the fact that you are there to help your boss be successful, you will become successful. . . . Think about your boss's challenge. What is their biggest problem? Go solve it."
—Kevin O'Leary ("Mr. Wonderful" on *Shark Tank*)

After a few embarrassing first jobs, we've gone on to become pretty mediocre businesswomen, all while keeping our full-time day jobs. On top of that, what we thought was going to be a little side-hustle passion project has become a second full-time job. We've made mistakes (lots of them), we've learned things the hard way, and each of us has brought our own unique set of skills to the LadyGang. We are not perfect by any means, but we do have some secrets that we've stolen from smarter people who have helped us along the way. First, and most important:

YOU HAVE TO START SOMEWHERE. And if that somewhere is in the mail room, or fetching coffee, or literally cleaning the bathroom floor, that's okay. Do the things that nobody wants to do, and do them with conviction. Keep your bitchcraft to a minimum and approach an entry-level position with the same passion, poise, drive, and attention to detail that you would a shiny, important job. Trust us, your superiors will notice, and you will move up the ladder exponentially faster than you will if you approach the same job carelessly.

STOP SAYING "JUST." We learned this nugget of wisdom from Erin and Sara Foster when we asked them to share their best piece of business advice with us. You should never apologize for doing your job or simply taking up space. The first and easiest step toward doing this is to start taking the word "just" out of your emails. You would be shocked to realize how often you use "just" in your professional vocabulary . . . we sure were: "*just* following up," "*just* checking in," "*just* circling back." We tend to apologize *by default* for taking up someone's time, taking initiative, or simply *doing our jobs*. At first, you might feel like your emails are abrasive or even rude without "just," but trust us, omitting it will make you feel direct and powerful.

LIMIT THOSE EXCLAMATION POINTS!!!! Always go through an email and take out at least one or two exclamation points. It's important. As women, we tend to sugarcoat difficult conversations, and we want to leave a good, friendly impression. Plus, maybe we're excited about a new project or connection or deal! But when every sentence ends with an exclamation point, communication starts to sound too conversational and super unprofessional. You're hereby allowed to use one exclamation point in any business-related email, so choose your placement wisely. You don't have to be sweet all the time; you can just be smart. And, more important, DELETE ALL EMOJIS IMMEDIATELY.

GO GET THAT MONEY. Be proactive and aggressive about it. Work your ass off, and don't let anyone get in your way. Ask for the raise if you truly think you deserve it, because you'll never move up the chain if you don't show your worth. Don't take it personally if you're offered something lower. Because, guess what, everybody wants to pay everybody less money for the same job. It doesn't matter if you're in an entry-level position or you're Bill Gates—someone at some point wanted to pay him less than he deserved.

KNOW YOUR WORTH. And know your value in your professional life. Don't get ahead of yourself and think you deserve raises and bonuses and a great salary and benefits if you're not qualified. There are a lot of people fighting for the same jobs these days, and things aren't going to be handed to you if you're not equipped for the position. Be realistic about what you're asking.

LISTEN TO MINDY KALING. She once tweeted: "'Why the fuck not me?' should be your motto." And she's right, it's a fantastic life motto. *Someone* is gonna get the gig. What if Michael Phelps woke up one morning and didn't think, *Why not me?* Sure, he has the wingspan of a pterodactyl, but he could have very easily been like "You know what? Training all those hours sounds pretty hard, and the likelihood of me getting this is pretty slim, so I'll just let someone else do it." There are a lot of people out there with enormous talents that go wasted and unnoticed every day.

A gift is absolutely useless without drive behind it. The biggest achievers are the people who think, *Why the fuck not me?* Be that gal.

MAKE BETTER MISTAKES TOMORROW. The truth is, you're gonna make mistakes no matter how hard you try. You're gonna fuck up more times than you can count, you're gonna feel cuntstipated, and you're gonna cry on the subway home. And, hey, that's just a part of life and putting yourself out there. But remember: They are only mistakes if you don't learn from them. If your boss yells at you, it's not the end of the world. You still get to go to work the next day, and they are eventually going to forget about it. Just like no one is thinking about your divorce, your boss isn't thinking about the minor mistake you made last week. They have way bigger fish to fry, so try not to be mortified for weeks on end about it. And listen up: Don't ever make the same mistake twice. You're gonna make new mistakes, you're gonna make other mistakes, but always, and we mean always, make better mistakes.

TAKE OWNERSHIP OF YOUR SHIT. If you piss someone off or you do something the wrong way, take the blame and admit it was your fault. Acknowledgment and responsibility go a long way. Pointing fingers and making excuses will only dig you a deeper hole. The discussion should end with "I know I messed up, and this is how it won't happen again." Don't let something small snowball into something huge because you don't know how to apologize. As long as you are growing, learning, and evolving from your mistakes, you're doing it right. Another Ryan Murphy nugget: "In your darkest moments of pain and rejection, if you can just get still enough to let it land, and you can feel it and try and understand what it was about and move forward, comes great things."

LOOK LIKE YOU HAVE YOUR SHIT TOGETHER EVEN IF YOU DON'T. Remember, no one knows what they're doing. Everyone is overworked and underqualified. Charles Bukowski said it best: "What matters most is how well you walk through the fire." You're constantly going to be thrown curveballs left and right at your job. But at the end of the day, how well can you problem solve with grace?

DRESS FOR THE JOB YOU WANT. That's why Jac is always in bikinis on exotic beaches: She wants to be a professional international drinker.

But for real, no matter how much society evolves, everyone is still judging your outfit. Human beings are visual and shallow creatures. This doesn't mean you need to wear expensive shoes or designer clothes. You don't need to wear tight pencil skirts or uncomfortable heels, or spend three hours getting ready in the morning. It's pretty simple: Show up as a chic, put-together version of yourself. It can be as easy as ironing your shirt or putting your hair on a slicked-back ponytail. Present yourself in a respectable way.

Shoe Size Six:
A Blessing and a Curse

During my time as a broke dancer in New York City, I had several odd jobs. I babysat for rich neighbors, I worked in a gift shop, I modeled shoes . . .

"What the hell is a shoe model? Is it like a foot model? Are people just going to be taking pictures of your feet? Is it sexual?!" Those are all the questions my mom had when I told her about my exciting new gig. I can't blame her, because it did sound fucking creepy.

Let me enlighten you. When shoe designers go to market to show off their new collections for store buyers, they hire some skinny, broke-ass girl with a "sample size" foot to be there to try on the shoes and show what they look like on the foot (essentially, you're a mannequin). Most sample sizes are a size six, so any dancer living in New York with a small foot was golden. Sort of.

They would fly me out to Las Vegas for the big conventions for retailers, and I would report to a hotel room that was set up as a showroom for the weekend. It was a twelve-hour day, and the appointments with buyers were stacked from morning until night. I rarely got a lunch break, and I was paid about $200 for the entire day. Back then, I felt like I had hit the jackpot. I fucking LOATHED the job, but I walked away from a weekend with $600 in my pocket, and that felt pretty great. It's the broke bitch's version of golden handcuffs, if you will.

I would be on my feet all day, shoving my (closer to a size-six-and-a-half) foot into the world's ugliest shoes so that some fat, sweaty man whose family owned department stores across the Midwest could decide which styles to buy for his shops (because middle-aged white men really have their fingers on the pulse of women's boot trends for the fall).

The buyers and sales reps would throw pair after pair in my direction, never make eye contact with me, and make comments about how the shoe would probably look better on a slimmer leg. As the day went on, my feet would swell, and I would develop lesions and blisters all over my feet from shoving them into cheaply made boots with no socks over and over. (There was no time for socks.) By the end of every day, I would be covered in sweat, my bladder would be filled with urine, and my self-esteem would be pretty much depleted. I would go back to my shitty hotel room every night and cry to my mom about how much I hated this fucking job, and I would vow to never take another one again, no matter what.

Guess what? I went back six more times. Why the actual fuck would I do that, you might ask? I needed the money, I refused to give up on my dream (another deposit in the Universal Energy Bank), and, at the end of the day, a girl's gotta eat . . . thanks to her feet.

Break a (Chicken) Leg

I've always loved the idea of having a job. I'm a workaholic by birth!

Playtime as a child usually involved some sort of "job," and one of my first experiences working was going to work with my dad. I'm pretty sure there was a childcare issue and I was "going to work for fun" for different reasons than the ones presented to me, but I was READY TO WORK. My only job was putting invoices in numerical order, and even though I slayed those invoices, I remember being severely pissed off when I was not allowed to answer the phones, use the checkout till, or swipe the fancy credit cards through the machine. It made me even more upset when, at the end of the day, some secretary checked my work like I might have made an error (I didn't) and shoved the invoices away into a pile like they didn't actually matter to the business (they most likely didn't).

As I moved into my teenage years, my dad found some more important work for me to do at his shop on Saturday mornings. I would drive into work with him and, for $20, I would clean the toilets, the disgusting urinals, and the coffee stations.

But my first *real* job was in the ninth grade. I couldn't drive, so I needed to work somewhere within walking distance of my house and close enough that I could get there quickly after school. The only place that returned my inquiry for work was Liam's Famous Recipe Chicken. It was run by Mr. Liam, an old man who barely spoke English, and I was hired as one of his two employees who never had shifts at the same time. As the bone-breaker (more on this later), I was paid $4.14 an hour for three hours at a time, two days a week. I wasn't allowed to speak to customers, and I was painfully alone while I was working. Mr. Liam would simply write the hours he expected me on the back of a little dry-erase calendar taped in the doorway, and I would show up.

I had two responsibilities. One, pour giant plastic bags of "gravy" into huge vats to be heated. Two, stand at a huge double sink, unload bag after bag of raw chicken parts, and fish through them to find the chicken thighs. Once I found a thigh, there was a specific way I had to crack the bone in half so that it would cook completely in the deep fryer. After cracking the thigh, I sorted all the chicken parts by type. Legs, breast, thigh, and "unsure." Then I rinsed them all with hot water and made sure that THERE WERE NO FEATHERS LEFT.

This is a real job. I was on feather watch for your chicken sandwich. There were an alarming amount of feathers left on the chicken parts, and when I found one, I had to pluck it out. Fun fact: It's actually not easy to pluck a feather whose base feels more like a porcupine needle out of an almost frozen, slimy, slippery, dead chicken follicle. After removing all the stubborn feathers, I laid my chicken pieces on huge silver trays and dusted them with some sort of flour seasoning from a shaker, put them onto big metal stands, and stored them in the freezer. I was very particular about how my chicken pieces were laid out on the tray. I liked them to be perfectly aligned, all facing the same way, with the same amount of space around each piece. I'd also try to match up similarly sized pieces, as if to show that these pieces all came from one chicken and I wasn't separating families.

At the time, there were only two chicken joints in my town: one KFC on the other side of town, and my Liam's Famous Recipe Chicken. We were very busy. Just imagine how many chicken thighs and feathers I had to sort through to make just one family's twenty-four-piece bucket of chicken.

There were some really great things about the job. It helped me save up to buy clothes I wanted at the mall, and it made me realize that I could save my secret work money and bribe eighteen-year-olds to buy me booze, instead of stealthily stealing it from my parents' liquor collection. I got unlimited soft drinks during my shift. Plus, the alternate chicken breaker was a guy in my class named Shawn who would leave his Tragically Hip CD in the crappy little CD player when he wasn't there, and I listened to it on repeat during my shifts. This helped me fall in love with one of the greatest Canadian rock bands of all time and the icon that is Gord Downie . . . RIP.

A couple things really bothered me about the job, though. First, I didn't get to wear a uniform. I love a costume! Because I was hidden way in the back, gruesomely breaking bones, and no customer ever saw me, I could wear whatever I wanted. I was dyinnnggg for a work outfit. I once bought a Subway branded polo shirt at the secondhand store and wore it around the trailer park where one of my good friends lived when we had sleepovers. I tried to impress the neighborhood boys with the lie that I "had a job" and I worked at "Subway," and I would even wear the Subway shirt out on Friday nights . . . but I digress.

Second, I really, really wanted to use the deep fryer, but I wasn't allowed to. Commercial-grade deep fryers are scary as hell and endlessly fun. I got no joy from breaking the chicken bones, or making the gravy, but I was obsessed with dropping any available food into the wire basket and then watching it bubble up and cook in the fryer. Once in a while, we would get so busy that Mr. Liam would call to me to drop an order in the fryer, but 99 percent of the time, I was forbidden from frying. Sometimes, when Mr. Liam was not looking, I experimented by attempting to fry condiments: cheeses, tomatoes, lettuce, or any other toppings—just to see what happened. So fun!

The third, and most important, hardship of my first job was that a year or so before I became employed by Mr. Liam, I became a vegetarian. It's a long story, but I had been deep in eighth-grade ballet classes when I pulled my hamstring. The same night, my mom happened to cook a ham for dinner, and when she pulled it out of the oven, I realized, for the first time, that when I ate meat, I was actually eating an animal's muscle (like that of my sad hamstring). I decided then and there that I was no longer going to eat anything that had feelings. And other than one small exception during my first marriage and a period of time when I didn't realize that French onion soup is made with beef broth, I haven't eaten anything that has feelings since. Obviously, all land animals have feelings, and any sea animals that have played major roles in Disney movies also have feelings. Some fish have feelings (the pretty ones), and some don't (here's to you, delicious, ugly-ass tuna). Anything that seems more like an insect than a cuddly animal can also be eaten, i.e., lobster (looks like a spider) and scallops (I don't believe they have a brain). Disney rules come into play with crabs—because Sebastian in *The Little Mermaid* has such a cute little personality, I just can't eat him.

So, chicken-bone-breaker was my first job, and I've had many terrible, gross, and barely paid jobs since. Working hard from a young age taught me to have a good work ethic, professionalism, and humility. On my way to my "dream job" I learned how hard show business would be. I learned that I would have to do a hundred terrible jobs to support myself. To be honest, one of the main things I learned during my twenties, while trying to be a professional dancer, was that being in the arts is an impossible fucking way to live. I trained my entire life to chase a career that was basically less than livable, even when you did book a job. Even when I was dancing with Beyoncé, I wasn't being given health insurance or being paid what someone in the upper echelon of any other profession would make.

Even though I eventually became one of the most in-demand dancers in New York City, I still did what they call a "side hustle" almost every night just to get by financially. I've listed just a few of my esteemed positions here, and I'll add that I've spent a large portion of my life in a sparkly costume or bikini doing something very random and odd and got paid to do it. Eventually, I got really burned out from making it and yet . . . still not making it—and that's when I chose to make a major pivot and retire from dance altogether. For my next chapter, the universe chose to throw me mouth-first into being a television host, a career that my dancer work ethic and drive served beautifully. After working my ass off for another decade, I've managed to make this second act work because of the hustle that's been in my (excuse the pun) bones since way back at Liam's Famous Recipe Chicken.

A Complete List of Keltie Knight's Jobs

- pizza maker at Little Caesars Pizza
- waitress
- hostess
- line cook
- beer tub girl at a bar
- shooter girl at the same bar
- showgirl on a cruise ship
- art auctioneer's assistant
- librarian
- dance teacher
- New Jersey Nets dancer
- synthetic grass model at a trade show

- perfume sprayer
- go-go dancer
- magician's assistant
- Knicks City dancer
- motivational dancer at bar mitzvahs
- backup dancer for Taylor Swift
- Radio City Rockette
- bride in Disney's *Enchanted*
- backup dancer for Beyoncé
- TV correspondent
- and, most important, HBIC (head bitch in charge) of LadyGang!

Never Trust a Trust Fall

When I was a kid, my dream job wasn't to be a big powerful LadyBoss. There's a video of me sitting on my cousin's steps when I was five, and in it, my mom asked me what I wanted to be when I grew up. I jumped up, wearing uneven pigtails and thick red-framed glasses, and I shrieked, "I want to be a mouse!" Not like the Chuck E. Cheese's mascot—I wanted to be an actual rodent. I wonder what the psychology is behind that one. When I finally understood what a "job" was in my preteens, my dream was to work at Hollister, a.k.a. the beachy California version of Abercrombie & Fitch. Just as dark, stinky, and douchey as A&F, but they had a punk-rock playlist and more edgy shirts that said things like "I'm with the band" and "I kissed the lead singer." I literally fantasized about standing out in front of the store next to a shirtless dude, spraying people with their god-awful perfume. Ah, what a dream.

During my early high school years, my parents wanted me to focus on getting good grades. I think the only time I was grounded was when I got a B+ in AP Physics in tenth grade. In my defense, my teacher was an alcoholic who spent the entire class talking about how good his "root beer" made him feel, and one time he congratulated me on a hickey I had on my neck. That definitely wouldn't fly these days.

As my sophomore year came around, my mom realized that I spent all my free time taking brooding artsy self-portraits, so it was obvious that I had time to get an actual job. Hollister, my dream workplace, was overflowing with job applications because it unironically *was* the cool place to work, and apparently I wasn't the only one intoxicated by the overbearing stench of cheap cologne in the store. So I decided to apply to work at Hollister's dorky step-cousin, Old Navy. They hired me immediately, without any work experience whatsoever, because . . . it's Old Navy.

I'll cut right to the chase and admit that I lasted there for eighteen days. During those eighteen days, we had more team-building exercises than I ever thought existed. We tossed around a beach ball and shared "fun facts" about ourselves (my fun fact was that I hated team-building exercises). I accidentally dropped my coworker during a trust fall because I saw a hot guy walk through the door. Do you know how rare it is for a smoke show to walk into Old Navy?! We had to deal with internal theft (I hope those $2 flip-flops were worth it, Susan), and I was promptly fired when I went to Denver for spring break because I failed to tell them I needed my shifts covered. Oops. I was an unreliable teenager . . . what can I say?

During this time, I was positive that I was going to be a music photographer, so I convinced my mom to let me intern at different music-related jobs rather than spend my time at a random store that wouldn't teach me any real skills related to my chosen "line of work." (The fact that I said "line of work" as a high schooler is embarrassing, but, you know, I *was* pretty embarrassing.) I interned at two different indie-rock record labels where some of my favorite bands were signed: Fearless Records and The Militia Group. Instead of teaching me any useful skills, they used my extra set of hands to mop the floors and organize office supplies—and one time I even had to help some guy craft a plan so that his girlfriend wouldn't catch him cheating on her. After a few weeks of scrubbing toilets at each record label, I moved on to bigger and better things: interning at our local rock radio station, KROQ. This was where I actually used some of my skills to create flyers and ads for upcoming shows. In between creating graphics for the radio station's next giveaway, I used my time to teach myself photo editing on Photoshop, and to browse my favorite punk-rock news website, absolutepunk.net.

From new releases to leaked songs to scandals to straight-up gossip, AbsolutePunk was your one-stop shop for everything in the punk-rock music community, and I devoured that shit like it was going out of style. When I wasn't scrolling through the endless abyss of new records and band drama, I was bringing my dad's fancy Canon 10D camera to concerts and taking pictures of bands from the crowd. I was teaching myself aperture, shutter speed, and more by trial and error, and for a sixteen-year-old, I was pretty damn good. As soon as I had a decent portfolio of live photos, I sent in my résumé to AbsolutePunk to apply for a staff photographer gig. To my surprise, they hired me immediately! Well, I mean, "hired" is a stretch, because this was an unpaid internship, but for me it was a massive accomplishment and a dream come true. I was the youngest "employee" there, and one of the only girls in a sea of dudes working for the website. I had an "admin" username (which is when I started going by Jac instead of Jacquelene, and everyone thought I was a guy) with a super important avatar and everything.

AbsolutePunk was my entry into a world I always wanted to be a part of, and the very first step I took in my career. I finally felt like my time was spent working toward a tangible goal that I was actually passionate about. It was the first time I experienced professional competition, received professional praise, and had to deal with professional sexism. This job gave me my first taste of the sweet highs and bitter lows of trying to pave my own professional way, and the rest is history.

"It's Show Business, Not Show-Fun"

If you're a host stuck between being a nobody and being a star, the entertainment world will label you as "green" or as a "cub reporter."

To the outside world, I looked like I was crushing it. My name was appearing alongside a big, network-syndicated show title. My parents could watch me every once in a while on TV. I had a fancy agent. I had a lawyer to do my contracts. I was being paid(ish) for the first time as a host. The most telling thing was that, at this time of my life, random people I had known at some point in my past—an old ballet teacher, someone who used to be in my class at school, a friend of a friend—were all coming out of the woodwork to "reconnect" because they saw me on TV. Proving that, up until now, I was not deemed worthy of their efforts. Notoriety is a really weird thing, because it started way before I had felt any inkling of "making it," and if I'm completely honest, I still get the Sunday Scaries every week and wonder if this week I will "make it."

As a cub reporter, I put every ounce of energy into my job. I was working twelve to sixteen hours a day, every single day, pitching at least twenty-five stories a week. I was learning what made a great interview, what made a great story, how to get good TV ratings, how to dress on camera, and how to talk on camera. I was figuring out how to play in the major leagues and look like a million bucks when I had about twenty bucks. Mostly, though, I was trying to please my absolutely unpleasable boss.

To put things in perspective, I grew up as a ballerina, trained by a woman who makes *Dance Moms* star Abby Lee Miller look like a saint. I went on to become a professional dancer and was either constantly rejected or criticized in rehearsals. Finally, I went on to dance with the Rockettes, and my boss was a Bob Fosse protégé who never smiled, always wore black, and would stand in front of me during most kick lines, screaming my name until I was kicking and crying at the same time. During my stint as a Rockette, before *every* single show I did, I would receive a long list of notes from our dance captain, detailing basically everything I had done wrong in the previous ninety minutes. So I've never been precious about getting feedback or having a tough boss. I thought I had thick skin.

Boy, was I wrong.

This boss would give me hives whenever I saw his name light up on my phone. I would get emails that said things like "Come see me this afternoon," and I would spin like a top, counting down the hours, thinking of all the reasons I had messed up, only to be greeted with something as simple as "I'm sending you to New York again this week." One day, I was his favorite; the next day, I was inches away from being let go. I never knew which version of my boss I would get. Because I'm a people pleaser at heart, this yo-yo destroyed me. One time, my boss called me on the phone and yelled at me so awfully that he only stopped yelling when he rear-ended the car in front of him. Another thing this boss used to do was have me sit on the side of our show's stage and then "test" or "audition" other people who were exactly my "type" in front of me while I waited to film the show. I was never sure where I stood, and I was always on my tiptoes, even when I wasn't standing in a four-inch heel.

One day, I was requested to be part of a big cast photo shoot. I was thrilled that I was included in the new pictures day for hosts. It meant that my boss might be keeping me around a little longer. Why would they spend money on photos of me if they were going to replace me? Emails confirming the time and place of the photo shoot had gone back and forth, with my boss copied. I was excited! The hair and makeup department had confirmed with me that they would be there. I had gotten a call from our wardrobe team about the shoot, and they asked what I wanted to wear. I picked out a few of my favorite dresses and handed them over. Next, I got a call from another part of the show's team, letting me know that my boss wanted to preapprove what I was going to wear in my new photos. Wardrobe called again to say that I was meant to bring my dresses to my boss in person and let him choose what I would wear.

I walked into the conference room, as requested, with our wardrobe team, surrounded by eight of the senior producers and staff from the show. I didn't even dare to speak. Wardrobe held up a red dress and a yellow dress on hangers and said, "Here are the dress choices you wanted to see for Keltie's photos."

My boss took one look at the dresses, one look at me, and then stated loudly, so that everyone in the room could hear, "I never asked for pictures of Keltie. I don't need to see these dresses. Whhhhhhy would I need pictures of Keltie? What for?" He then turned back to his computer in silence. No one said anything. The wardrobe woman gave me the side-eye, and we tiptoed out of the office. I did what any woman would do, and I ran into the bathroom stall and tried to muffle my tears with five back-to-back flushes. I was mortified and heartbroken.

I never found out why my boss had humiliated me in this way. I'm not sure if he was trying to take me down in front of others, if it was a bad time to ask about the look, or if he simply forgot about the shoot and/or that I worked for them. Hours after this conference room debacle, it was decided that I would wear the red dress. The photo shoot went on exactly as planned. There were many more little heartbreaks with that boss, and also times where he championed me and made my wildest dreams come true. I've had good bosses, hard bosses, and amazing bosses between then and now and while I'm very thankful for him, I still get hives when I hear his name. Since this time, I've also become a boss, which has given me perspective and a master class on the way I communicate with people.

I've learned two lessons. First, never take anything personally. Keltie the worker and Keltie the human being are two different entities. I have to keep those people separate. When something goes terribly wrong at work, it doesn't mean that I am a waste of space. It just means I wasn't my best at work that day. When I come up with a bad idea and it falls flat and fails in front of a room of my peers, I am not a failure. My idea was bad. I've realized that 99 percent of the time, when something really crappy happens at work and someone says something hurtful, it's rarely actually about me. When an A-list celebrity curses me out on live TV because she says I put words in her mouth, even though I was just doing what I was told to do, and I want to crawl into a hole, I remember that this A-list celebrity doesn't hate *me*, she hates "TV host Keltie Knight," and it's not the same thing. I can still watch her movies and laugh (but I'm petty, so I won't).

In the same vein, I've been short with people at work for a variety of reasons: I'm tired, I'm stressed, I have something else on my mind, I'm not fully present, I'm pulled in too many directions. If Jac or Becca took it personally every time I was short with one of them during LadyGang when I'm in "get shit done mode," we would be the Real Housewives of Los Angeles, pulling out one another's hair and fighting. I'm kind of a dick sometimes at work. I'm not great at handling stress. I can see now that almost everyone is in the same boat. Besides the actual work stuff, we all have real lives that we're trying to deal with and navigate in this new world where work is 24-7. We're all a little extra stressed because the pharmacy closes at five but we work till six, you know? So I try my best not to see it as a personal attack when things go poorly at work.

My mom always said to me, "Keltie, it's show business, not show-fun." It reminds me that I don't have to be best friends with everyone, and that not everyone is going to like me, and that a bad day at work doesn't equal a bad life. Also, we are imperfect human beings, not robots, and that means we are going to make big mistakes sometimes. I've made plenty.

The second lesson I've ever learned is to take the blame when you need to. Own up to making a mistake. Make it clear that you know why it was wrong, and then never make the same mistake again. Being self-aware is one of the most important tools I use at work. Read the room's energy, and try to learn from the things your coworkers and bosses might not have the courage to say to your face. Remember my rule of thumb: The first time you fail, it's a fuckup, but if you make the same mistake again, "You're fired."

CONNECT THE DOTS

SALLY WANTS TO FOLLOW HER DREAMS, BUT THE BASTARDS ARE TRYING TO GRIND HER DOWN. WHAT SHOULD SALLY SAY TO THEM?

Fuck the Man!

**Figuratively, not literally.
Well, maybe literally.
Is he hot?**

Boss babe. She-E-O. Girl boss. Fempower. Boss bitch. LadyBoss. There are a lot of buzzwords about professional female empowerment floating around the zeitgeist these days, and we are HERE. FOR. IT. While it feels powerful as hell to be able to call the shots, owning your own business or being your own boss—no matter your gender—is stressful, risky, and straight-up *hard* sometimes.

But now is your time to shine. You've done all the terrible first jobs. You've gotten the coffee and been the grunt. You've worked two day jobs and a night job to be able to pay for what one good job could pay you. So whether you are a Jac, who started her own business in college, or a Becca, who just wants to be given lines to read and told where to stand, know that work life is never going to be perfect. You now have a huge decision to make: Are you going to have a boss or be the boss?

What they don't tell you in all the "Be Your Own Boss and Make $40k a Month, It's Easy! ;)" articles is this: the highs are high, and the lows are lowwwwwwww. You're investing *your* money, *your* time, *your* energy, and *your* emotions into something that is statistically destined to fail within the first year. You're going against the odds, usually with little to no experience, crossing your fingers that you're making the right choices and investing your life savings correctly. It's beyond stressful, emotionally draining, and all-consuming. Have a backup plan? Doubt it. There's no time for that! So get ready for sleepless nights and endless cups of coffee (with a side of dread) that everything is going to come crashing down before your very eyes at any moment.

But if you're one of the lucky ones (and by "lucky" we mean the ones who work their butts off and finally get a break) who finds success in your entrepreneurial journey, it tastes real sweet. And we're here to tell our stories.

Good Things Come to Those Who Work Their Asses Off

When you picture your typical twenty-three-year-old, you probably think of keg stands, all-nighters, and Cup Noodles for breakfast, lunch, and dinner. The last thing you'd probably envision is a CEO of a successful self-made business. But in 2011, I found myself in charge of my own company, dealing with employees and inventory, attending trade shows, and learning about business contracts. I was blindly navigating my way through this terrifying unknown landscape, having meltdowns at every turn, all while doing Jägerbombs and chasing boys with girlfriends.

I'd be lying if I told you that I always had an "entrepreneurial spirit" as a child. I was a weird, creative kid, but I was never the girl carrying a briefcase, boasting to people about how I'm "gonna be the next Steve Jobs." I was super smart, but I was also super artistic and quirky. I was always doodling on the sides of my school notebooks, and I took sewing classes so that I could make my own clothes, since I could never find what I imagined was the perfect outfit. I think I still have the cowhide bell-bottoms I sewed in fourth grade. I sold lemonade on the side of the road like everyone else my age, but mostly because I liked drawing cute little sketches on all the cups we gave out. While other kids were making messes with finger paints, I was in the corner, quietly drawing intricate, imaginary worlds filled with tiny creatures. I was hyper-focused, hyper-critical of anything I did, and just hyper-weird. After puberty hit and I discovered the opposite sex, I turned into a boy-crazy and music-obsessed teenager, and those two things, on top of my innately creative brain, drove pretty much everything I did in my young adult life.

Once the teenage hormones set in, music became my primary entertainment, my therapy when I was feeling low, and my inspiration when I felt creatively blocked. I started attending so many live shows in high school that I ended up making friends with a lot of bands and their touring crews along the way. While my classmates were attending high school football games on Friday nights, I was partying with Skrillex or The Used. At eighteen years old, I left my senior prom early for every emo girl's dream: working a paid gig photographing the guys in Taking Back Sunday for a magazine.

While I was living my rockstar-by-proxy life, in 2004 I started documenting my experiences on a website called *LiveJournal*, which was one of the very first online blogs (before the term *blog* even existed). I wrote about going to concerts, sneaking backstage, and kissing boys in bands. I shared my brooding teenage ramblings about how nobody understood me. Most important, I posted artsy self-portraits with emo lyrics plastered all over them. The more I overshared, the more people gathered at my journal to follow my everyday life. My followers were living vicariously through my emo adventures.

Along with *LiveJournal*, I was one of the first people to join MySpace (the cooler version of Friendster, RIP) and was in everyone's Top 8, from Katy Perry to Jeffree Star. Kids started "role playing" me in fictional stories involving other members of my music scene. Girls from around the world copied everything from my raccoon tail hair extensions to my SideKick cell phone to my AOL away messages. I was dubbed a "Scene Queen" by my peers, and the term really fit the strange phenomenon my life had become. Somehow, I found myself ruling this niche corner of the internet.

Ironically, back in my peak scene queen stardom days, having a huge online following came with absolutely *zero* professional respect. Influencers today run the damn world, but if you were "internet famous" in the early 2000s, you were looked at as . . . kind of a joke. Thankfully, I had the foresight to see the potential of my online popularity.

Because I was exposed to this whole new, exciting world with endless possibilities, high school life seemed so limited and trivial. My new band friends were traveling the country, living their dream, and having a fucking blast doing it. I was getting little glimpses into what this crazy, touring world looked like, and that excitement was all I wanted for myself. I didn't have any musical talent, but what I did have was a pretty substantial following on the internet and a degree in progress in Design and Media Arts at UCLA. I'm not going to lie to you and make up some frilly inspirational story about the inception of my brand. The drive behind starting my business was never to be a big powerful boss lady, or to pave the way for the internet generation, or to "stick it to the man." The drive behind starting my business was to earn the money to do my own thing, travel the world, and party with my friends while I was young and free.

When I was a junior in college, my spending money was running low, and my parents were putting pressure on me to get a job to help pay for my time at UCLA. You read about my Old Navy experience—I knew deep inside that I wasn't meant to work for anyone else. Around this time, the yellow rubber Livestrong bracelets were having their moment, and my mom threw out the idea of me making thicker rubber bracelets with different sayings on them to sell to my internet "fans." We did some research online and found a semi-legit-looking company that produced rubber bracelets overseas in a large, one-inch-thick format. I had to borrow the $200 to pay for my first round, and I crossed my fingers that it wasn't a complete scam. I truly felt like I had just flushed that money down the drain, so that same day, I walked into Forever 21 to get an application (for a "real" job) to pay my parents back for the loan.

To our total surprise, the first round of JV bracelets arrived at our doorstep as ordered. They were black rubber, one-inch bracelets with the word RUTHLESS embossed on them in Helvetica type (inspired by my favorite song by my favorite band, Something Corporate) and the Jac Vanek logo on the back. E-commerce existed then, but it wasn't widely accepted or trusted. Kids felt more comfortable ordering things online, but no sane adult would dare trust the internet with their credit card information at this point. My dad was still paying for everything with cashier's checks, and I honestly don't think I even knew what Amazon was yet. So, instead of setting up an online store, I started selling my bracelets from bulletins on my Myspace page. I'd announce that the bracelets were available, ask anyone who wanted one to email me their order, and then send out a Pay-Pal invoice for payment. It was a long, drawn-out process that my mom and dad helped me with, and it took ten times longer than it ever should have. All of the orders were then mailed out of my parents' living room, which I continued to do for YEARS after I started. My parents' entire house was almost filled with my products! It was 100 percent DIY, and 100 percent a huge pain in the ass.

I decided to put twenty bracelets aside from my first order to give to a few of my friends in bands. My band friends would wear them onstage, and their fans would see them, think they were cool, and want a matching bracelet to emulate their favorite rock star. I was actually "seeding product" and doing "influencer marketing" before that was even a thing. Certain band members would request different words or sayings that resonated with them, and because of this, kids were finding a sense of identity and connection to their music idols through these simple rubber bracelets.

The bracelets took off at the speed of light. After selling them out of my backpack at concerts for a year, I was finally respected and trusted enough to jump on tours all over the world representing my own brand. I went on the Warped Tour for the next six years, working grueling sixteen-hour days for two months straight and loving every sweaty, dirty, partying second of it. I traveled all over the United States, to Australia, and to Europe as the face of my brand, meeting the coolest kids and slinging merch out of my booth. Anytime I popped open my Jac Vanek tent, I knew I was going home with enough money to live my unconventional, adventurous lifestyle, all while having one of the best experiences of my life.

With the success of my own brand from this single item, the bracelets began to catch on in the scene. Some of my besties, like All Time Low, Cobra Starship, and other bands asked to collaborate on bracelets, which was an awesome and validating opportunity for me. But it wasn't long before virtually every band on tour started making their *own* JV-style bracelets. I was bummed that the concept was being knocked off, but I couldn't really get mad because I knew the bracelets weren't some amazing invention, like a miracle cure for cancer or flying cars. It was cool seeing a simple idea of mine blowing up to such epic proportions, though. Those bracelets were everywhere. There was a ripple effect that moved outside of our scene and into the mainstream world, with everyone from John Mayer to Lady Gaga releasing their own JV-style bracelets.

Like any other good business idea started by a single individual, my merchandise, especially my T-shirts, was ultimately knocked off by large corporations left and right. Trademarking sayings is an expensive process, and so is trying to sue big companies for violations. The little guy never wins. I had to sit there with my tail between my legs, watching products with verbatim sayings I had used on my merch sold by big, corporate "hipster" clothing companies. People would send me pictures of items they saw for sale at these retailers, and not only were the phrases identical, but so were the typeface and the word placement on the shirts. These corporations were making millions off my original designs. To this day, they're selling a complete rip-off of my SORRY FOR PARTYING tank tops at the Jersey Shore. You're welcome, Snooki.

A few years went by, and the bracelet fad was exploding to the point where the market became extremely oversaturated. Something that had been super niche and special to a very focused group of people turned mainstream, basic, and eventually stopped being trendy. Because of this, the value of my bracelets, and ultimately the value of my brand, started to dwindle. As it is for most small businesses, staying relevant and financially sound has been a constant uphill battle. In recent years, nearly every brand I've looked up to, as well as many giants in the fashion industry, have gone bankrupt and gone out of business. That's why I decided to pivot, expanding into graphic tees, clothing, and home goods.

The transition went as well as one could expect after blowing up from a unicorn of a product and transitioning into the real world of commerce. My bracelets had a CRAZY high margin (the difference between the cost of making the product and the price at which you sell it to consumers), and there was virtually no other product I could sell to make that kind of profit ever again. Producing clothing and home goods was way more expensive, the inventory took up more physical space to store and cost more to ship, and ultimately the financial risk was way higher. But somehow, in some way, I managed to stay afloat . . . kind of.

Looking back at my sales from my Jac Vanek brand over the last ten years, I see a total mess. There was no rhyme or reason to anything. Some years profits were huge, and then they were minuscule. Some years I made good decisions and netted a lot, and some years I made some dumb decisions and walked away with nothing. I lived in a constant state of anxiety about my brand for an entire decade. Every night, as I closed my eyes to fall asleep, every single possible way to fail completely engulfed my consciousness. I was putting all of my eggs into one really unstable basket, praying that it wouldn't all come crashing down. I had absolutely nothing to fall back on. I had no plan B. My brand was my livelihood, and it was my only source of income. I started it as a kid, after all. It was all I knew, and that was really terrifying.

My entire experience with my brand was one long string of trials and errors. This was my first rodeo, and I messed up so many times. I ordered too much inventory countless times and sat on dead cash for years. I tried my hand at making cut-and-sew garments that almost sent me into bankruptcy. I rented warehouses that were way too expensive, I went on failing tours that sucked me dry, and I hired employees that I couldn't afford. But for all the times I fucked up, I succeeded just a little bit more. And as long as I continued to move forward, that was all that mattered.

I honestly and unabashedly attribute a lot of my success to luck. I took advantage of a silly little idea, and I was in the right place at the right time. The other part of my success I attribute to being creative, listening to my gut, and being perceptive and flexible enough to pivot when things felt uneasy or stale. In the last ten years, I've never had an investor or taken out a loan (minus that $200 from my parents). To this day, I still own 100 percent of the Jac Vanek brand, it is still the little engine that could, and I am still extremely protective of it. My mom always tells me that I'm too hard on myself and I never give myself enough credit—so here I am, giving myself some credit.

At the end of the day, I'm thankful for how things transpired with my brand. I would never have had the space in my life to join a podcast called the LadyGang with two of the most incredible, inspiring, and hardworking women I've ever met. The Jac Vanek brand gave me experience, it gave me knowledge, and it let me have a blast during my twenties. But it never gave me purpose. And now, with the LadyGang, I have that.

BECCA

#BOSSBABE or Nah

We are living in an incredible time, right?! There are more women in charge in the workplace than ever before, and it's fucking BADASS. But, as on all parades, I must shit on this one as well. (It wouldn't be on-brand for me if I didn't.)

When we started the LadyGang podcast four years ago, I felt a humongous sense of gratitude for finally being in charge of something in my own career. As a performer, I've been at the mercy of other people's opinions, moods, and visions for longer than I can remember, and my job title started to feel more like "dancing monkey" than "actor." I was ready to have more control in my life, so having the podcast, something that was all our own, felt fucking spectacular. I felt empowered, inspired, and extremely excited.

When we started working on the TV show, we became not only the talent on the show, but executive producers as well. This was when I started to notice that I was extremely stressed out most of the time, resentful of my position some of the time, and more emotional and anxious than ever before (and as an actress, that's a shit ton). This brand was our baby, so *some* nerves were normal and to be expected during this transition, but the kinds of anxiety and stress I was experiencing were different than I had ever felt.

It took months of living in it for me to finally acknowledge something about myself that I felt very insecure and even embarrassed to admit. I didn't enjoy being the boss. Yes, I realize what I have just admitted. I'm sure there are tons of women reading this and cursing my name for taking the women's movement back fifty years. However, I believe it's more important now than ever before to vocalize these feelings.

Here's the reality: not *every* woman (or man) wants to be the boss, and that's OKAY. I felt a lot of shame and guilt for not really enjoying this new (and highly sought-after) position of power. I grew up my entire life striving to be at the top of the food chain, only to get there and find out that I didn't want it (which, in turn, made me sort of suck at it, too). Talk about a slight identity crisis and a major bummer. I figured I would just stifle these feelings forever and keep pretending to love my new title at all the dinners with my equally or more successful girlfriends. "Look at us! We're doing it! Pour more wine! Let's make it rain!" we would exclaim. But deep down, I felt like a bit of a fraud.

It wasn't until a therapy session where I felt like I wouldn't be judged (or stoned) for making these admissions that I really unloaded. I explained that I hated the stress of being other people's boss. I talked about how emotional I was after every single meeting or slight disagreement in a conference room. I admitted to panicking anytime my phone rang and it was the office calling. I didn't enjoy the aspect of the job that required me to "bring work home with me." By that, I don't mean actual work, just the inability to stop my brain from constantly living in it. I had always had a job where I could hang up my costume in my trailer at the end of the night, go home, and just *be*. I hadn't realized how much I needed and craved that as a working woman. The work I did at home as an actor was learning lines, reading scripts, character studies—a.k.a. the fun stuff. I wasn't worrying about ratings or whether I had communicated clearly enough with a segment producer about what I wanted to change without offending them or insulting their work. I also realized that sure, I could work harder at being the boss, but guess what? I didn't want to. There were so many amazing women out there (like Keltie and Jac) who were up for the challenge and genuinely loved it. Why not leave it to those badasses?!

During this conversation/venting session with my therapist, I suddenly realized something super important that would help me with my dilemma of feeling like an anti-feminist. Turns out, I had this entire feminism thing ass-backward. A true feminist is someone who champions women and respects their decisions. A true feminist accepts that even though we have many similarities, we are also dynamic and complicated creatures and are far from all being the same. There is power in admitting what you want, no matter what that thing is. The moment I realized that, I could breathe again, and, most important, I could vocalize my feelings for the first time since this whole TV show started. I told anyone who would listen that I hated being the boss and couldn't wait to pass those duties on to Keltie and Jac, who love being in charge. It felt fucking liberating.

So here's the moral of the story: Find out what *actually* makes you tick. Figure out what doesn't. Take a look inward and decide what position *truly* makes you happy, not what the most impressive thing to tell other people is. And the absolute most important thing is to respect the girl who admits she doesn't want to be the #bossbabe, because we are still pretty fucking rad.

WORK HARD TO PLAY HARDER

Whether you want to be an entrepreneurial powerhouse or you want to have a secure and predictable career path, *you* get to decide where you shine the brightest and what brings you the most joy and validation in life. You want to be a LadyBoss? Good for you! Go get it, girl, but you shouldn't feel like a failure if you don't have your own LLC by the time you're twenty-five. Everybody measures success differently, and that's totally cool with us.

You don't have to be the boss to be important to a company. You can be a cog in the wheel where you don't have to bear the stress or the weight of an entire corporation on your shoulders. You can have health care and benefits, and leave work on Friday at 5:00 p.m., and have your weekends be stress free. And while doing this, you can still take pride in your work.

So, whether you want to own your own company, be an employee for a big corporation, be a stay-at-home mom, try something new every year for forty years, date a sugar daddy, or you still don't know what you want to be when you grow up . . . at the end of the day, it really doesn't matter what you do. No job or career is going to be perfect. There are going to be ups and downs and pros and cons to everything you do. We know it might look like everyone on your social media feed is a travel blogger, drinking Aperol spritzes in Italy, and making $10,000 per Instagram post, but the reality is that most people are on the grind just like you are. All that matters is that you're doing something that fulfills you when you lay your pretty head down to sleep every night.

Realistically, for most of us, your job is your job, and your fun time is your fun time. In our 24-7, all-consuming lives, it's hard to balance the two sometimes. You will have a broken heart if you think your job is going to fulfill you in the same way that Christmas morning fulfills you. Your free time is just as valuable as your job. So work hard to play harder.

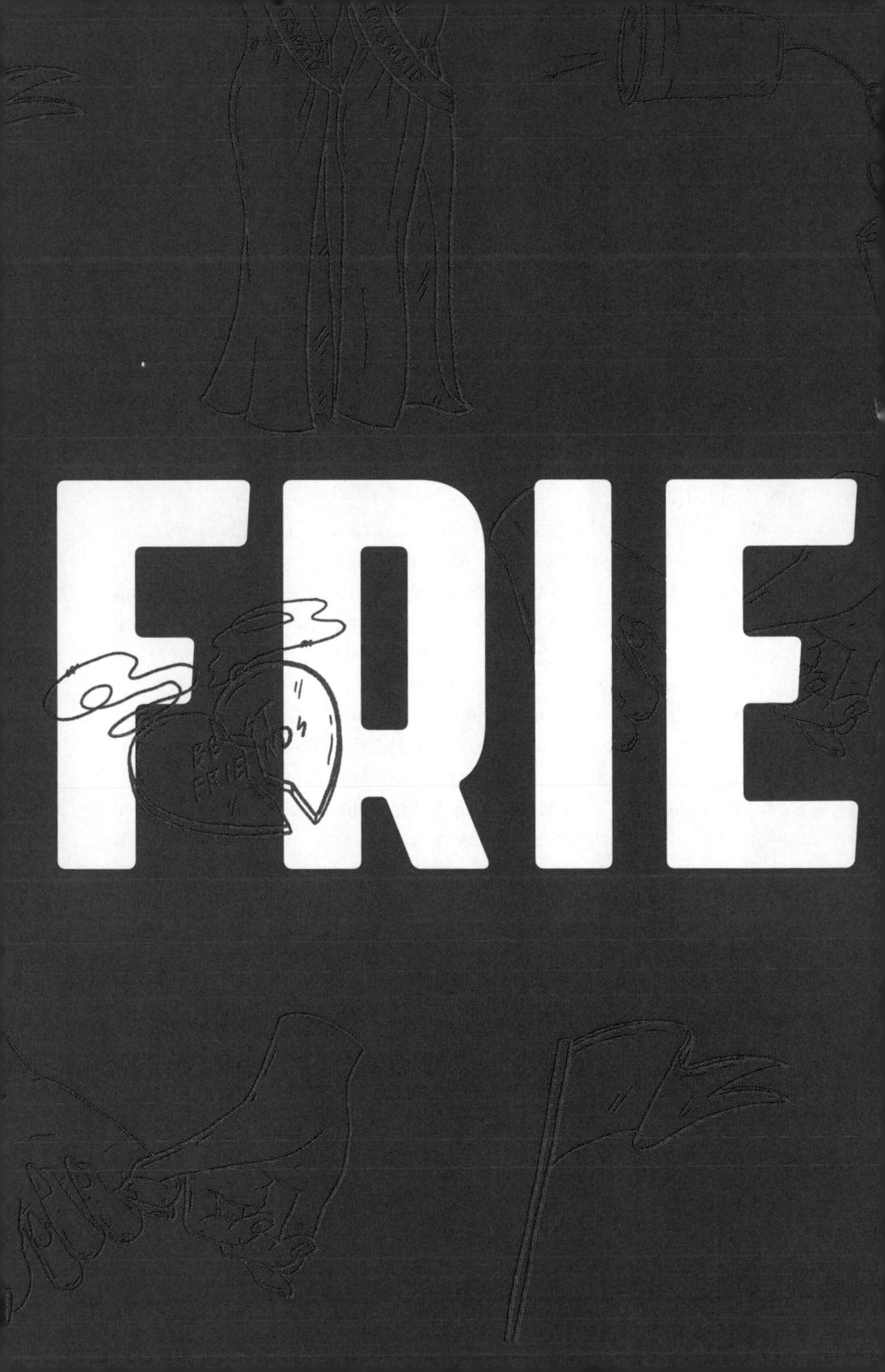
FRIE

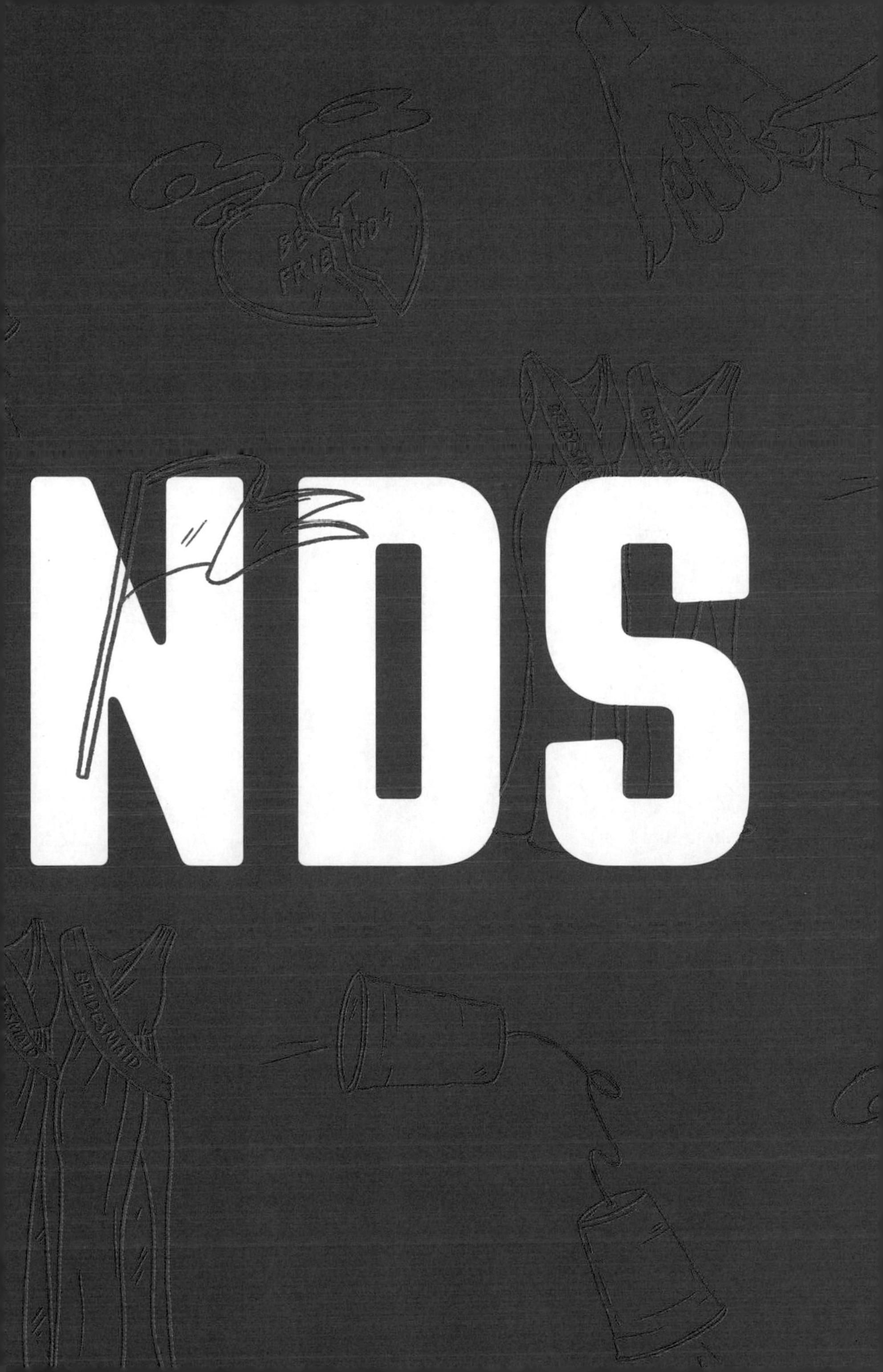
NDS

What Doesn't Kill You Makes You Weird at Parties

Why the hell is it so hard to make friends as an adult?

Maybe it's because we're already so set in our ways. We've got our go-to spots and our crazy work schedules and a serious lack of spare time. Maybe we've already outgrown so many other friends and we don't have the time to take on anyone else's bullshit. Maybe we've gone through so much drama that we've completely lost faith that anyone new can just be normal. Maybe we've realized how nutty people are and how hard it is to find a reliable person that we can actually count on. Or maybe it just seems impossible to think anyone could genuinely care about us without trying to get something out of us.

Finding new saltmates is a complicated task. You're looking for someone who likes to bitch and gossip about the same things as you, but it's hard enough to work around your busy adult schedule to squeeze in even one new happy hour. The older we get, the more we just want to be old hermit ladies who never leave the house and watch people out the window. That might be why we started our podcast. We can talk to and engage with millions of people every week, but actually be face-to-face with no one.

The truth is, you don't need a million friends. Popularity is overrated, and adulthood isn't high school. You don't need everyone to vote for you to be student president or prom queen or most likely to succeed. If you have one friend that you can call if something gets truly messed up and that you can rely on to love you and support you through thick and thin, then you have more support than most people do.

But we can't stress this enough: it's extremely important to have friends *outside your relationship.* Everyone wants their lover to be their "best friend," but you are also going to need someone to put you back together during a fight, a breakup, a stolen credit card, infidelity, or divorce, y'know? So don't put all your eggs in one basket.

The fewer friends you have, the less you can fuck up a friendship. It's actually harder to have a lot of friends and constantly be dragged in a million different directions. The older you get, the more life happens to you, and the less free time you have to hang out. If you're too busy to see or text a friend for a month, you should be able to pick up from where you left off, whenever that may be. Friends are supposed to be your support system, to put you back together, and to be your unwavering rock. Friendship should never suck you emotionally dry, and it should never be too difficult. You should never have to make excuses for a friend, fight for a friend, or resent a friend.

Most important, friends are *not* like beach cover-ups. They are not "one size fits all" for all aspects of life. We have certain friends for different seasons and occasions in our lives, we have certain friends we turn to for specific problems, and we rely on certain friends in different ways.

The best kind of friends are childhood friends, the ones who have known you the longest. They can look at you and say, "That's such a *you* thing." They might know you better than you know yourself, because they've been watching you grow and evolve for a lifetime. They'll love you no matter what, even if you live in different states, have grown apart, and only check in once every few months. This kind of friendship is a deep sisterhood. It's a bond that can't really be replicated, and you understand each other on the most basic human level.

Then there are your ride-or-die bitches. These are the friends who will answer your call at three o'clock in the morning. These are the friends who will pick you up at the airport. These are the friends who will help you move. And, most important, these are the friends who will call you out on your bullshit. They are the only friends you can accept the truth and criticism from. Your ride-or-dies can say, "I still love you, but here's why you suck right now." But they will also let you puke in their clutch in the back seat of an Uber. That's how much they love you.

There are your work friends. They might know more details about your everyday life than your ride-or-die bitches, but you'll never see them outside of work except during a happy hour. They would rather listen to you vent about your shitty boyfriend than do their actual job, so take advantage of this fun objective perspective. They'll never meet anyone really significant in your life, so they're kind of like free therapists.

And there are your party friends. These are the friends you want to get blackout drunk and forget about life with. They're not reliable at all for any real-life shit, but they're a damn good time. They're probably more immature than you, but they know the fun bars and will always be great wingwomen for an eventful night. You can cry to them after a few tequila shots, but don't expect them to ask how you're doing on a Tuesday afternoon.

As you get older, your friends become more and more circumstantial. Friendships stop being about bracelets and matching tattoos, and more about . . . are we in the same place at the same time? Maybe you have a two-year-old and you meet someone who also has a two-year-old, and you need someone to bitch about mom life with while your kids eat Play-Doh. Maybe you spend a bunch of time with your husband's best friend's wife because they live two blocks away. Maybe at the gym you meet a new acquaintance who has the same days off as you and also loves a dry rosé. But don't be fooled. Keep your friends in their respective lanes, and don't try to turn your party friend into your ride-or-die. Doing that will always lead to disappointment and heartbreak.

At the end of the day, in order to hang on to a couple good friends, you have to be a good friend in return. The best way to be a good friend is to be sure you and the other person have similar expectations for a friendship. If you're emotionally high maintenance and always need a nine out of ten from a friend, you can't expect a chill independent gal who only requires a two out of ten to be on your level. Your neediness levels have to be equal, or one of you is going to be bummed out. But if you're on the same page, communicate and understand each other, then your friendship will grow into a beautiful flower.

(Not) Sleeping with a Friend

I've been pen pals with a man for twenty years. This sounds like the plot of a romantic comedy in which a young Drew Barrymore would play me (obviously) and I would eventually end up giving up my "big-city life" to settle with this man at a lake cabin, where we would cozy up under blankets and he would wear turtleneck sweaters while he chopped wood for the fire. But no, it's just three cheap notebooks, twenty years of writing, and thirty-plus years of friendship.

Besides my dad and my brother, he's been the most constant man in my life. I've shared my deepest, darkest secrets and my biggest fears with him. We've shared clothes, a subway card, meals, and countless pots of tea. We've attended a Halloween party in a couples costume (Janey and Jeff from the '80s dance movie *Girls Just Want to Have Fun*), and we've even shared a bed (we both love flannel sheets, even in the summer).

This is the part of the "my best friend is a guy" story where I get asked if we've slept together, kissed, were in love with each other once, or where my friends are convinced that he is somehow in love with me and has been waiting all this time for me to come around. The answers are: nope, never slept together, never kissed, never wanted to sleep with or kiss each other, and this guy was never waiting around for me to be in love with him. No one believes us, but this is 100 percent true.

My best guy friend and I have known each other since we were five or six years old. We were family friends, and his sister was in all my childhood dance classes. He also took dance at the studio (like a lot of kid brothers), and he ended up sticking with it into his professional years, with multiple comparisons to a young Fred Astaire. For the first thirteen years or so of our friendship, we sort of hovered around each other's worlds. Once he got his driver's license, he would drive me home from our classes, and we would listen to Tori Amos on full blast because we were "artists" and no one understood us. I would talk about boys I liked, and he would

WHAT KIND of FRIEND do YOU NEED?

CHILDHOOD FRIEND

YOU JUST FOUND OUT A CLOSE FAMILY MEMBER IS SICK

 YOU'RE GOING THROUGH A DIVORCE FROM YOUR HIGHSCHOOL SWEETHEART

YOU WANT TO GO TO A BACKSTREET BOYS CONCERT & ACT LIKE YOU'RE 14 AGAIN

RIDE or DIE

 YOU NEED SOMEONE TO BAIL YOU OUT OF JAIL

YOU CAUGHT YOUR S.O. CHEATING ON YOU

YOU NEED SOMEONE TO HOLD YOUR HAIR WHILE YOU PUKE IN THE TOILET FROM TOO MUCH TEQUILA

WORK FRIEND

YOU NEED TO VENT ABOUT YOUR HUSBAND BEING A DICK

YOU WANT AN UNBIASED OPINION ABOUT YOUR MOTHER-IN-LAW'S SUFFOCATING BEHAVIOR

YOU JUST STARTED A NEW DIET & NEED TO STAY MOTIVATED OMG HELP!

PARTY FRIEND

YOU JUST STARTED A NEW DIET & YOU NEED SOMEONE TO SPLIT FRIES WITH YOU WITHOUT MAKING YOU FEEL GUILTY

YOU JUST GOT DUMPED & WANT TO GET SMASHED

YOU NEED A WINGWOMAN FOR A MUSIC FESTIVAL

talk about girls he liked. He was the first person I ever told about eating only apples for weeks on end in preparation for a big ballet exam. He was the first person to tell me that my first serious boyfriend was a "bad guy." We had this really special honesty with each other from the start. We never defined our friendship, and we always had other friends.

When we both launched into professional touring dance careers as adults, in a time without email, Facebook, or cell phones, he came up with the idea for our shared journal. Instead of writing letters and mailing them to each other, we would share a journal. We would write entries for a few months and then send it to the other person. Inside, we taped ticket stubs, photos, and stickers. It was like a scrapbook of our lives, just for the two of us.

The first entry ever was December 22, 2000—he was telling me that he had broken up with his girlfriend—and in my first entry back to him on February 2, 2001, I talked about how much weight I had gained in my new professional dance job. We both used a ton of quotes from the musical *Rent*.

2002: I met my future first husband, my friend almost moved to Toronto, and I was told to lose seven pounds in a week because I was too fat to be a dancer.

2003: We both moved to New York City, and I wrote some very angsty poetry called "The City Is Calling Me." Insert eye roll.

2004: An entry in which I admitted I didn't like being married (I had been married for four months at the time). My friend told me my marriage was hard because I was a dynamic person. He said to me, "You live hard. It's not just something you do. It's who you are." Basically, marriage number one was doomed to fail, and we both knew it but neither of us was saying it. I became a Radio City Rockette, and my best friend wrote a beautiful note in the journal congratulating me. "I'm so proud of you for your passion and the beautiful way that you dive into life." I felt seen in a way that no one else in my life understood me.

2005: There's eating cheap pancakes at the Moonstruck Diner in Manhattan, days we both need hugs, and a love triangle with a girl he was nutty about and a girl who was safe and loved him back. Gavin DeGraw song lyrics from the CD I listened to on repeat and his response back in Damien Rice lyrics. I discovered my first wrinkles, and at the end of the year, life got so hard that I drank for two weeks straight.

2006 (VOLUME TWO): A WILD year. I dated a Christian folk musician with a studio apartment, and my friend wrote, "This guy is going to hurt you, Keltie" (and he did). There was more about me being broke, and I was deeply into glitter pens. I danced on the VMAs for the first time and wrote pages about how small all the celebrities were: Jessica Simpson, Fergie, Jack Black. I wrote about how my best guy friend came from Queens to help me move into my new Manhattan apartment and we ate Rice-A-Roni at 2:00 a.m. I had flown to Europe on a whim to make out with some other music guy (he wrote, "This seems like a questionable idea, Keltie"). We celebrated my best guy friend's birthday and decided his mouth was crooked and that our favorite quote was "If at first you don't succeed, see if the loser gets anything." In June, he wrote a message that started with "Let me get this out of the way, I am shit-faced right now." WILD.

2007: I found my first gray hair and plucked it out and taped it inside the journal. I used the quote "Nothing heals a broken heart like an ex with a stupid haircut." I watched *The Secret* for the first time. There are many many entries from me trying to come to terms with the fact that I had a boyfriend at the time who would say things like "She's not really my girlfriend" when I wasn't around. My best guy friend would constantly call out this idiot, and I would know that he was right but still dig my heels in deeper anyway. Young love. There is a big letter I wrote to the guy after we broke up that I never sent, because I just had to get all my feelings out, but the only person I trusted to read it was my best guy friend. He was dating a redhead at the time, and his entries were mostly about that. There was my first time trying magic mushrooms, and I wrote some poetry.

2008: He lived in New York City, I was on tour, and we talked a lot about airplanes, airports, and James Blunt.

2009: When the relationship my best guy friend knew was bound to fail miserably actually failed, he flew out to be my date for the opening night of my big Las Vegas show. We wrote about that. I talked a lot about heartbreak. I promised to quit drinking Diet Coke.

2010: My best guy friend went to Japan, I started dating online using Match.com, and I moved to LA. I made a large and embarrassing post about my celebrity crush on Matt Nathanson, I promised to stop drinking Diet Coke (again), and he got his first ever set of "naughty pictures" from a lady friend. We got to hang together in NYC and we wrote about that. His sister almost died in a car wreck.

2011: My friend shared his idea that a woman isn't a woman until she turns thirty (I now agree). His grandpa died. It was St. Patrick's Day, so he wrote in green ink. I was depressed and without health care and wanted antidepressants. I wrote about wishing I didn't hate myself so much.

2012: I was writing about getting over my need to make "impossible things possible," and he was trying to convince himself he was in love with a girl who I knew wasn't his forever person.

2013: My best guy friend was leaving NYC forever, and I flew to New York to spend one last epic week drinking tea, writing, and drinking beers in his apartment with him. I couldn't stop crying. I felt like I wouldn't know how to function when I came to NYC if he wasn't there. I held on to the journal for a long time during this year. I moved, got married, and got a new job. My next entry was on November 30, three days after his birthday, and the first time in my life I had forgotten it. I behaved really selfishly this year. At Christmas, my best guy friend and my husband took a guys' trip to climb Mount Everest. I was slightly jealous that I had to share him, and also worried that my friend would tell my husband some of my secrets or things from my past that only he knows.

2014: My best guy friend signed up for online dating. I received my first entry about his eventual wife. He was introducing her to his family. I was excited because I only worked from 5:15 a.m. to 3:30 p.m. (Ten hours was considered a short day.) I complained a lot about being tired. Our entries this year were six months apart.

2015: The first entry of the year started with my best guy friend saying, "Keltie, I am really worried about you" (I was spiraling), and then he bought a new house in our hometown.

2016: My best guy friend got engaged. I toured Africa. I ended the year by admitting that the better we become at being adults, the worse we become at journaling. I was writing at the time because I was the most hungover I had ever been in my entire life. He got married. I admitted that I tried to drive my car into a wall during a breakdown.

2017: I had to put my beloved dog Hobo down, and my best guy friend wrote me the most incredible journal entry about her and grief. I went to an adult rehab program to quit sugar, and I wrote admitting that I stole an apple on day five of the juice cleanse because I was so hungry. I wrote that I'm not ready to talk about my dog because I'm in denial that she's gone. I ended 2017 by calling it the year of death. I buried thirteen people and one dog. I was so over 2017.

2018: I was in a terrible car accident and learning to write again, so my handwriting was terrible. My husband was also having a terrible year, and I wrote about not being sure we were gonna make it. I couldn't stand him. My best guy friend had a baby girl and recounted every detail of her growth.

2019: There's a series of entries about how busy we are, our responsibilities, and how excited we are to spend some time together again soon. I'm nostalgic for the days we used to get a tea and sit in Central Park for hours.

So, basically, we have written for twenty years about nothing and everything.

These journals are my most prized possessions. I recently wrote a will and, besides my diamonds and some money, they were the only thing I cared about. Hundreds of pages filled with mostly pointless musings on twenty- and thirty-something life in New York City and all the other places we've been. Lovers, sex, confusion, and regret. Strength, memories, song lyrics, and poems. Photos, backstage passes, ticket stubs, and subway cards. A hundred types of pen ink and a hundred different versions of myself. These journal entries show me that life is mostly pointless, but at the same time, life really only matters if you have people beside you to witness that you were alive at that time. After twenty years, the memories of the way things happened and what I was feeling at the time have faded into the past and become less important. Mostly they have become the stories I tell at dinner parties, the stories that inform who I am as a person now.

My parents knew me until I was a teen, and then I moved to New York. I've had a handful of loves in my life that have known me for spans of years. I've had friends at different stages. I've had work friends, dance friends, castmate friends, and internet friends. But having someone in your life who has witnessed it all, even the terrible and embarrassing parts that you wouldn't dare tell anyone else, is really meaningful. When I see this friend, it's like coming home in a way that couldn't possibly exist with a lover or even a family member. We didn't stay in touch because we had to, or because we had the same last name. We are each other's chosen family. I have a deep love for this man, and I am in love with all of him, but he's not my lover.

People have a hard time understanding how this could be. When we were young, it was like having an older brother to confide in. When we got older, it was like having a nonsexual backup boyfriend who actually treated me nicely, who was there to dry my tears when whatever asshole I was dating and sleeping with broke my heart. As an adult, he's been a sounding board, a voice of reason, and a supporter. He's the person who doesn't care at all about anything I am accomplishing in my career, and who also doesn't care about any material possessions. I don't even really think he knows what I do for a living. It's a friendship of the soul. When he told me my husband, Chris, was a good man, it was the only opinion that really mattered to me. When I met his now wife, I instantly knew that the twenty years of crushes and the handful of one-night stands were meaningless in the story of his life. He had found his forever.

For all these reasons, I know that girls and guys can be just friends. I know that it's possible to have lifelong friends if you invest in them. I know that it's meant the world to me to have my best guy friend at my back. And I know it's important to keep friends around who knew you before you had it all figured out.

RIP, Girlfriend

People always say that you find out who your real friends are when life gets complicated . . . or when someone dies.

After my boyfriend passed away in 2014, I was definitely shown who my forever friends were and who it was time to let go of. Don't get me wrong, no one majorly fucked up—not even the cast member who joked with me at my boyfriend's memorial that he was only there for the free food. (Yes, that actually came out of someone's mouth. But, hey, people are awkward as fuck around you after your boyfriend dies.) It's not like Matt passed away and I expected everyone to handle it perfectly, because there's no rule book out there stating the perfect things to say and ways to act around a grieving individual. Some things that may be comforting to one person may be extremely offensive to another. Believe me, I understood that my friends and family were navigating a minefield, so I tried to be understanding.

I realized that I wasn't allowed to write off people who loved me during this time just because they couldn't read my mind or gauge exactly what I needed, but their responses when they *did* (unintentionally) hurt me were when their true colors really showed.

Here's a story of two of my closest friends and how I became even closer to one of them after the tragedy, while the other is now dead to me. Okay, kidding, that was harsh. But, in all seriousness, she had to go.

ELLEN

Ellen and I had been friends for about eight years. She was the friend who gave great advice and pep talks when I needed them. She was my biggest champion and cheerleader. It felt good to be friends with Ellen. Of course, Ellen had her flaws (as we all do), and sometimes she would get a little too self-righteous and judgy, but I just always aimed to be on her good side when those qualities presented themselves.

A couple weeks after Matt passed away, I started to get very overwhelmed with the constant check-ins from my friends and family. I knew all these people loved me and were just worried about me, so I was never annoyed or resentful, but I simply needed a break and didn't want to feel obligated to respond instantly or feel guilty for not responding to everyone. My best friend, Kat, offered to send out a simple text to everyone and just ask that I be given a little time-out from the attention, and that I would reach out if I needed any of them and when I was ready.

About a week after that text was sent, I received an email from Ellen. It was addressed to me and a few other close friends. Ellen had gotten married four months earlier, and she decided to resend us the photos from her wedding because, as she stated in the email, "a few of us had asked her to send them again." There was also some other bullshit in there about how she wanted to "relive such a magical weekend."

So here I am, the sad, grieving, chain-smoking disaster of a human that I was at the time, being sent a gallery link of my dear friend's happily ever after. I felt like I was being metaphorically punched in the gut by another shitty reminder of how I would never be so lucky to have such a "magical weekend" with Matt. But this reminder wasn't the same as the Hanes commercial with the adorable couple rolling around in bed that DIRECTV didn't know to shield me from during this difficult time. It was an email sent specifically to me, by someone who cared about me, which I had to open, and it caused me to feel the sinking pain that comes from the reminder that you're alone and the person you wanted to spend the rest of your life with is buried six feet underground.

I knew that Ellen had a tendency to be a little self-centered and a little too much of an exhibitionist at times, but I never thought it would equate to (what I felt was) such blatant insensitivity toward one of her best friends. I decided I needed to take a time-out from this friendship and that this cheery, self-obsessed newlywed was not who I needed to have in my orbit at the moment if I was going to survive the hardest experience of my life. I made the decision to take some time away from the friendship without wanting to get into it with someone who was so obviously tone-deaf.

Now, Ellen is the type of person who can't really handle ever being "put on ice," so I should have known that this approach wouldn't go well, but I was stupidly optimistic. She came barreling back into my life a couple months later with a voicemail that basically demanded attention and an explanation for my sudden need for space. I emailed her this:

Ellen,

My intention with this email is simply to explain my actions in recent months. I don't want to vilify anyone or cause any more pain than either of us have already suffered. But I have to be honest about what triggered my distance in our friendship. I can actually pinpoint one specific event, and everything sort of snowballed from there.

Back in September, I went to New York for work and stayed with Kat. While I was there, I had, for lack of a better word, a major meltdown. I was literally hanging by a thread. Kat noticed that, on top of everything else, I was getting very stressed out about returning everyone's calls and texts. She explained to me that I needed to take care of myself and that she would let all my friends know that I was taking some much-needed time.

It wasn't more than a week later that I opened up an email from you in which you were resending the link to your wedding photos to some friends and family. To be completely honest, opening that email was like a slap in the face. It not only made me question your forethought, but it felt incredibly insensitive. I'm sure you can understand how the photos were a glaring reminder of how I would never have that day with Matt, as I thought I would when I was sitting at your wedding.

I don't wish unhappiness for you or anyone. I want all my friends to be happy. But I thought that my closest friends might use a little more discretion in the short months following such a tragedy. I never thought that any of your actions were malicious or done on purpose to hurt me, but even without meaning to, you did hurt me. In order to get through this chapter of my life, I am surrounding myself with people who are aware and willing to make sacrifices in order to avoid causing me any more pain.

And in order to salvage our friendship, I simply need time.

Becca

One would send this email and hope to hear something along the lines of "I'm so incredibly sorry! I never meant to hurt you, but I understand how I did, and I hope you can forgive me."

Instead, I received a string of texts justifying her (very stupid) reasons for sending the wedding photos, saying how she couldn't believe I would ever think she would do something to hurt me, and asserting how hurt *she* was that I didn't come to her sooner to let her explain herself.

At the end of the day, I realized that I had a friend who couldn't admit when she was wrong, and I just didn't have the space for people like that anymore. Ellen lacked the ability to swallow her pride and simply say "I'm sorry." Sometimes excuses aren't appropriate after apologizing. And sometimes, to be a good friend, you can't ask the person who's hurting the most to take care of *your* feelings and emotions. Unfortunately, those have to take a backseat when the other person is dealing with insurmountable pain and loss.

SARAH

Sarah and I had been friends for about the same amount of time as Ellen and I had when Matt passed away. I actually met Matt through Sarah and her boyfriend at the time. The four of us had talked about taking a big European vacation together the summer I lost Matt. Before his death, we had all decided the trip would be too complicated, so they planned their travel and we planned ours. Both trips, though, were scheduled for about two weeks after he passed away.

After the funeral, I needed to get the hell out of LA, and I went to Atlanta to be with my family. So instead of heading off to Paris with the love of my life, I was going to Georgia to sit on my sister's couch and try not to take pills and lie down. (Sorry for the darkness, but we get real in the LadyGang.)

I stayed off social media for a while, for obvious reasons, but I picked it back up again in Atlanta because the depth of a fashion blogger (or lack thereof) was just the escape I needed at the time from my own depressing existence.

One day, I was scrolling through my feed, hoping I could gawk at the obnoxiously skinny New York City blogger, when my friend Sarah's photo popped up. It was a picture of her and her boyfriend on their beautiful, romantic European vacation. I was officially triggered. I'm not saying it was justified, but for whatever reason, the slew of photos that continued from their fabulous trip felt like hell for me.

After a number of these posts, I decided to send a text to her. I said something along the lines of "I know you would never ever want to hurt me, but seeing these pictures is breaking my heart. We were all supposed to be in Europe this week, and I can't help but feel devastated by these pictures." Whether or not I was entitled to these feelings (and, in hindsight, it doesn't feel like I was), I still felt like I really needed to put them out there.

Her response? EXACTLY the one I needed. She was devastated that she had done something that hurt me, and she said she was so sorry and loved me very much.

What Sarah did wasn't bad or wrong or even insensitive if you ask most people, and she probably had every right to defend herself like Ellen did. But she didn't. Taking care of her friend who was in excruciating pain was more important in that moment than her pride or desperation to "be right."

If I could go back in time, I would step up and tell Ellen as soon as she hurt me, like I did with Sarah. But I didn't. I think it's because, deep down, I knew she would require me to take care of her instead of the other way around. Maybe I was too harsh, and maybe Ellen deserved a second chance, but her reaction spoke volumes to me about the type of friend she was and would probably always be. When your friends show you who they are, pay attention. And when you're down, surround yourself with those who will pick you up. I love you, Sarah.

It's Never "Just Friends"

There is nothing that makes me wanna puke more than when people refer to their significant other as their ~*BeSt fRiEnD*~. WE GET IT, you actually like each other. I mean, I would fucking hope so. This sentiment always made me want to roll my eyes into another dimension, and then . . . something happened to me.

I'll preface my story with the fact that my early twenties marked the very peak of my emotional instability. I was insanely insecure and extremely fragile, and I could crumble into nothingness at the drop of a hat. A stranger could look at me the wrong way, and I would burst into tears. I felt completely misunderstood, and the only place I felt comfortable was in my room pounding out brooding stream-of-consciousness writings on my vintage typewriter while drinking Johnnie Walker Black Label and listening to Mumford & Sons on vinyl. I know, I was SoOoO edgy and super deep and not a stereotypical wannabe hipster doofus at all.

Looking back, I laugh because I have always had such a solid group of girlfriends who are still my ride-or-dies to this day. But, for some reason, I kept looking for something more, something deeper, a connection that tugged at my heartstrings. Okay fine, I'll admit it. I was totally masochistic and I yearned for something painful.

So, like everything else in my life, this story starts on the Warped Tour (which you are familiar with by now) in the summer of 2009. While lugging 150 pounds of merchandise into my pop-up tent in Bonner Springs, Kansas, on the first day of the tour, I met a guy named Jared, a stocky, strawberry-blond guitarist in a band called The Maine. Jared was wearing neon-green sunglasses, an ugly pink T-shirt with a flying pig on it, and a swoopy emo haircut that was actually almost a mullet. As embarrassing and unattractive as that sounds, he looked like a SNACK to me. Jared and I exchanged a short hello, and I continued on my way to work. We kept bumping into each other in the following days, and the short exchanges turned into longer conversations.

You've heard me talking about Warped Tour before, so you know the drill. Hundreds of people traveling the country on a punk-rock music tour together, working and partying 24-7 for two months straight. And since I was one of the only girls on the tour, the whole summer was constant ADD-boy-filled heaven for me. Even though there was an endless supply of band dudes for me to flirt with, Jared and I started slowly but surely gravitating toward each other. Neither of us were really doing anything on purpose. I would just . . . take the long path to my tent so that I could nonchalantly pass his tour bus. And Jared would just . . . coincidentally happen to walk by my tent twenty times a day. Our subtle efforts soon turned into pretty shameless and obvious acts. We were both trying to find any and all excuses to accidentally bump into each other.

And how could you blame me? Jared was the literal best. He was goofy and thoughtful and lighthearted and an all-around fun-time guy. He was super smart, quick-witted, and extremely talented. He was sensitive and had lots of deep feelings, and he wasn't afraid to talk about them. He never took himself too seriously, and he was always a good sport when I poked fun at him. We always joked that he was "the blurry guy" because none of his band's fans cared about him, and he was always standing in the back of their photos, out of focus. I always thought that was so funny and ironic because he was one of the most interesting people I had ever met.

And Jared just got me. It felt like he understood me immediately and completely. Without saying a word, I could just look him in the eyes and know that he could read exactly what was swirling around in this messy little head of mine. He listened to me bitch about work and gossip about friends and gush about music and cry about boys. He talked me through heartache and held me through anxiety attacks. He made me believe that all of my feelings were valid, no matter how dumb I felt about them. He valued my intelligence and trusted my opinions. He made me feel like the most important person in the world. On top of that, he just made me feel *good*. He was like my human Xanax. He was everything my lonely, frustrated little emo heart was yearning for.

But there was one little problem. Jared had a serious girlfriend. So, from the very beginning, we both knew our fun little relationship ended at friends only. I respected his situation, and there were enough lead singers to satisfy my make-out needs for the summer. No biggie. I was grateful for my new best bud. But no matter how hard we tried to pretend it didn't exist, our connection was magnetic and undeniable to anyone who knew us.

We spent more time together in those two months than you would with a friend over the course of two years. We learned about each other on the most basic and complex levels. We stayed up countless nights talking about life and love and everything in between. We had the quickest banter and would fire comebacks at each other nonstop. We had comfortable silence, never awkward silence. We pushed and challenged each other, and we saw each other at our best and at our worst. We never ran out of things to talk about.

That was one of the best summers of my life. Not only because I had a blast getting drunk and traveling around the country with my friends for two months straight, but because it was the first time I felt like I'd met someone who truly understood the inner workings of my heart. As much as I wished that we could have had something more, I was just as happy to have a best buddy I could turn to for anything and everything. But, of course, nothing is ever that easy.

Even though we had this undeniable connection, Jared wasn't the greatest friend to me over the years. When that summer ended, our friendship became extremely inconsistent, and he would jump in and out of my life without notice. Even though we traveled around the world together numerous times after the Warped Tour, he ultimately became flaky and unreliable—and understandably so. I wasn't dumb. Even though we were "just friends," there was an obvious and unquestionable bond between us that was not appropriate given his relationship status. Because of that, he was fighting his own internal battle about his feelings for me, and my physical presence in his life didn't make things any easier.

As I grew older, I started to walk away from lukewarm friendships that didn't serve me anymore, so I started ignoring his random "Hi, how are you?" texts, and I bailed on hanging out with him when he was in town. I didn't have time to waste on fair-weather friends, no matter how much he "got me." I deserved better.

After our friendship crumbled, I had hopes that I would find that kind of twin-flame connection again. I was only in my early twenties, after all, and I had so much life left to experience. All I had to do was get back out there and meet some more people. But the older I got, the more I realized how special my best buddy really was to me. But, alas, he was dead to me. Whatever. RIP Jared.

Fast-forward five years and, out of the blue, I got a text from my old bud Jared.

"A little birdy told me you were coming to Warped Tour this weekend, is that true?"

It wasn't true at all. I had no plans to go to Warped Tour, and it turned out Jared had just made that up as an excuse to text me because his band was playing. Pretty sly, dude. Lucky for him, he wrote me during happy hour on a Friday afternoon. After a few rosés, going to the very last Warped Tour at thirty-one years old sounded like the *best idea ever*. But first, I had a very important question, so I texted him:

"So . . . are you single?"

He immediately responds, "Yup," with that snarky winky-face emoji, and my response was, "OH BOY." We both knew what that meant. Shit's going down.

At this point, so many years had passed since I'd last seen him. Any resentment that I had for him bailing on our friendship had dissipated, and honestly, my memory of that magical bond had faded a lot, too. I was at a point in my life where I was finally fully healed from my last disastrous relationship, I truly loved the person I had grown into independently, and I was *actually* excited to be single and able to explore my options. So, what the hell? Your girl was ready to sing along to her favorite emo songs and smooch some middle-aged band dudes!!! I decided to go.

To backtrack a little bit, the night before Warped Tour, I went on a date with a guy named Shad. Yes, SHAD. S-H-A-D. Chad with an S. He was actually really cool—and way less douchey than you would think someone named Shad would be. We made out and drank wine and played cornhole, and I was hungover as balls the next morning but super excited for a nostalgic day with my good old bestie, Jared.

When I got to the venue and saw Jared for the first time, I was already a little bit tipsy from bottomless-brunch mimosas, and I was feeling especially sassy. The first thing I noticed was his terrible fuckboi hair cut. You know the one. Buzzed pretty much to skin on the sides, and long and gelled back on top. Once I got past the strawberry-blond catastrophe on his head, I felt warm. Physically, because it was 105 degrees outside, but also emotionally, because I had really forgotten how good this person made me feel. We spent the day drinking Bud Lights and reminiscing about the glory days, and it was like no time had passed at all. We sang our hearts out to The Used, ate cheeseburgers from the after-party BBQ, and made out until 2:00 a.m.

I left that night drunk and happy about seeing my old friend, but I didn't really think anything of it. To be honest, I spent the next day texting Shad. Over the next few months, though, Jared fought for me day after day. He spilled his guts and made it very clear that he would walk on broken glass to be with me. Because I had been burned and bamboozled so much in my last relationship, I was hesitant at first and skeptical to the millionth degree. But Jared was patient and understanding and persistent, and he was hell-bent on succeeding at the task of proving himself to me, no matter how long it took. We have moved slow and steady, and let me tell you that the tortoise really does win the damn race. He has finally won me over.

It has been ten years since I first met that floppy-red-haired, neon-sunglass-wearing goofball. In those ten years, we both had a ton of work to do independently to even put us in a place where we could be ready for a healthy, long-lasting relationship. In those ten years, I've become less of an emotional mess and more of a stable, secure, independent gal. And in those ten years, Jared has grown into a pretty fantastic man himself. The coolest part of my relationship with Jared now is that I know him to his very core. I've seen him as a dumb kid, I've watched him make a bajillion mistakes, and, thankfully, I've seen that he has learned and grown from each and every one of them. Through it all, I can really appreciate the wonderful person he truly is today.

Jared is my security blanket, my big teddy bear, my shoulder to cry on, and my warmth. He still knows exactly what I'm thinking, which is annoying because I can't be mysterious AT ALL anymore. He still listens to me bitch and vent and gush and cry, but now he has the tools to actually support me. He watches *The Bachelor* with me (and doesn't complain!), he rubs my feet, and he knows when to stop cuddling me so I can fall asleep. He still holds me through anxiety attacks, and he adores me and tells me every day that I am the most important person in the world. He is stable and reliable and consistent and true to his word. He won't bail. He'll never be the blurry guy to me. And we still never run out of things to talk about.

Who knows what the future holds for me and Jared, or for anyone really. All I know is that life comes at you fast. And damn it, sometimes you do end up with your ~*BeSt FriEnD*~. Maybe your guy really is right in front of you. You just need to give him ten years and a new haircut.

Supportive Sally

>

Bitter Betty

When you're single and your best gal is single, you seem to spend all your free time getting happy hours and having sleepovers and watching shitty reality TV together. You can't imagine a time when you won't be attached at the hip, doing all of the fun things best friends do together. But, unfortunately, unless you have a sexual relationship with your best friend, you can't possibly be everything to each other for the rest of your lives. Eventually, your bestie is going to find another bestie, but one who goes down on her, and things are going to shift. When your friend finds love, she's gonna start ditching you. Even if she's the best friend in the world, she's still gonna start ditching you. And she most likely isn't doing it on purpose. Maybe she just won't feel like going out drinking until 2:00 a.m. to find dudes anymore. Or maybe she's busy on *Bachelor* Monday because her boyfriend surprised her with a cute date night. It might feel like a big change in your dynamic, but please be happy for your person when they find their person.

When your bestie finds love, she's going to retreat into her little love bubble. This is normal, but it's also annoying to anyone who is not currently in a love bubble themselves. Remember that your love bubble is coming, too, and until then, you need to lower your expectations for your starry-eyed friend. She's not going to be around as much. She might drop the ball. She might forget to text you back. But that doesn't mean she's a bad person or a bad friend. Even the best relationships take a substantial amount of energy, and she's probably doing the best she can with the time she has. But there's good news: She will come back around! If you don't burn the bridge and guilt her for simply being in love, she will eventually find a healthy balance between you and her new dude. If you have the right friends and you find the right man, everything will work itself out in the end.

Just Because You're Miserable . . .

During the eight hundred years I've been navigating friendships, I think I've finally figured out the key to having (and being) a good friend. It's a very simple yet very important question that I ask myself. The question is: Does she seem genuinely happy for me when I'm happy? It seems pretty simple, right? Think again.

In my twenties, I always assumed that the girlfriends who showed up for me during breakups, failed auditions, and lost jobs were the true ride-or-dies. It was so nice to have that one girlfriend who would drop anything to be with you in your time of need. We all know the type: She brings you ice cream, a bottle of wine, a pack of cigarettes, and all the energy in the world to trash-talk whoever or whatever hurt you . . . and it feels like true ecstasy.

That friend for me was Heather. Heather was like a superhero who swooped down at the first sign of trouble and didn't leave your side until justice was served (or, in other words, until we had thoroughly destroyed some cheater's life inside and out). There was a period of time when life just wasn't going great for me in any department, and that's when Heather and I really bonded. It was when Heather could showcase her superhero abilities and truly shine in the friendship department.

It wasn't until 2015, when I started dating Zach, that I saw a different side of Heather. She would do weird things like fish for his flaws during our conversations about him. She would be quick to jump on anything he did wrong as a potential "red flag," and she would constantly make comments about how it was a great "rebound" relationship for me. It was confusing to me that I would have only positive things to say about this man I was falling more and more in love with, yet this best friend of mine seemed to want to make me feel like there was something I was totally missing and that he couldn't possibly be "my person."

A year went by, and Heather finally calmed the fuck down (a little) because it was clear that Zach wasn't going anywhere. During Zach's and my courtship, Heather dated a string of guys who were truly terrible, and she was MISERABLE. I couldn't blame her—she had hit a really rough patch, and I desperately wanted my friend to find herself a Zach. I felt a lot of guilt for having such a loving relationship while one of my best friends was lonely, so I gave her a lot of passes for her occasionally rotten behavior.

When did the shit *finally* hit the fan, you ask? When Zach proposed, naturally. This was the beginning of the end for Heather and me. I couldn't believe how someone who said she loved me so much could become the worst, most negative part of this wonderful period of my life. She would constantly ask our mutual friends if they thought Zach and I were "moving too fast." She made any and every event leading up to the wedding about her. I barely even saw her at my actual wedding because she spent the entire night in a corner, sulking. She officially turned into a sad, pathetic, emotional vampire.

I realized after that period of time that Heather never actually cared about me. She cared about having someone in a shittier position in life than her so that she could feel better about her own situation. She loved me when I was sad and weak, and she resented me when I became happy and strong. I never realized how important it was for me to have people in my life who not only showed up for the shitty moments but who would cheer me on during the great ones.

Now Heather has a baby and a fiancé she loves and (SHOCKER) is a complete joy to be around. Heather and I are still friends, but I definitely had to reevaluate our friendship after what happened. I put her in the "fair-weather friend" category, and that's okay. She's still really fun to get drunk with.

Sorry for What I Said When I Hated Your Husband

My friend married a total asshole, and we all knew it but couldn't say anything to her.

She was cuckoo-for-Cocoa-Puffs crazy about this dweeb from the moment they met. They started as friends, and her life quickly started to revolve around him. She changed her work schedule so that they worked the same shifts and offered to repaint his apartment, buy his groceries, and watch his dog. They were going to the same event "as friends" and having deep talks "as friends" and having meaningful sex "as friends who sleep together."

Eventually, she followed him across the country (with separate apartments, of course, because they were "just friends") and somehow wore him down to committing to her. I came to her rescue and scowled at him when their on-again-off-again thing would become off again. I begged her to have some self-respect and walk away from this selfish asshole, but there was nothing I could say. My job as her lifelong friend was to love her, be suspicious of him, and try to talk some sense into her. We've all been in this position, and honestly, I've been the cuckoo one before, too. She was smitten, and getting treated like absolute garbage only intensified her obsession with him.

To my surprise, they moved in together, introduced each other to their families, and got engaged. By that point, although I was wary, I just wanted to be there for my bestie and support her. I embraced him. I got his phone number, and I texted him here and there to try to deepen our friendship. We became Facebook friends. I would see them out together and ask about his life. We went together to the place where he was a chef, and I gushed over his mac and cheese. (Like, how hard is it to make mac and cheese, though?) When she asked me to be her maid of honor, I accepted. But as the wedding day neared, I began to be pulled aside by members of her family, our mutual friends, and even my own mom. "She's not really gonna do this, is she?" they would say, or, "Ohhhh, I don't know about him," and, "She's so different when she's with him." I felt the same way, but I felt like I couldn't say anything to her because she was in so deep and because she really did love the guy.

The morning of her wedding was intense. No one really knew what to say. She was stressed, like most brides are, and was somehow convinced that a perfect bouquet and a beautiful updo could make her growing doubts go away. Off we went! The wedding itself was actually sweet. She looked gorgeous. They seemed really happy. He held her hand and was really loving to her. I remember riding with them in the limousine and looking at them and wondering if I had been wrong all along.

It came time for my speech, and I couldn't say what I really wanted to tell him and the rest of the room: "If you hurt her I will murder you." So I gave my speech focused 100 percent on how great she was and how lucky *he* was to have her. I spoke of her kindness, her loyalty, her sense of adventure, her beauty, her selflessness, and her sense of humor. I secretly hoped that he would hear it and a light bulb would go off in his heart and he would realize just how lucky he was. I was legit trying to convince this man that my friend was great—on their wedding day.

The first year of marriage went smoothly. She got pregnant, and then she got pregnant again. He stopped working, and out of nowhere, I saw my best friend working two jobs to support her family, with two kids under the age of four, while her dude hung out at home doing I. Do. Not. Know. What. The kids went to daycare. Her calls became more infrequent, and the distance between us expanded. I knew what was happening. Her life was imploding, and she didn't want to admit it to anyone. I had been embarrassed and full of shame after broken relationships myself. I knew how it felt to have a righteous friend saying "I told you so." She was also, to everyone's horror, still really in love with this guy. She had lost herself completely. It was up to me, a friend who had known her since she was six years old, to remind her who she was.

I realized then that calling the man she loved "trash" wasn't actually the best way to be a supportive friend. So I changed my strategy. I focused on her. How she was doing? How was she setting up her future? Was she taking care of herself? I sent her books. Encouraged her to go to therapy. Sat on the phone while she smoked cigarettes and drank red wine. The only thing I kept saying over and over again to her was "You deserve someone who really loves you. You DESERVE someone who REALLY loves YOU." The cracks in their marriage appeared slowly. One day, it seemed like it could be saved, and another it seemed like a tornado of blame and lies and deception was pounding down on her. Some days she was strong, and on others she was a puddle of tears. I had a secret text chain going with my mom, her mom, and her sister-in-law where we constantly updated each other and made sure someone was there for her 24-7. It was ugly and hideous and childish and dramatic, but eventually she and her husband split up officially, for good.

Eventually, I got my best friend back. Her eyes started to sparkle. She started taking care of herself. She started saying things like "He is just saying these things to hurt me." She focused on her kids. She met a new, wonderful guy. She lost weight and started working out. We laughed and gossiped and chatted about everything in our lives, and not just the latest thing going on in the divorce. I helped her get a really good lawyer. Of course, months later, her ex backtracked and tried to manipulate her into coming back to him. (My proudest friend moment is when she walked away and refused to get sucked back in!)

We get a lot of questions on LadyGang about whether or not we should say something to our friends if we see them with someone terrible. I believe you can handle it however you want, and the outcome will probably always be the same. People have to live through and survive their own messy shit. You can't Bubble Wrap a friend when you know something is bad for them. All you can do is love them, hug them, and have a bottle of wine ready on the other side of their pain. It absolutely killed me to see my friend struggle to be loved in the way she did. But it was her heart that needed to heal, and my job was to just love her through it. That's what friends are for. You can pick your friends, but you can't pick your friends' loser husbands, y'know?

Bridal Party Rules

If there is one thing we wish we could get the ladies of the world to understand, it's this: Your wedding is the best day . . . of *your* life. No one else's. Not even your sisters'. Stop expecting people to freak out and care about your wedding as much as you do. Don't get us wrong, we are totally happy for you. We love you. You look gorgeous in that dress. But we didn't notice that the flowers in your bouquet matched the flower print on the napkins in the bathroom. Honestly, the only thing we really care about is the open bar. We don't feel comfortable going into credit card debt for a bachelorette trip to Cabo, a bridal shower in Nantucket, and a wedding on the Amalfi Coast. We're all adults, and we've got important shit going on in our lives, too.

Let's talk about bridesmaids. Bridesmaids are there to support you on your big day, but in no way, shape, or form are they required to drop their lives to help you plan your wedding for months on end. That's why you hire a wedding planner. Unless you are paying them with cash dollars, it is on *their* terms when and how they want to pitch in and help you out. The truth is, if you're going to have a wedding party and, God forbid, a maid of honor, their only job is to emotionally support you on your big day and wipe the lipstick off your teeth. They're not there to run your errands.

If you have a destination wedding, and people are buying flights and hotel rooms and something nice to wear to your wedding, and you *still* have a registry, you're a dick. Sorry to break it to you, but you don't deserve a wedding registry if you're asking people to spend thousands of dollars and take time off from work just to attend your goddamn wedding. We're positive they would rather spend that time and money on an *actual* vacation of their choice. Also, if you have a destination wedding and someone can't make it, you can't get mad at them. You can't write them out of your life because they didn't have enough vacation days, access to childcare, and dollars to get to the South of France.

A Tale of Two Bridal Parties

When I got married for the first time at twenty-one, I was under an immense amount of pressure to be the perfect bride. I was the first of my friends to get married because I was so young, and at that point, I had only been to one or two weddings in my life. One of them had been in a barn and the meal was a giant roasted pig. Not knowing what exactly I was supposed to do with this looming social event, I did what any ambitious pre-internet bride did in the early 2000s. I bought every wedding magazine at the supermarket, and I cut out all the ideas and pasted them into my own scrapbook for wedding planning (it was Pinterest before Pinterest existed). The only problem was that I was getting all of my wedding advice from wedding experts whose entire business was to stress you out about things that you would never actually worry about in real life. Was the ribbon on our invitations going to match the ribbon on the towels in the bathrooms of the reception? I had not given much thought to these types of details before my wedding magazine binge, but now that I was a bride-to-be, it was all I thought about.

My first husband was a New York native, and he was insistent that we have an NYC wedding. He had already planned out who his groomsmen would be before I had figured out how exactly I was going to get my broke-ass West Coast Canadian friends to New York City. Away I went into bridal party hell!

First, I asked my longtime best friend, Katie, to be my maid of honor. We had grown up together since we were six years old, and she is the person who 100 percent knows me the best on earth. From wearing matching Guess jeans to the mall in fifth grade, to holding each other's hair back when we were drinking underage at sixteen, we had been through it all. She instantly said yes, and on my next trip home, we took the day off to go to the mall and try on potential bridesmaid dresses. We landed on a collection of stretchy spandex, royal-blue, halter-top, v-neck gowns with fabric that was sparkly because of tiny little glue dots that are covered in cheap plastic glitter. I didn't even know who else would be in the bridal party yet, but we bought four dresses for (I think) $39.99 each and set off.

I had three slots to fill. I should have stopped there and explained to my future husband that I had left home twenty-four hours after graduating high school, had really only kept in touch with Katie and made some new friends during our cruise ship adventures, and that I couldn't fill the other slots. But I stuck to what the wedding magazine had said, that it was "important to have an equal number of maids and men so that the photos were evenly proportioned."

I dug deep. I asked my other closest friend from high school to come, and she said yes. She and Katie had had a tumultuous relationship throughout our teens, and there were definitely some weird vibes about who was my "best" friend. Nothing they couldn't work out through sharing a hotel room at a Holiday Inn on Long Island the day before my wedding, right?

Next I asked my closest friend from dancing. We had spent many late nights in the studio, driving to competitions together, and rooting for each other. She had been with me when we flew across Canada to audition for the cruise ship job that I had taken where I met my first husband, so I felt like she was significant in our story. She said yes, and, of course, she loved the blue dress I had provided because, looking back, it was more costume than dress.

I was out of friends. I was definitely out of friends I could ask to fly to New York City. My best guy friend had said he would come to the wedding, but this was way before I was confident enough to screw with the rules of girls for the bridal party and boys for the groomsmen. The acceptance of men in a woman's bridal party came a decade later. My first husband didn't think to ask my best guy friend or my brother to stand up with him. (Selfish to the core.)

As the wedding approached, Katie mentioned that a friend we used to waitress with in high school was thinking about taking a trip to New York. She was an acquaintance at best. But she was coming to NYC, so I got her number from Katie and asked her to be a bridesmaid. Pathetic.

My mom threw me a small bridal shower where I opened gifts and wore a white turtleneck. It was beyond ironic, because I had fooled everyone into believing that I was going to need a twenty-four-piece china set from Crate and Barrel with gold-rimmed plates, serving bowls, and glasses—when I couldn't even find four people to be in my bridal party. The next day, my dancer friend pulled out. She had booked her own cruise ship dance job and could no longer make it to NYC. A spot in the bridal party was once again empty.

I went deep into planning mode, and my first priority was showing my future mother-in-law the blue bridesmaid dresses so that she could help me match the balloons to the flowers to the table linens to the confetti to the favors to the menus to the invitations to the toilet paper—just like my beloved bridal magazines said. Her audible gasp when I pulled the stretchy glittery gowns out of a plastic bag made it clear. What was chic and special in my small town in Canada was tacky AF in New York. Laid out on her perfect marble kitchen island, in her perfect Martha Stewart house, in her perfect rich neighborhood, the dresses looked how I felt: like a complete piece of trash.

I couldn't worry about the dresses though. I had bigger things to do on my list. My bridal party was still sparse. I ended up asking my future husband's groomsman's girlfriend to be in my tribe, to round out the heartwarming assortment made up of one person who really knew me, one person who knew me but could kind of be a bitch, one person I knew in passing, and one person who I had spent less than four days with in my life. It felt forced and uncomfortable, but I knew I had to keep up appearances and make it work. After all, this was going to be the greatest day of my life, right?

I ended up getting new dresses for the bridesmaids that were black satin, simple, and up to NYC standards. We all came together in Long Island: my bitchy friend made trouble with my sweet Katie, and I never spoke to the waitress friend or the groomsman's girlfriend again after the wedding. Katie gave a beautiful speech, and we cried. In the end, a perfectly symmetrical bridal party photograph couldn't save what was a disaster of an arrangement. Eleven months later, my first husband and I divorced.

Fast-forward to a decade later and my second attempt at a bridal party. This time there was no fancy hall and no invitations that matched the flowers. We sent emails to invite only our closest friends. We got married in the backyard. I didn't worry about whether my people would come all the way to Los Angeles for a wedding, because we had spent the last decade being there in such major ways for one another. I was a (sort of) fully formed woman with beautiful and deep friendships. We had fifty-two people at our wedding, and I could have had seventeen bridesmaids from that group. Everyone in attendance was so very important to my life. Katie came to this wedding not as a maid of honor but as my lifelong best friend. She spent the night with me at my house and got ready with me in the morning. I didn't have a bridal shower, or a bachelorette party, although my LA friends did surprise me with a roller-skating party that had cake but no strippers or penis cups.

The love I felt at our wedding was so deep and real and full. All my favorite people on Earth were there, and not a single stranger or fairweather friend. There was no one from my work, or Chris's work, and there were no cousins or aunts we had never met. It was the exact opposite of everything a wedding magazine would have told us to do, and I couldn't have loved it more. Chris didn't have any groomsmen, and I didn't have any bridesmaids. Our beloved dog, Hobo, was our "dog of honor," and she spent most of the night sniffing around, eating scraps off the tables, and getting belly rubs. She was the most perfect bridal party ever.

What I learned from my two parties is that human beings and their love for you are not accessories for photos or assistants to the bride-inchief. It is not their J-O-B to spend all their money to celebrate you finding love. It's not their job to succumb to whatever princess/movie star/prom queen fantasy you have going on during your wedding day. Your wedding day is a big day for YOU, and it's just another day for them. You don't need to call out your most special friends by making them wear an expensive dress they can never wear again and dance with your nephew. But chances are, if that is your dream, the friends who really love you will show up for you and do just that. Bridal parties should be renamed "still my friend when I hate my significant other" parties, "I love you too much to make you wear matching dresses" parties, or simply "I'll still be around when you get divorced" parties.

You Can't Spell Friend Without "End"

The LadyGang friendship code is simple: You're significant, but you're not my significant other.

Friendship should be relatively easy. Of course, you should be there for each other when you need support, but there shouldn't be this constant guilt if you don't get together enough or text each other enough. Is there anything worse than that self-righteous friend who sends the text message "Are you alive?" when they know you're just overwhelmed and swamped with a million things?! The older we get, the more life happens to all of us. The time that used to be filled with girly sleepovers, drunken nights, and chasing boys becomes filled with crying babies, failing marriages, and aging loved ones.

The sad reality is that the older you get, the less you see your friends, so don't feel bad if you can't go out drinking because you're taking care of your toddler. You have 10 percent of the free time you used to have in your youth, so spend it wisely. Do you want to devote that precious energy to a few golden friends, or spread yourself thin to placate a dozen acquaintances? Take a good, honest look at who adds real value to your world. Life can get hard, and the last thing you want to deal with on top of all the real shit is a needy, petty friend making everything even harder.

SPOTTING A TOXIC FRIEND

We've all been friends with *that* person before. The friend who always makes everything about them. The friend who only reaches out when they need something. The friend who only asks how your day is so they can tell you about theirs. The friend who expects you to drop everything for them, but who wouldn't lift a finger in return for you. You can call them a narcissist. Self-absorbed. Jealous. Insecure. And it doesn't really make a difference how you classify them, because at the end of the day they're just . . . kind of a shitty friend.

There are obvious signs when a friend is having a negative impact on your life: They don't celebrate your victories, they're jealous when anything goes well in your life, and maybe they even try to hook up with your crush.

SIDE NOTE: We've all been young and dumb and smooched (or slept with) a friend's crush before. You are allowed to make this mistake once in your life. Don't beat yourself up about it forever, but let that mild guilt eat away at you so you never do it again.

Aside from these obvious behaviors, a toxic friend can sneak into your life so subtly that you might not even realize the impact of it until you're completely sucked dry. We cannot stress this enough: Surround yourself with people who have morals and values similar to yours. It may seem like a no-brainer, but we've all had to learn this lesson the hard way in our lives. If your friend's actions or words ever make your heart feel icky, even if it doesn't affect you directly, don't just let it slide. If you ever feel any ounce of pressure to compromise your character, chances are you're dealing with a sneaky toxic friend, and it's time to put them on the back burner.

SPOTTING A (SNEAKY) TOXIC FRIEND

Maybe you have a friend who talks *a lot* of shit about your other friends when they aren't around. We all vent to our friends during bad times, but if someone constantly offers you their unsolicited opinions about the people you care about, it's a major red flag. And we'll double down on that statement if they bring your family into it. *You* are the only person who is allowed to talk shit about *your* family, *your* significant other, and *your* kids. Sometimes we just need to get something off our chest, and a good friend knows the boundaries between harmless banter and trying to plant ideas in your head.

Maybe you have a friend who casually cheats on her husband. This is tricky, because we live in a progressive society with progressive relationships, and there can be a lot going on behind the scenes, so this really only applies if she is blatantly disrespecting a good, unsuspecting man. Sure, she might not be hurting you directly, but the respect she has for her significant other probably signals the respect she has for the other people in her life as well.

Maybe you have a friend who parties *way* too hard whenever you get together. If you're into that, party on, Garth and Wayne. But if every happy hour turns into a 3:00 a.m. coke bender and you find yourself puking at your desk the next morning, it might be smart to reevaluate your partying choices. It's easy to get swept up in a good time every now and then, but just make sure your fun nights out aren't negatively affecting your real life.

Maybe you have a friend who can't keep their mouth shut. You want to be able to trust your friends with precious information, right? We bet a million bucks that you've disclosed super important gossip to a seemingly trustworthy friend before saying "Don't tell anyone, okay?" And then they might go and tell ten people *immediately,* and you're totally screwed. Blabbermouths can still be good people, so you might choose to keep them in your life, but understand that you cannot disclose highly sensitive material ever again.

TO FIGHT OR NOT TO FIGHT? THAT IS THE QUESTION

Every once in a while, a friend will hurt you. Maybe it will be a small jab, or maybe it will be a deep cut. Maybe it will be an accident, or maybe it will be intentional. *You* have to decide how you will respond to their actions, and you have to decide what constitutes forgiveness, confrontation, or cutting them out of your life altogether. Listen, we don't expect everyone in life to behave perfectly, because we certainly don't, but we know that when we screw up, the best thing to do is to (in the words of Lisa Rinna) OWN IT! A sincere "I'm so sorry I did this to you" goes a long way. Someone who is incapable of admitting fault and apologizing is someone you can't have in your life. There will always be an excuse, or someone else to blame, with no lessons learned.

Friendship breakups can sometimes be harder, messier, and more painful than romantic breakups. If your friendship is on the chopping block, there are a few different ways to part ways without starting World War III.

THE MUTUAL GHOSTING. First, there is the slow, mutual ghosting. This is where neither party is really at fault for anything massive, but there's a breakup where you just . . . slowly drift apart. There's no major blowout, and there might not even be anything to pin it on, exactly. This kind of breakup is usually based on habits and values realigning as you get older and go through life changes. Your friendship might start to feel unbalanced, and this is most likely because one of you is maturing faster than the other. The mutual ghosting doesn't require a full-on confrontation, because there shouldn't be too many hurt feelings or too much resentment or pain.

Even though it sucks to lose a friend, you should both have some kind of understanding of the fact that you just aren't as close as you used to be. And you know what? That's okay. There is nothing wrong with being nonconfrontational sometimes. As you get older, your friend circle gets smaller and smaller, and you have less time to give.

THE ONE-SIDER. We hate those breakups where you're the only one who gets the memo that you're splitting up. You've tried to make your exit a dozen times, but your friend keeps obliviously texting and asking to hang out over and over again. If the ex-friend just doesn't seem to understand that they're getting dumped, we give you permission to tell a little white lie. Try one of these: "I'm taking care of me right now," "I'm drowning in work," or "I'm sooooo busy, maybe we can get together when everything calms down." Spoiler alert: Nothing ever calms down. Is this approach a little savage? Probably, but it works.

THE EXPLOSION. We've all had *that* friend breakup. There's screaming, crying, lying, blaming, and low blows. This is the friend breakup where both sides know *exactly* what happened, even though the story might be entirely different depending on who you ask. Chances are, you were both pretty awful toward each other at some point. There's no coming back from the explosion breakup. Words get said that you can't take back. The most important rule of this type of breakup is: DON'T MAKE YOUR FRIENDS TAKE SIDES. This is not everyone else's fault, so don't pull innocent bystanders into your drama.

This kind of friend breakup is very similar to a romantic breakup. Unfollow the other person on social media, and don't lurk. Don't talk about your ex-friend to other people. Ask your mutual friends to refrain from sharing information about your ex-friend with you. If you run into your ex-friend at a party, be civil or just pretend that your ex-friend doesn't exist. Don't make a huge scene (unless you're drunk, and then you know you will no matter what we say).

THE HEART WRENCH. This is the kind of breakup where someone *really* fucks you over. Maybe your friend slept with your husband, or stole money from you, or conspired to get your kid kicked out of their school. This is a one-strike-and-you're-out kind of situation. If you want to confront them and explain yourself, you can sit across from them at a table and air your grievances, Festivus style (for the *Seinfeld* fans). But, honestly, don't expect the reaction you're looking for. This ex-friend is most likely a narcissist and probably doesn't really care that they flipped your entire world upside down. You deal with the heart wrench the same way you deal with the explosion: They're dead to you now.

THE OMNIPOTENT EX. It's scary to break up with a friend who knows all of your deep, dark secrets. When you break up with a lover, it's different, because you've both seen each other naked and in really intimate moments, so there's a ton of ammunition on both sides. But a friendship breakup is different. This ex-friend could blackmail you. That's why we recommend saving every text, email, telegram, whatever. If you've recently cut someone out of your life who has a tendency to lie or twist the truth, don't delete your text chains! SAVE THOSE RECEIPTS. But at the end of the day, this strategy isn't foolproof. You can't make them delete all their secrets about you, and that's just part of life. Use this as a lesson, and be careful who you trust.

Finally, remember that nothing is forever. You can always forgive a toxic friend. We've all been toxic at certain times. If you catch somebody at the wrong time in their life, they can be a terrible person to be around. Keep your guard up, and be more aware of their behavior. You don't have to immediately fall back into being best friends again, but holding on to that resentment and negative energy, and being so mad at somebody for something that happened way back in the day, does you no good. Forgive, but *never* forget.

My Friend Adam

For the privacy of my good friend, I have changed his name for this story.

There have been two people I've met in my life who I have felt connected to in an all-encompassing, soul-mate type of way. One was Jared, and the other one was my friend Adam. I actually met them both in very similar circumstances during the same time in my life. But they each filled a part of my heart in very different ways.

Adam was the brightest light in any room he walked into, and the kindest soul I've ever known. He was unbelievably magnetic, his happiness was contagious, and he radiated this lightness onto anyone he met. He was hilarious, selfless, and infectiously friendly. He made anyone he talked to feel like the only person in the universe. He cared about people—and I mean *actually* cared. He treated everyone he met as an equal, with respect and compassion for their well-being, regardless of who they were or where they were on their life's journey. He was soft and gentle. And not only was he the most wonderful human to walk the planet, he lived a life of service and devoted himself to helping refugees in the Congo. COULD HE GET ANY MORE PERFECT? Ugh. What can I say? Everyone fucking loved Adam.

Why didn't I try to date Adam, you ask? Well, to be honest, at that time in my young life, he was too normal and stable for me. I wanted to chase after emotionally unavailable assholes who treated me like shit. And, truthfully, he was too good for me. While he was rebuilding houses in war-torn countries, I was stalking the singer of My Chemical Romance on Myspace. But goddamn, he was a great friend. When I was around Adam, I felt like the best version of myself. I felt like I could be unapologetically me, with all my quirks and flaws. He made me want to be a better person and a better friend to those around me. And because of that, I always wanted to be around him.

But I knew Adam. He would never admit it, but I knew that sometimes there was a small dark cloud behind his big smile and sparkly eyes. I knew there were cracks in his heart. He was empathetic to a fault, and he cared way more about his friends and family than about himself. His number-one priority was making everyone else happy. And his biggest fear was letting anyone down.

Throughout the years, Adam and I moved in and out of each other's lives, but our friendship had an unbreakable foundation. I could always call him up in the middle of the night for anything at all, even if we hadn't talked for months. He was always there for me. And a conversation that started in tears of heartache would end in tears of laughter. Every damn time.

One summer, I lent him my copy of *Extremely Loud & Incredibly Close*. This specific copy of the novel was one of my most prized possessions. Not only was it one of my favorite books of all time, I had marked the fuck out of those 368 pages. Highlighting, underlining, and annotating every idea that popped into my head. There was a lot of me in that book. He returned the copy to me two months later. Not only had he added his own thoughts and ramblings throughout the pages, he wrote me a beautiful letter hidden in the last chapter. He knew how much his notes meant, and he made that book so much more special to me.

Fast-forward a few years, and I had been dating a boy for a year and a half when I ran into Adam one day. Adam and I talked and laughed and drank and reminisced. Nothing exceptional or memorable happened that day, but when I left, I felt like I had been hit by a bus. Seeing Adam that day turned everything upside down. My whole body was tingling. It finally hit me: I loved him. I had always loved him, but I was too busy chasing garbage band dudes to realize that this perfect man was right in front of me the whole time. In that moment, it finally became clear that the feelings I had for Adam were hundreds of times stronger than I had felt for anyone in my entire life, including my current boyfriend.

Because I had a semi-decent conscience, I broke up with my boyfriend the next day. Oh God, it was fucking embarrassing. I picked him up from the airport and immediately dumped him in the car. He cried, blew a snot rocket into his sleeve, and threw a stuffed animal at my steering wheel. We almost rear-ended a semitrailer on the freeway because the stuffed animal got stuck underneath my brake pedal. I dropped him off at his house, and he showed up at my doorstep at 6:00 a.m. crying and sweating. I had to physically remove his sweaty body from my apartment so that I could leave for work.

It was now crystal clear to me that Adam was my person. I was 110 percent sure, and now that I was single, I was finally free to express my true feelings! Because I'm a hopeless romantic, I gathered all of my thoughts and put together a handwritten letter on beautiful tea-stained paper. I sprayed the paper with my perfume and sent it via snail mail. To this day, it's the most honest collection of words my little hands have ever created.

Writing that letter and confessing my love to someone who may not have felt the same way wasn't the easiest thing in the world to do, but for me, it was necessary. I didn't want to look back on my life and regret something I was too afraid to do or say. I didn't want to think *what if* when I thought of him. I didn't want him to be the one that got away, or the one that could have been if I just had gathered up a little bit more courage.

When he texted me that he had received my letter, my stomach dropped. IT'S REALLY HAPPENING. *It's finally our time*, I thought to myself. He told me he was going to take his time reading and processing it so that he could give me the response I deserved. So I waited. Hours turned into days turned into months. And I was ultimately just left with . . . nothing. He never responded. I spilled my guts on the floor, and I got nothing in return. I felt worthless. And I'm not going to lie: I was furious. I was so fucking mad that he didn't love me back. I was so mad that I just cut him out of my life altogether. Cold turkey. That letter totally ruined our friendship. And I never talked to him again.

He tried to reach out to me a dozen times over the next few years, and I ignored all of his texts and calls. I never really forgave him for leaving me high and dry. And the part of my heart that Adam filled was empty from that point on, but I was too proud to let him back into my life.

A few more years went by. Every couple of months, I would look at his Facebook page to see what he was up to. He moved to Austin, got an awesome job, and married a beautiful girl. Both of our lives had changed so much since I sent that letter, and it looked like Adam had found everything he was looking for. He looked so happy. Because of that, I was happy for him from afar. And then, one day, I woke up to one of the worst texts I've ever received: Adam took his own life.

It felt like hours to process the text. I read it over and over and over again, not comprehending the words I was staring at. It read like gibberish. There must be a mistake. *My* Adam loved life harder than anyone I'd ever known. *My* Adam radiated joy. *My* Adam was happy. It must be . . . someone else. Then I looked at my bookshelf, and my eyes locked on to my copy of *Extremely Loud & Incredibly Close*. And then I just cried.

I woke up with a stomach flu on the day of his memorial. If that wasn't my body trying to tell me I can't handle heavy shit, I don't know what is. Because of that, I've never been able to fully process or properly grieve losing my friend Adam. Maybe writing this will bring me some clarity.

Adam's death rocked me to my core. It still doesn't make sense, and I don't know if it ever will. I feel devastated that such a bright light was put out. I feel honored that I was able to experience his warmth. I feel fucking horrible that our last texts were him reaching out over and over and over again. I feel helpless for not knowing he was hurting so deeply. I feel guilty that I wasn't there for him when he obviously needed it. And I feel massive regret that I walked away from one of the most important friendships of my life over a stupid letter.

Adam now lives within the pages of my copy of *Extremely Loud and Incredibly Close*. One day I'll have enough courage to open it up again. There's a lot of him in that book. If I've learned anything from this experience it's this: please, don't write people out of your life over stupid shit. Check in on your "strong" and "happy" friends from time to time. Sometimes, they are the ones who need it most.

FIGHT LIKE A LADY

Women are emotional beings. We are psychological destroyers, we act out of impulse, and we fight with our words. That's why men are terrified of us. Because of this, you need to be extra careful when you find yourself in an argument with a girlfriend. Pause and get your emotions straight instead of just blurting out the first thing you feel. You should write your feelings down, or even sleep on it. Get an outsider's perspective. Don't let a stupid moment destroy a meaningful friendship because you didn't take a deep breath before speaking.

We all learn how to be a good friend as time goes on: How to be supportive. How to forgive. How to not be a judgmental asshole. How to refrain from talking shit even if you're pissed. How to *actually* keep a secret. We have a tendency to judge other women for not acting or reacting to a situation the way *we* would. But over time, we realize that we're all just doing the best we can with what we have. It's okay if your friend doesn't handle every situation the way you would. You don't have to judge them too harshly for it. Honestly, it probably doesn't even affect your life. Having some empathy and understanding makes friendships a hell of a lot easier to maintain.

LEARN HOW TO APOLOGIZE. Stop beating around the bush. Stop placing blame on other people. Stop finding excuses. If you fucked up, be straight up and honest, and own your mistake. Honesty is going to resonate the fastest, easiest, and deepest with the person you wronged. Acknowledge the hurt you caused. There is nothing worse than an empty apology, so when you say "I'm sorry," you'd better mean it. Never, and we mean *never*, end your apology with a "but," because that "but" is just displacing your own responsibility. If you would like to explain yourself, you can add "My intentions were never to hurt you," or explain "Here's what I meant." But the truth is, if you hurt someone, that's the most important thing to accept, and it doesn't really matter what your intention was.

It's hard to not take things to heart, but it's important to learn how to separate what feels like a personal attack from honest, constructive criticism. Be mindful of the company that you keep. If you have a sensitive, nonconfrontational heart and you can't handle criticism well, your feelings will probably get unintentionally hurt by no-nonsense straight shooters with super thick skin.

Here's a good rule of thumb for the next time you want to vent about a friend: If they were to read your texts or overhear your conversations about them, would you care? Would you stand by your words and say it to their face, or would you be mortified if they found out what you were saying? If you can say what you're thinking about somebody to their face, it's probably justified and really bothering you. But if you feel like you got caught, you are probably just talking shit. Listen, we love a good gossip session. Give us all the scoop on Jessica's divorce and Megan's hot new boy toy, and OMG, did Tanya *really* say that?! Inject that drama into our veins! But there's a huge difference between fun innocent gossip and detrimental shit-talking.

We know, sometimes it stinks to hear the truth about yourself from your friends. When someone calls you out for bad behavior, it's embarrassing. But you have to realize that your friends care about you. It's awkward to be confrontational with people you love, so if someone brings some uncomfortable stuff up to you, chances are that it's pretty valid. Plus, if your friends don't call you out for being an asshole, how will you ever grow and become a better, less-of-an-asshole person?

On Wednesdays, We Wear Pink

I know it's hard to believe, but there are people out there in the world who do not like me. Sure, it's offensive, because I am such a lovely, caring, and perfect human being, but some people have bad taste and do not want to be my friend. This is especially shocking because I am a pretty good friend. What I lack in the way of actual human contact, I replace with remembering birthdays, giving gifts, throwing parties, knowing the Enneagram number of everyone in my life, and connecting my friends with the person who will change their house, career, hair, and life.

During this incident I'm about to recount, I was in the middle of a rough year. I was in my mid-twenties and I had just had my heart really epically broken after a long-term relationship exploded. I was homeless and sleeping in a friend's guest room, working full-time at a high-pressure, physically demanding job, and not treating myself very nicely. I wasn't sleeping or eating much. One day, during rehearsals, I took a bathroom break and felt so light-headed and sick that the only thing I wanted to do was lie down on the cold concrete floor and close my eyes. I woke up in the emergency room after having passed out.

I am a highly functioning, ambitious woman, so the fact that I had let down my cast and myself in this way over a stupid boy rocked me. I was beyond embarrassed. Adding to the stress was the fact that between the fainting episode and generally not being my best self, I became a target for the gossip and cruel intentions of my castmates. Being in show biz, we love drama. Theater casts become families in a way that anyone who hasn't existed in a showmance could never understand. More than friends.

Some of my cast members were supportive, tried to give me tough love, and helped me put my heart back together. Others were horrible to me. They talked about me behind my back, and whenever I walked by, they would mock me by falling to the ground and "fainting" like I had done in rehearsals. One girl in particular—let's call her "Regina George"—was the ringleader. Regina George took pleasure in making life even harder for me. I would show up to work with my eyes down, avoiding contact even though we were sharing the same dressing room. It felt like I was in junior high school again. She was the beautiful popular girl, our director's favorite, and I was the little heartbroken shadow girl with a bit part and a mullet getting tripped by her every day.

Over time (the only thing that really helps heartbreak), my heart began to heal, I started eating again, and I finally started to feel like myself. I moved out of my friend's spare room and into my own apartment. I went to therapy and did a serious amount of personal work. But the one thing I could never live down during that contract was the fainting incident. When I finally quit the show to go back to New York, I didn't say goodbye to Regina George or any of the other horrible humans who had made my time extra difficult. I'm sure they cackled and clapped when I left the building. Good riddance! I was ready for the next chapter of my life.

For the next decade, I didn't really think about it. I never had to see those people again. I learned that even though my people-pleasing heart really wanted to be well liked and be friends with everyone, you don't actually have to do that. You can choose who you want to be friends with, and you can just be "meh" about everyone else. I learned that friendship was not something I had to give away to anyone who was breathing, but a special and sacred bond that I would commit to and work at and put my time and energy into for worthwhile people. Being the most popular person or the one invited to all the parties and all the events stopped mattering to me. My heart got stronger. I met my husband, and I found real love and happiness. I changed careers to hosting, and I got dream jobs. I bought a dream house. My circle of friends got smaller and smaller but stronger than ever.

I'd hear gossip about Regina George here and there. She's been married and divorced. She'd been in this show and that one. Over time, I forgot altogether that the fainting had happened. When I saw people from that time in my life, I was able to roll my eyes at myself and make jokes about how pathetic I was back then.

Then, one day, my husband went to see an off-Broadway show with a friend, and they hung out with the cast afterward. Regina George happened to be in the cast, they had been introduced, and a mutual acquaintance had explained to Regina that Chris was my husband. He came home from that work trip and casually mentioned that he had met someone I knew, but I didn't give it a second thought.

Until a message popped up in my DMs.

"I'm sorry if I was ever unkind in the past. When I met Chris, he said, 'Oh, Keltie will be so happy to hear that I met you!' And it made me think, 'Hmmmmm, I don't know,' and that made me sad. Just wanted to clear the air and any old lingering bad vibes. I look back at my old behavior, and I'm like, 'Ewwwwwww.'"

Regina George had come to me for redemption. I wrote something back like "Don't worry about it," and I deleted the message. It did feel nice to hear the apology, even though it didn't change anything about that hard time or any of my life moving forward. But it was a great lesson that even though people can be cruel, the people who hate you will one day hate you less. The person you couldn't stand at twenty-four might be someone you follow on Instagram at thirty-four and kind of enjoy. A friend or an acquaintance who you think is a jerk might not actually be a jerk at their core but just going through a jerk stage in their life. Hold tight to the actual good friendships in your life, and stay loyal to the people who are good to you even when you are not at your best. Finally, realize that having two good friends is better than having an entire table full of Regina Georges.

LADYFIGHTS

We are constantly getting asked how the three of us manage to work so well together. You probably won't believe us, but in the years we've been business partners, we've never fought once. Sure, there have been times where we've disagreed, or when two of us want to do something and the third one doesn't. There have been times when Hurricane Keltie spiraled so hard that Jac and Becca secretly plotted her murder. We have each individually felt raw, unhinged, or overwhelmed, and we've broken down in tears over something along the way. But we've never fought, and this is why: We are extremely straightforward with one another. To be honest, we never really discussed how we would handle conflict, but somehow we got lucky and ended up on the same page about how we operate. If we don't like something or we feel uncomfortable about something, we'll say something. This kind of honesty is an impossibly easy rule to preach, but it can sometimes be a difficult one to practice.

We have unintentionally set healthy boundaries with one another from the very inception of the LadyGang. We always have girls tell us, "OMG, you're so lucky you get to work with your best friends!" But the thing is, we've never been best friends. Sure, we were friendly acquaintances, but none of us were *besties* when we started this thing. The LadyGang started as a professional relationship, and it has stayed a professional relationship over the years. Our *literal job* is to gab about our lives to each other, so we probably know more about one another's menstrual cycles and ex-boyfriends than our actual besties do. We've obviously grown close over the years, but there is still a distance among us. And that distance has been one of the most beneficial things to keep a fresh, healthy synergy flowing between us.

A huge reason why we work so well together is that we are all so different. We have different personalities, different viewpoints, and different strengths and weaknesses. We are all determined to get to the finish line, but we each have our own individual way of getting there. The way Keltie makes a list isn't the way Jac makes a list. The way Becca talks in a meeting isn't the way Keltie talks in a meeting. But we have learned to trust in one another and embrace our differences, because our magic comes from just being ourselves. As far as LadyFights go, if you make a mistake or hurt someone's feelings, the easiest way to deal with it is just to get on the phone and talk it out. The distance that a text chain or communicating via hearsay puts in the middle of a fight can be devastating to the outcome. Talk it out, offer a sincere apology, understand that no one is perfect, and move on. At work, realizing you can be friendly with everyone without needing to be best friends with everyone is a powerful lesson. Finally, be careful who you complain and gossip to. Even when we are pissed about something, we try our best not to complain about each other to each other. We take it to our partners, moms, or friends who don't run in the same circles. We all love to vent and spill the tea, but remember that tea stains, so be careful where you pour it!

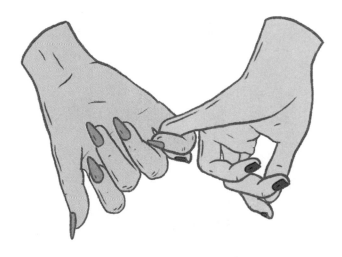

Every Maverick Needs a Goose

If you claim that you're the "best wingwoman ever," you're probably not. A good wingwoman doesn't even want to be a wingwoman, because her worst nightmare is putting on makeup and going to a bar and being around a bunch of guys she's *not* gonna hook up with. The main mission of a wingwoman is to hype up her friend, make her feel like a goddess, and let her have her choice of the dick buffet.

To be a good wingwoman, you need to support your girl subtly and solidly. Do not—we repeat, do not—flirt with the guy she's into for your own personal validation. We all have *that* friend who loves to flirt even if she has a boyfriend, who will steal the attention of anyone's man just to boost her own ego. If your girl needs a wingwoman, chances are she might be a little timid or shy. If you're the type of gal who goes up to all the guys and is overly chatty, chances are the guy is going to end up liking you instead of your friend. If you really want some extra wingwoman points, maybe forget to wash your hair or to put on makeup that night. Also, you need to know when to make your exit. Don't overstay your welcome and become an annoying third wheel when your friend is trying to give you a sign to get the hell out.

If you're going to take your wingwoman responsibility one step further and play cupid, tread lightly. Setting up two friends can really complicate your friend circles when things go south (which they most likely will), and then you have to start picking sides and avoiding people. When you tell your girlfriend you want to set her up with her soul mate, you start planting unhealthy seeds in her mind that will probably never amount to anything more than a one-night stand. If you think two of your friends are meant to be, don't say a word. Instead, throw a party or organize drinks, and conveniently invite both people. If you sense some romantic vibes, approach each of them separately and say, "Isn't John so cute? I think he might be into you!" and "Oh, isn't Sarah such a catch? She's one of my best friends, and I feel like you two would really get along." Boom! You did your work, and now you walk away.

A Dozen Red Flags? I Love Them!

Your wingwoman duties don't just end when your friend finds her guy. We all have to stay on high alert and say something when we see a big red flag in our gal's relationship. It's real easy to get stuck in the **DICKSAND**, and it's almost impossible to think logically with love goggles on. But this doesn't give you the go-ahead to talk about your friend's guy every time he makes a grammar mistake. How red is that flag? If he's hitting on your other friends, or you, or if you saw him out cheating, *that* is a red flag. If he's gaslighting or disrespecting your friend, *that* is a red flag. If he just likes to drink, is a dumb bro, or is kind of a douche canoe, that's not a red flag. When men get together with "the boys," even the greatest guys somehow lose their last brain cell. Sometimes men do and say gross things when they're left alone in groups without women. Forgive them and think about the fact that women can be so much worse.

However, the hardest time to be a wingwoman is when you have to tell your friend that she is the one in the wrong. It's time we stop biting our tongues when our girlfriend complains that she doesn't understand what went wrong in her relationship. *We* know what is wrong: She is acting like a brat, or her expectations are too high, or she is being clingy and annoying. We need to be cautiously honest with our friends and call them out, because we want our friends to call us out on our bullshit, too.

Sloppy Seconds

Keltie Knight and I dated the same guy. Well, I dated him first, and she took my sloppy seconds. We now refer to him as our "mutual ex." Here are our stories.

I never had boyfriends in high school. While the rest of my cheer-leading squad was swapping spit with everyone on the football team, I was chasing after shitty band guys who were too busy swapping spit with different groupies around the country to ever want to actually date me. That was until one fateful day, a month before I turned eighteen, when a cute, anonymous emo boy from Las Vegas commented on my LiveJournal. Because the internet never forgets, I was able to track down the exact day this happened and the exact message that started this whole thing:

April 28, 2004, 8:37 PM

> whoa. hot. i like your style =)

This was around the time that my little scene queen star was rising in the weird emo corner of the internet, and kids all around the world were intently following my life under a microscope. I was like Kim Kardashian, if Kim Kardashian wore pounds of black eyeshadow, studded belts, and expressed her feelings through brooding AOL away messages. Back in the day, I replied to pretty much every comment on my LiveJournal, so I said something generic back to his comment and didn't think much of it. But he was quite determined, and after that initial outreach, he occasionally posted semi-cringey and semi-flirty comments on my entries over the next few months. Oh, and he kept begging me to listen to his band's demos, but I was too busy smooching his role models to get around to it.

He finally piqued my interest when he rearranged lyrics from a bunch of different bands into his own original composition to express how his heart was feeling. And, boy, did that Third Eye Blind–Counting Crows mash-up *really* turn me on. We started chatting outside of my journal, and I learned that his band was recording an album with some mutual friends of mine in a band called Fall Out Boy. Okay, so he's not a *total* stranger. I'm in.

After a few months of online flirting, we met in person for the first time. And we went from a digital-digital-get-down into a full-blown relationship in no time (I seemed to have a pattern in my youth, I know). We immediately plastered our love all over the internet, and everyone was *eating it up.* The untouchable "scene queen" was dating the lead guitarist of the "next big thing." It was a match made in emo heaven, and our fans either loved us or loved to hate us. Regardless of whether the attention was positive or negative, it sure blew things up. Kids all over the world were making fan accounts and "role-playing" us in a fictional online fantasy world, to the point where we almost became exaggerated caricatures of ourselves.

Fans were following our every move, and that's because we were naïvely blasting our every move on our respective online journals. This dynamic only intensified when the singer of his band started dating another popular scene queen, and we immediately became a powerful foursome. Two best friends dating two best friends—what could go wrong?!

Well, a lot could go wrong. The fall was just about as fast as the rise, and I won't bore you with the in-between. We dated for LITERALLY THREE MONTHS, but three months feels like three decades when you're eighteen. If you've made it this far in our book, you know that I never slept with him. I don't think I ever even saw his penis. We definitely never said "I love you," but it's safe to say that when we broke up, it crushed my immature heart to its absolute core.

Just like we plastered our relationship all over the internet, we also passive-aggressively plastered our cryptic post-breakup feelings all over the internet. Here's a fun excerpt I found from an interview he did after we broke up:

WOW, I FEEL PERSONALLY ATTACKED. Oh, how times have changed. Half of the people who are idolized these days "don't do anything," and *literally* all you need to be a photographer is a digital camera and Photoshop. But, man, did that sting back in the day.

I was single for five years after our breakup, but it only took him a few months to find his next adorable blonde love interest.

Enter Keltie Knight.

Mutual Ex and Keltie's relationship catapulted into internet fame just as fast as ours did. Of course I stalked Keltie, of course I was jealous of Keltie, and of course I secretly hoped Keltie's relationship with Mutual Ex would crash and burn like ours did. I was young and immature and totally left in the dust. And she was living the exciting, rock-star life I had always dreamed of. Somehow, she was even more of an oversharer than I was, so I knew every little detail of their relationship just by googling her name. In my mind, he had just found a better version of me. She was more outgoing, more bubbly, and more talented than I could ever be. And because of that, I felt insecure, insignificant, and lesser than.

The internet didn't help. Fans of Mutual Ex's band were *obsessed* with their personal lives, so somehow I immediately became the villain, even though I was the one who had been dumped. His fans *hated* me, but they *loved* to publicly compare me to his hot new girlfriend. Our looks, careers, personalities, weight, whatever—you name it, and it was used as a weapon to pit us against each other. Before I knew it, I *hated* this girl who I had never met before. Little did I know, she was a kind, hilarious, and wonderful person who was just as insecure as I was.

Keltie and Mutual Ex's relationship came and went, and she and I ended up running into each other a few times after that. Thankfully, enough time had passed so that the run-ins weren't too awkward, and, to our surprise, we got along pretty damn well. We ran in the same circles and became friendly acquaintances, but that would all change when she called me out of the blue one day and asked me to start a podcast. The rest is history. Mutual Ex is the sole reason Keltie and I ever even knew the other existed in the first place. So, thank you, Mutual Ex, for unintentionally changing our life paths forever.

Mutual Ex is now our favorite (not-so-)inside joke, and part of our quirky, dysfunctional bond. Not because either of us truly cares, but more so that I can make fun of Keltie for taking my "sloppy seconds." Neither of us has feelings attached to the situation, but those superfans are still lurking around the dark corners of the internet, trolling us any chance they get whenever we crack a joke about it. To this day, Keltie and I *still* both get hate mail and death threats. (We're both on the edge of our seats, waiting for the "OMG, IT WAS TEN YEARS AGO, GET OVER IT" messages after this book comes out. Look, we're over it—it's just funny!)

That was my first real relationship with my first real boyfriend, and even though it only lasted for a measly ninety days, I learned a lot. Things aren't always as they seem on the outside (or on the internet), and you're truly doing a disservice to yourself by judging someone you've never met before. Last of all, people are assholes.

To conclude, I always pride myself on the fact that I've never gone back to an ex before. But that's a lie. A few years after Mutual Ex and I broke up, I happened to be in Las Vegas for a show, and we happened to fool around one night. I remember that it was around the time he dated Keltie, but I could never actually figure out if he cheated on her with me or not. The only detail of the night I remember was that we were watching the newly released music video for Incubus, "Dig," so Keltie and I recently did some recon and discovered that he was, in fact, single at the time. So, at the end of everything, I guess I took Keltie's sloppy thirds.

Sloppier Seconds

There are actually very few things that Jac Vanck and I have in common. She's a seven on the Enneagram, "the Enthusiast," and her personality type is described as "spontaneous, versatile, and scattered." Jac is a crop-top-wearing, day-drinking, game-loving, "don't worry, it will get done" kind of human, and I am a never-drinking, games-without-purpose-are-dumb, "worry until you finish it" type of person.

The one thing we do share is our mutual love of musician men. We both love a guitar-playing, skinny-jean-wearing, weird-haircut-having, tour-bus-smelling man. We love concerts and being backstage at concerts. We love men who are emotionally unavailable, need saving, and write us poems.

This is probably why we have a mutual ex-boyfriend. At this point in our adult lives, this person has become a weird character in our story. Every time we bring it up and laugh about what complete idiots we were, I try to picture myself with that person and I can't even remember what his face looks like. Over time, he has become a caricature of a person, and a summation of every terrible choice I made in my twenties.

While Jac was busy on the Warped Tour, actually hanging out with bands, I was a struggling dancer in New York City. I remember booking the audition to be a backup dancer for our mutual ex-boyfriend's band, and being in Ripley-Grier Studios in New York with the choreographer, watching a VHS tape of his band's performance and figuring out what we were going to do. The dudes were wearing full-on makeup. I thought to myself, *This is such weird shit*. I had no idea who they were.

I was a backup dancer at MTV's Video Music Awards for the band, and I ended up meeting Mutual Ex, dating him, living with him, crying over him, and eventually being pathetic enough to write an entire section of a book about finding myself again after him. There is this really weird thing that goes along with trickle-down fame. When you run in the circle of someone who has "made it," you start to feel like you've made it, too. Only, when the fame, and success, and money, and lifestyle are not really yours to hold, when it ends, you've gotta do some serious soul-searching. For me, that soul-searching led to therapy and the start of a second phase of my life, in which I really invested in myself and worked hard to understand that I was deserving of love and success on my own terms. Once I truly started investing in my own happiness, my entire life flourished.

I've since closed the goddamn door, literally, on that section of my life, and I've married a rocker turned businessman (who, by the way, still wears skinny jeans and takes me backstage at concerts—just in a different way). Nonetheless, it was a really meaningful series of events, and I think that's why it's so easy to bring up and talk about. I'm not sure how much the version of him I invented in my head actually existed. I really didn't know what kind of person I wanted to be, what I wanted out of my life, what I needed in a relationship, and, to be honest—I didn't think I deserved much.

I know that I certainly did not deserve the amount of hate I received on the newly birthed internet during this time. There was a bizarre corner of the internet that was devoted to bands and their girlfriends. I only knew of Jac because we were pitted against each other regularly. I would see her "modeling pictures" and cool, scene-girl hair, and I would have that comparison be the thief of my own self-worth. She was the ultimate cool girl, and I was and still am an oddball loner who would rather spend time with a book than with a human. We were labeled instant enemies for no real reason, and to be honest, there were times when I thought of this woman I had never even met with disdain. I wasn't a fully formed human yet, and I tended to believe all the one-sided bad things that Mutual Ex would say about her. It's such an easy narrative to pit an ex against a new gal, and I still to this day feel bad about the time I passive-aggressively posted SCENE QUEEN < DANCING QUEEN on my Myspace page. Sorry, Jac.

Here is what I do know. The internet is a cruel place for Emo Jac and Dancer Keltie and their mutual ex-boyfriend. The photos, the blogs, the passive-aggressive tweets, and the overall immaturity of the entire era will haunt me forever. But dating Mutual Ex, and finding out who Jac was, eventually led me to realize that I did not hate this girl—in fact, I thought she was pretty dang cool. I went on to silently stalk and admire her for years afterward, which led me to forcing her into my life.

I wanted to work with her, so I texted her randomly one day. Jac, being the enthusiast that she is, said, "Yes, sure!" And it has been one of the most fulfilling things I've ever done. LadyGang wouldn't be the same without Jacquelene Vanek. I have never met anyone who can literally have no idea what is going on in the world but also know exactly where the smush-face dog convention is happening on Friday. She's a special human. So, while our mutual ex-boyfriend might not have been the greatest actual boyfriend to either of us, he brought us together, and I do want to thank him for having such incredible, flawless, perfect taste in women.

GOODBYE: A LADY WOULD NEVER

It's probably pretty clear to you by now that we are questionable women and that we gave you some pretty questionable advice. It's not easy being a lady, especially when society's expectations can be so unattainable and ass-backward. We started the LadyGang to empower ourselves, to be our own bosses, and to make women everywhere feel less alone. We never really imagined that anyone would actually listen to our constant ramblings, but our gang of ladies is now a worldwide tour de force, with millions of connected women giving us the confidence and courage to fearlessly and unapologetically be ourselves.

We aren't afraid to pluck a nipple hair at the beach, eat a rotisserie chicken with our bare hands in the car, or bawl our eyes out to a Rascal Flatts song in the middle of a bar . . . again. We've been pathetic and desperate in love, and we've puked from a hangover at our desk at work. We've bought designer purses we absolutely couldn't afford, we've dyed our hair every color of the rainbow, and we don't wash our legs in the shower. We will continue to fuck up, make bad decisions, and have a cheat day that turns into a cheat month. We don't have all the answers, and we usually just drink a bottle of wine when all else fails. Lady life is messy, after all.

As you close this book, take a deep breath and try to remember that everything is temporary. Bad weeks will turn into good weeks, eventually. Timing is everything. Don't let people be reckless with your heart. Be gentle with yourself and with others. Don't be a dick. Try to act confident, even when you don't feel it. You are better, smarter, and prettier than you think. Stand up for yourself, because you deserve it. Wear sunscreen every day. Do no harm, but take no shit. There's room for everyone at the table. Whatever is breaking your heart right now won't break your heart for much longer . . . because something else will! And that's okay, because life's a bitch, and then you die. But in between those two things happening, remember that you're not alone.

So if you are already a LadyGang member, it's good to see you again, friends. Thank you for making the LadyGang so incredible. We couldn't do this without you. And if you are new to us, welcome to the gang! You now have thousands of new best friends.

In the immortal words of Kris Jenner, *"You're doing amazing, sweetie!"*

LadySlang Dicktionary

Askhole (*n.*) A person who constantly asks for your advice yet always does the complete opposite of what you tell them to do.

Bitchcraft (*n.*) The art of being a total bitch for no reason, often practicing acts of upsetting people just for the hell of it.

Cuntstipated (*adj.*) Experiencing emotional or spiritual blockage caused by having to deal with too many cunts in one day.

Dicknotized (*adj.*) Starting to catch feelings for the guy because the dick is so good.

Dickpressed (*adj.*) Being sad or depressed from the lack of dick in your life.

Dicksand (*n.*) The female version of being "whipped." Much like quicksand, dicksand is what girls get caught in when they're obsessed with their crush, boyfriend, husband, or anyone giving them dick.

Fuckening (*n.*) A day of reckoning that occurs when things have been going too well and then some shit finally goes down.

Garbae (*n.*) Your bae, but he's trash.

Hangxiety (*n.*) The feeling of overwhelming guilt, stress, and worry you experience after a night of binge drinking. Hangover-induced anxiety.

Hatfish (*n.*) A person who is attractive only when wearing a hat.

Highdea (*n.*) An idea or insight you have when you are high. For the duration of being high, it is a truly profound, original, and genius idea, but it makes zero sense the next day.

Hoement (*n.*) A moment when a lady renders herself a ho.

Hoetivities (*n.*) A collection of hoements.

Jactivities (*n.*) Activities Jac loves, such as day-drinking, adventuring, and traveling.

Justache (*n.*) Justin Bieber's mustache.

Keltdown (*n.*) A Keltie-style meltdown.

Mimbo (*n.*) A male bimbo.

Porkfolio (*n.*) A collection of dick pics that girls save for later hilarity.

Rolodicks (*n.*) A phone directory of male cohorts who can quickly be contacted for sexual activities.

Sadsturbation (*n.*) Masturbating while sad.

Saltmates (*n.*) Two like-minded people who, like soul mates, enjoy being salty as fuck together.

Screwvenir (*n.*) A souvenir you steal from someone you sleep with.

Sexico (*n.*) Any tropical destination where couples go annually to reignite their sex life.

Sexorcism (*n.*) The act of having intercourse with someone in order to move on from an ex.

Tampnesia (*n.*) Forgetting a tampon inside of you for an extended period of time.

Trashback (*n.*) A flashback to a trash ex.

Vag-enius (*n.*) A man who is highly educated in the workings and art of the vagina.

Vajourney (*n.*) Any sexual adventure led by your vagina.

Yesterbae (*n.*) An ex-boyfriend, ex-girlfriend, ex-crush, or former hookup.

Acknowledgments

Diana Baroni, for giving us a platform and believing in our stupid Lady-thoughts; our editors Michele Eniclerico and Danielle Curtis, for editing a book written by one college graduate and two morons, along with the rest of the team at Penguin Random House.

Andy McNicol, the book agent with the best taste in the biz, and the entire WME team: Meghan Mackenzie, Justin Ongert, Marcus Levy, and Jenni Levine Michener.

Our lady lawyer, Carolyn Conrad; Derek Kroeger; Sue Madore; manager and hypeman extraordinaire, Ricky Rollins; Debbie DeCorte; Elena Garcia, a.k.a. the OG LadyGanger; Norm Pattiz, a.k.a. Daddy Normbucks; Kit Gray, a.k.a. the man who fields all of our emotional emails like a champ; Peter Morris and the entire kick-ass sales team at PodcastOne.

Our partners at Hello Merch: Sam Means and Tom Cook. Brand Like That's Natalie Pirzad and Lainey DePompa. BeSocial's Ali Grant, Sarah Burns, and Haley Henning. Something Social's Calli Choldonenko, Erin Dykstra, and Amanda Apgood. Our funny friend Justin Martindale; Wesley Bird, for her badass illustrations; Alexandra Ingber, for being the only person who actually knows what they are doing and has the lists to prove it. Ket Nejat-Thompson for making us sound a little less dumb. And lastly, thank you to the LadyGang community worldwide. You *are* the LadyGang. Without you we'd just be three lone LadyLosers.

BECCA: To Zach, for letting me exploit, humiliate, and make fun of myself in front of the entire world and never asking me to stop. To my sister, Jessica, for always answering my calls and making me feel normal no matter what. To Orly, you are my everything. Lastly, to my parents, who let me curse and chase my dreams without doubting my ability.

KELTIE: To Chris, the most private person in the entire world, whose life got blown open when he met me. Thank you for laughing at the pathetic human being I was, and at all the terrible choices I made before your love made me cool, and for loving my workaholic tendencies. To my parents and brother, for never listening to our podcast; and finally to my Emmy Award, for being the reason I get up every day.

JAC: To my parents, for being my best friends in the entire world, for boldly supporting every crazy life venture I have ever taken on, and for putting on invisible earmuffs when listening to our podcast and coming to our shows (you're not a regular mom and dad; you're a cool mom and dad). I am SO proud to be your daughter. To all of the assholes I dated, for treating me like garbage and teaching me how to fully appreciate my person when I found him. To Jared, for loving me fearlessly, and for letting me roast him every day.

Published in the United States by Rodale Books, an imprint of
    Random House, a division of Penguin Random House LLC,
    New York.
rodalebooks.com

RODALE and the Plant colophon are registered trademarks of
    Penguin Random House LLC.

Library of Congress Cataloging-in-Publication Data
    is available upon request.

ISBN 978-0-593-13644-7
Ebook ISBN 978-0-593-13645-4
Premium edition ISBN 978-0-593-23232-3

Printed in the United States of America

Cover design by Jac Vanek and Britt Rohr
Book design by Jac Vanek
Illustrations by Wesley Bird

10 9 8 7 6 5 4 3 2 1

First Edition

About the Authors

The LadyGang began with a podcast with the mission to make women feel less alone. Since 2015, the show has boasted over 100 million downloads, topped the podcasts charts, and spawned a television series and an entire network of like-minded podcasts. *LadyGang* the podcast was a People's Choice Award nominee and a Webby Award nominee for best series, has been featured on *Entertainment Weekly*'s coveted "Must List," and was judged "Podcast of the Year" in 2016. The creators—Keltie Knight, Becca Tobin, and Jac Vanek—have been featured in *People, Forbes, Variety, Who What Wear, Hello Giggles, Daily Mail, Entertainment Tonight, The New York Times,* and *The Hollywood Reporter.*

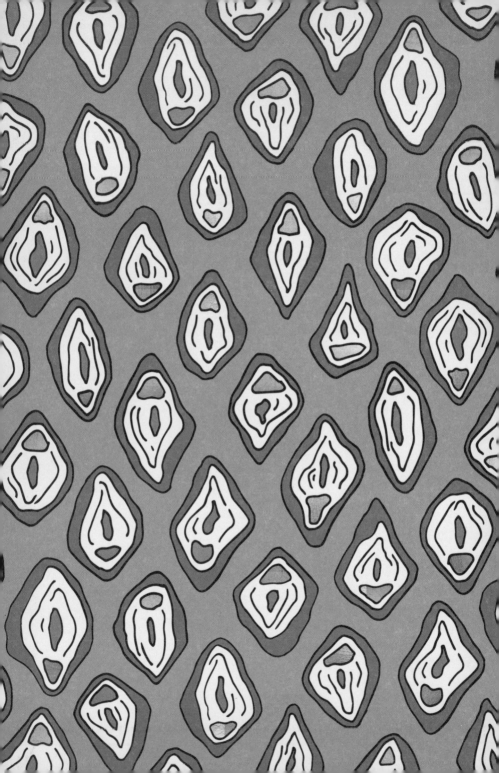